SOCIAL WORKERS AFFECTING SOCIAL POLICY

An international perspective on policy practice

Edited by John Gal and Idit Weiss-Gal

First published in Great Britain in 2013 by

The Policy Press
University of Bristol
Fourth Floor
Beacon House
Queen's Road
Bristol BS8 1QU
UK
t: +44 (0)117 331 4054
f: +44 (0)117 331 4093
tpp-info@bristol.ac.uk
www.policypress.co.uk

North American office:
The Policy Press
c/o The University of Chicago Press
1427 East 60th Street
Chicago, IL 60637, USA
t: +1 773 702 7700
f: +1 773-702-9756
sales@press.uchicago.edu
www.press.uchicago.edu

British Library Cataloguing in Publication Data
A catalogue record for this book is available from the British Library.

Library of Congress Cataloging-in-Publication Data
A catalog record for this book has been requested.

ISBN 978 1 84742 973 5 hardcover

Cover design by Qube Design Associates, Bristol
Cover image: © 2008 California State University, Fullerton Volunteer & Service Center. Image
designed by Nathan Leiva for Students ACT's Social Justice Summit.

Printed and bound in Great Britain by MPG Books Ltd, Bodmin
The Policy Press uses environmentally responsible print partners

MIX
Paper from
responsible sources
FSC
www.fsc.org   FSC® C018575

Contents

List of tables and figures

Tables

Figures

Notes on the contributors

Editors

John Gal is professor and dean at the Paul Baerwald School of Social Work and Social Welfare at the Hebrew University of Jerusalem. He has published extensively on social policy in a comparative perspective and in Israel, and on policy practice among social workers.

Idit Weiss-Gal is associate professor at the Bob Shapell School of Social Work at Tel Aviv University, Israel. She has published extensively on the professional ideologies of social workers, on social work as a profession, and on policy practice.

Contributors

Annamaria Campanini is professor of social work at Milano Bicocca University, Italy. Previously a coordinator of the thematic network EUSW (European Platform for Worldwide Social Work) and former president of European Association of Schools of Social Work, she is now president of the Italian Association of Teachers in Social Work and is responsible for the dialogue between Europe and China in social work education in the context of the Europe–China Forum. Her research interests include social work education in Europe, international social work, systemic approaches, evaluation in social work practice and policy practice.

Carla Facchini is professor of sociology of the family at Milano Bicocca University, Italy. She is dean of the Faculty of Sociology and coordinator of the BA in Social Work. Her research interests include family transition, ageing, social policies and social professions.

Richard Hoefer is the Roy E. Dulak professor for community practice research in the School of Social Work at University of Texas, Arlington, USA. He is the author of numerous articles on social work advocacy and his book, *Advocacy Practice for Social Justice*, recently came out in an expanded second edition. He also edits the *Journal of Policy Practice*. Other areas of interest include programme evaluation and nonprofit management.

Elena Iarskaia-Smirnova is a professor in the Department of General Sociology at National State University, Higher School of Economics, Moscow, head of the Department of Social Work at Saratov State Technical University, and academic adviser at the Center for Social Policy and Gender Studies, Russia. Research interests include the public sphere, gender, disability, social work, and visual studies.

María-Asunción Martínez-Román is professor of social policy in the Department of Social Work and Social Services and at the Research Institute on Social Development and Peace, University of Alicante, Spain. Among her research themes are social exclusion, gender, ageing, health, and disability inequalities. She is editor of the social work journal, *Alternativas: Cuadernos de Trabajo Social.*

Philip Mendes of Monash University, Australia, is associate professor and the director of the Social Inclusion and Social Policy Research Unit in the Department of Social Work. His key research interests include young people transitioning from out-of-home care, welfare states and globalisation, social work and social activism, and Indigenous social policy.

Pavel Romanov is a professor in the Department of Socio-Economic Systems and Social Policy at National State University, Higher School of Economics, Moscow, and director of the Center for Social Policy and Gender Studies, Russia. His research interests are the welfare state, ethnography of professions and organisations, social inequality and representations.

Tapio Salonen is professor in social work and dean of the Faculty of Health and Society at Malmö University, Sweden. His main research interests include poverty, marginality, participatory strategies and social policy. He has been research leader for multi-disciplinary research groups and been responsible for a number of externally funded research projects at both national and international level. He has served as an expert in public inquiries, commissions and government committees.

Graeme Simpson is a senior lecturer at the University of Wolverhampton, UK, where he teaches on the BA and MA social work awards. His research interests include children and families and learning disabilities. He has been involved with international social work for many years. He also teaches in Germany, and has publications in the field of international social work, sociology for social workers and, latterly, social policy for welfare professionals.

Katarina H. Thorén is assistant professor in social work at the School of Social Work, Stockholm University, Sweden. Her main research interests include social policy and social work practice, especially social workers' engagement in policy practice. Her research focus is on social assistance policies, unemployment, activation and labour market policies, and the street-level implementation of social policy in social work organisations.

Acknowledgements

We are very grateful to Emily Watt, our commissioning editor at The Policy Press, for encouraging us to undertake this project and to the anonymous reviewers for their comments on the proposal and final manuscript. We would also like to thank the rest of the team at The Policy Press, particularly Laura Greaves, for moving the book forward so efficiently. This volume is, of course, the result of a very fruitful and ongoing collaboration with the chapter authors. Without exception, they were original, cooperative, and committed to this effort to put policy practice on the social work agenda worldwide. Finally, we would like to acknowledge the hard work that our doctoral student and research assistant, Talya Tayri, put into this project. Hopefully, this is only the beginning of a very fruitful academic career for her.

ONE

Policy practice in social work: an introduction

John Gal and Idit Weiss-Gal

The notion that social workers should seek to influence the policies that affect the societies in which they work has existed for nearly as long as the profession itself. Indeed, the history of the social work profession is replete with examples of social workers seeking to influence policies in the societies in which they lived. In the United Kingdom (UK), through her participation in various national committees social worker Eileen Younghusband was party to the formulation of policy in a wide range of fields during the 1950s and 1960s (Lyons, 2003). The much-acknowledged social activism of Jane Addams during the early decades of the 20th century in the US and her efforts to mandate children's education and to protest at the conditions of immigrants and women exemplified the commitment of social workers to social change (Reisch and Andrews, 2001). Similarly, the involvement of US social workers such as Harry Hopkins, Frances Perkins, 'Molly' Dewson and Aubrey Williams in the formulation of New Deal policies during the 1930s epitomised this commitment to policy involvement (Trattner, 1984).

Elsewhere also, social workers have been at the forefront of efforts to further social change and progressive legislation. In Australia, the social advocacy activities of social workers such as Marie Coleman, who was affiliated with the Victoria Branch of the Australian Association of Social Workers, influenced health and social policy, particularly during the late 1960s and early 1970s (Mendes, 2003). Swedish social workers Gerda Meyerson and Agda Montelius founded the Central Union of Social Work (CSA) in 1903 and played a major role in inducing the government to change the Swedish poor relief system. In Israel, social workers were key actors in the introduction of a national income maintenance programme in the early 1980s, adopted as a result of criticism among social workers of the previous locally administered programme. The minister of labour and welfare at the time, Israel Katz, as well as the academic who formulated the programme, Abraham Doron, and the National Insurance Institute official chosen to establish it were all social workers (Weiss-Gal and Gal, 2011).

This tradition of social worker involvement in social policy formulation reflects values and assumptions that lie at the very foundation of social work. The key values of social justice and social change that are so strongly embedded in the thinking of the social work profession (Craig, 2002; Hare, 2004; Marsh, 2005; Banks, 2006) form an obvious motivational basis for this involvement. Although defined in a variety of ways (Reisch, 2002), social justice is generally perceived as including, among other things, a vision of a society in which all people have equal access to social resources and basic social goods, and in which they enjoy equal social rights and cultural respect. It seeks to further a society in which cultural injustices and unacceptable inequalities in income, wealth and opportunities are reduced (Fraser, 1995; Barker, 2003). Indeed, a commitment to furthering social justice through social change is a constant in a profession that has changed much over the last century or so.

Beyond this generalised commitment to furthering social justice, there are a number of additional assumptions that better clarify this commitment to social policy formulation. Central to the social work ethos is the understanding that society is often the source of individual distress. As Bill Jordan (1990, p 77) once famously noted, 'clients are not isolated individuals, nor are their problems theirs alone'. The 'person in environment' approach that is often portrayed as the organizing principle of the social work profession (Weiss-Gal, 2008) echoes this assumption that the problems faced by individuals very often derive from economic, social and cultural sources. This approach views the individual and his/her multiple environments as a dynamic, interactive system in which each component simultaneously affects and is affected by the other (Hare, 2004). It perceives the individual and his/her environments as forming an ecosystem consisting of the individual, all the systems with which the individual has reciprocal relationships, the wider environment in which the individual acts and all the mutual interrelationships that occur between the individual and the various subsystems. Within this ecosystem, individuals are both influenced by, and influence, their environments through their actions (Johnson and Yanca, 2001; Kondrat, 2002).

Social policies are the means by which states, and the various authorities operating within them, seek to deal with social problems. These policies concern the distribution of societal resources, both material and symbolic, in the social welfare fields and affect the wellbeing of individuals (Weiss-Gal and Gal, 2011). In welfare states, social policies constitute a major part of what governments actually do, are implemented by all the levels of government and by numerous non-governmental entities working on behalf of the state or regulated by it. Typically, the resources devoted to these policies make up about a fifth of all of a society's resources (OECD, 2009). Not surprisingly, then, social policies are a crucial component of the ecosystem in which citizens exist; they can have an enormous impact on communities, families and individuals, and can thus be a means for furthering social justice. Obviously, some policies can help alleviate distress by facilitating better access to resources and services, while others may aggravate existing problems or create new ones. Thus social workers seeking to improve clients' wellbeing will engage in the policy process, either in promoting new policies, changing (or at times defending) existing policies, and fighting new policies that are perceived as detrimental to clients (Jansson, 2008).

Another assumption, which is less explicated in the professional discourse but nevertheless is crucial to a better understanding of why social workers seek to influence policy process, relates to issues of governance, certainly in liberal democracies. Here, the assumption is that the policy process, where social problems are identified, policies are formulated and then implemented, is open to outside influence to a certain degree. As such, social workers (and other individuals and groups) can have an impact on the issues discussed and the policies adopted. Social workers, if in the context of their place of work or in other settings, have opportunities to affect those policies that have an impact on the problems faced by their client groups and that are considered worthy of change.

A final assumption is that social workers have a moral duty to engage in social change and an opportunity to participate in this, but are also uniquely placed to do so. This is because they have a special role in the social policy process. Social workers are often those expected to implement social policies or, at the very least, to coordinate the implementation of them and to identity those eligible for the services and benefits provided by them. More important perhaps, the fact that social workers are faced with situations of oppression, injustice and abuse of rights and are required to deal with the economic disadvantage and cultural disrespect suffered by individuals and families in society as part and parcel of their occupation enables them to have first-hand knowledge of the problems and the needs of clients, and the impact of policies on them (Ellis, 2008).

Given the prevalence of these assumptions and values within social work, it may come as no surprise that influencing social welfare policy is depicted as an important task of social workers in social work Codes of Ethics in various countries (BASW, 2012; ISASW, 1995; NASW,

2008) and in the definitions of social work (CSWE, 2010). Furthermore, the idea that social workers should influence policy is supported by a large number of social work practitioners and scholars around the world, including the US (Figueira-McDonough, 1993; Stuart, 1999; Ezell, 2001; Schneider and Lester, 2001; Pearlmutter, 2002; Haynes and Mickelson, 2003; Jansson et al, 2005; Hoefer, 2006; Jansson, 2008), Australia (Zubrzycki and McArthur, 2004; Gibbons and Gray, 2005), the UK (Dominelli, 2004), South Africa (Mazibuko, 1996), and Israel (Korazim, 1985; Doron, 1989; Weiss-Gal, 2006).

Despite the profession's tradition of involvement in social change and social work's formal commitment to engaging the policy process, until recent decades the social work discourse and the actuality in most national settings tended to delegate the role of involvement in social policy to a small group of social policy experts and to community social workers.

The notion of policy practice

Policy practice, which is the focus of this volume, challenges this traditional distribution of labour within social work. It endeavours to affect the social work discourse and refashion the way in which social workers view their professional role. More specifically, policy practice seeks to reinterpret the very limited existing interpretation of the social work commitment to social justice and social change and to expand it significantly.

The term 'policy practice', first coined by Bruce Jansson (1984), is not new, but until now has been in common use in only limited parts of the world. It has, for the last two decades, been employed by many of the participants in the social work discourse (particularly in the US) on engagement in policy formulation (Rothman and Tropman, 1987; Wyers, 1991; Figueira-McDonough, 1993; Rocha and Johnson, 1997; Pierce, 2000; Saulnier, 2000; Keller et al, 2001; Ellis, 2008; Jansson, 2008). An increasing number of books and articles deal with the normative, theoretical, practical, empirical and educational aspects of policy practice in social work (Holosko and Au, 1996; Haynes and Mickelson, 2003; Jansson et al, 2005; Hoefer, 2006; Figueira-McDonough, 2007; Colby, 2008; Ellis, 2008).

Policy practice refers to

> activities, undertaken by social workers as an integral part
> of their professional activity in diverse fields and types of
> practice, that focus on the formulation and implementation

of new policies, as well as on existing policies and suggested changes in them. These activities seek to further policies on the organizational, local, national and international levels that are in accord with social work values. (Weiss-Gal and Gal, 2011, p 12)

Three primary characteristics of policy practice or class advocacy (as it is sometimes called) can be identified in the literature (Wyers, 1991; Figueira-McDonough, 1993; Pierce, 2000; Hoefer, 2006; Jansson, 2008). First, policy practice refers specifically to activities undertaken within a social worker's professional setting and does not include the voluntary civic involvement of a social worker in other non-professional settings (see the discussion later). As such, secondly, there is general agreement that all social workers, not only a small number of specialists, should and can be involved in policy practice. Regardless of the focus of their professional activities or field of practice (be it direct or indirect practice), all social workers should incorporate this type of practice in their repertoire of intervention strategies. Finally, policy practice seeks to influence social welfare policy at various levels, ranging from social workers' workplaces through the wider community (for example, other agencies and local government) and at national and even international levels. Policy practice seeks to influence policies that are directly relevant to the population groups with which a social worker is engaged; it is perceived as a professional undertaking and does not encompass his or her political participation as an involved citizen.

Policy practice comprises a variety of tasks and strategies. Social workers involved in policy practice will be commonly seeking to engage in agenda setting, problem analysis, policy enacting, policy implementation and policy assessment (Jansson, 2008). They will adopt strategies such as legislative advocacy and lobbying, social action, policy analysis, information dissemination and reform through litigation (Figueira-McDonough, 1993; Haynes and Mickelson, 2003).

Policy practice and other types of social work practice

In order to understand better the contribution of policy practice to the social work discourse and the profession's practice, it is perhaps useful to distinguish this type of practice more explicitly from other practices and intervention strategies common within the social work profession. First, policy practice should be very clearly differentiated from political participation. Political participation is a broad term that encompasses various types of civic political participation on the part of citizens, among them social workers. This participation covers a wide spectrum of activities, ranging from running for political offices, participation in political activities such as demonstrations and rallies, and in election campaigns organised by political parties or movements and on behalf of candidates running for office, financial contributions to political bodies, membership in political parties and simply voting in elections. While social workers can, and clearly should, engage in these types of activities, the crucial difference between political participation broadly defined and policy practice is that the latter term refers only to those activities (included within the wider spectrum of political participation) that are undertaken as an integral part of the social worker's professional activities and directly linked to furthering the welfare of his or her clients. Put simply, policy practice refers to tasks undertaken by social workers who, as part of their professional responsibility, seek to change policies in order to better the lot of their clients. This may take place within the framework of their workplace or outside it, as part of formal or informal activities.

Policy practice should also be distinguished from community social work, which is a distinct field of social work practice in many countries. Though many of the social workers that engage in policy practice tend to be community social workers, the difference between these terms helps better explicate what we mean when we employ the term 'policy practice'. Obviously, policy practice and community social work are very closely linked and there is a degree of overlap between them. This is often true of the professed goals of the two types of practice (such as furthering social change), their underlying values and vision (social justice and democracy), as well as some of the strategies employed by social workers engaging in community social work or policy practice (legislative advocacy and social action). However, the divergences should also be noted. While policy practice identifies social policy change or contribution to policy formulation as its ultimate goal, community social work tends to regard community building or furthering the organising of individuals as its goal. Community social work seeks to develop the capacities of communities and groups, to strength solidarity and to enhance social capital as goals in themselves (Rothman, 2001; Butcher et al, 2007). In the case of policy practice, policy change may derive from community organisation but it may also be due to legislative advocacy, media efforts or litigation carried out by caseworkers with or without the participation of their clients. Similarly, a direct social worker publishing an op-ed article on a policy shortcoming that has a detrimental effect on clients or contacting a legislator to discuss policy issues will be engaging in policy practice though not in community social work. While community solidarity and empowerment are worthy causes and are often crucial in achieving policy change, they are not perceived as necessary conditions for such change in policy practice nor are they the goals of this type of practice.

Social policies affect client groups in a myriad of ways. They determine the types of social welfare services that exist, the way they are run and the access of individuals, families and communities to services and benefits. Social workers devote time and effort to facilitating the access of clients to these services (Weiss-Gal and Gal, 2009). This type of practice has been termed 'case advocacy'. This is defined as practice that seeks to promote clients' access to services, entitlements, benefits and other social rights to which they have a legitimate claim (Hepworth and Larsen, 1993; Bateman, 2000; Schneider and Lester, 2001). It also attempts to ensure the availability and relevance of provided services (Herbert and Mould, 1992) as well as to represent clients' interests (McGowan, 1978). As such, case advocacy is crucial to improving the living standards of clients and providing responses to their needs. While case advocacy links social workers to social policies, it should also be distinguished from policy practice. This is because this type of practice does not seek to change policies or introduce new policies, but only to facilitate access of clients to the services that existing policies have created (Jansson, 2008).

In contrast to political participation, community social work and case advocacy, policy practice is very similar to what is often described as 'social advocacy'. This type of practice is generally described as interventions on behalf of the large groups of individuals who share a common problem or belong to the same social class (Hoefer, 2006). It involves efforts to influence the policies of organisations, local authorities, services and national-level bodies (Hepworth and Larsen, 1993). Such efforts are typically exerted through lobbying, litigation, research, community action, public awareness campaigns, negotiation and persuasion (Litzelfelner and Petr, 1997; Schneider and Lester, 2001; Hoefer, 2006). Despite the obvious similarities between social advocacy and policy practice, the difference lies in what most social workers would regard as a critical and inseparable component of social advocacy, which is the need to involve service users, communities and groups affected by problems and policies in efforts to induce policy change. While policy practice is often undertaken with the participation of service users as a reflection of both good tactics and ethical behaviour, this is not always the case. The notion of policy practice, as distinct from that of social advocacy, implies that any effort on the part of social workers (as part of their professional activities) to affect policy (with or without the cooperation of client groups) is to be encouraged. In short, social advocacy is certainly a form of policy practice but policy practice is a broader term that encompasses engagement in policy change with or without the involvement of clients. As such, social advocacy with its (welcome) emphasis on empowerment and client involvement is not the only form that policy practice can take.

Between vision and practice

One central claim of the policy practice literature has been the observed gap between the discourse that has actively encouraged involvement in policy practice and the actual engagement of social workers in the policy process (Figueira-McDonough, 1993; Reamer, 1993; McInnis-Dittrich, 1994; Jansson et al, 2005). More specifically, it has been claimed that social workers often tend to distance themselves from those arenas in which social policy is formulated (Haynes and Mickelson, 2003). Although the number of studies that have sought actually to study the involvement of social workers in policy formulation as part and parcel of their professional roles is limited, they do appear to lend support to this claim. In Mark Ezell's 1994 study it emerged that while most social workers devoted a number of hours a week to advocacy activities, only 25% of this was devoted to policy practice (termed class advocacy in the article), while the rest was devoted to case advocacy. Also studying social workers in the US, Koeske et al (2005) found that, despite a desire to advocate for social justice and engage in policy development, social workers engaged in policy practice activities very rarely. Weiss-Gal (2008) found that social workers in Israel reported working most at the level of the individual, followed at a considerable distance by the level of the group, the family, the community, the organisation, the couple and, last and at some distance, social policy formation.

Nevertheless, anecdotal data indicate that there is a surge in the policy involvement of social workers in some nations in recent years. In Australia rank-and-file social workers engaged in a successful campaign to defeat a government proposal that would have limited access of low-income earners to mental health services by removing social workers and occupational therapists from eligibility for Medicare. During the first decade of the new millennium, social workers in the US played a major role in the struggle for a livable wage in Nevada through the writing of an influential report on the subject and legislative advocacy (Chandler, 2009). In Israel, front line social workers were dominant in campaigns for revising the qualification conditions for infants with developmental disabilities to access to rehabilitative childcare, community social workers were instrumental in leading a struggle for improved benefits and services for elderly Holocaust survivors, while in recent years social work academics participated in state commissions dealing with policies on the reintegration of welfare recipients into the labor market, the reform of local social services and with state intervention to deal with food insecurity.

This apparent upsurge in policy practice may be linked to contemporary welfare state transformations in these countries, which have had a marked effect on the roles and stature of professionals (Hugman, 1998; Malin, 2000; Farrell and Morris, 2003; Noordegraaf, 2007). In particular, 'New Public Management' has led to professionals, such as doctors, teachers and social workers fulfilling administrative roles. Not surprisingly, social workers have been the subject of much of the literature concerning the impact of welfare state change on professionals (Lymbery, 2000; May and Buck, 2000; Webb, 2006). This is a consequence of the identification of social work with the functions of the welfare state and the fact that these changes, especially in the case of the UK (due to radical changes introduced in community care in that country), have had a negative impact on members of this profession. Yet these developments and others may conceivably also offer new opportunities for professionals, and particularly social workers, to be able to engage in policy formulation rather than only in policy implementation (Alavikko, 2008; Campanini and Fortunato, 2008). As administrators in social services, social workers may play a role in the process by which the nature of services is discussed, access conditions are decided on, priorities identified and the forms of provision and funding are determined. Finally, when they serve as high- or intermediate-level bureaucrats, social workers are clearly directly involved in setting social policies.

At the same time, outsourcing of services and the establishment of quasi-markets has led to a growing role for non-state organisations in social care provision (Grimshaw et al, 2002; Forder et al, 2004). A widening of access to the policy process has provided these organisations with new opportunities to influence social policy formulation (Bode, 2006; Schmid et al, 2008). As these are potential employers of social workers, it can be assumed that they may facilitate enhanced social worker involvement in the social policy formulation process. Similarly, the growing impact of advocacy organisations in the social policy process in different countries (Mendes, 2006; Potting, 2009), offers opportunities for the involvement of social workers in policy formulation. Social workers' unique knowledge and qualifications should provide them with the credentials that enable them to play a major role in this process (Hoefer, 2005; Jansson, 2008).

Our conviction regarding the importance of policy practice within social work and our sense that the conditions for increasing the involvement of social workers in the policy process now exist are the impetus for this volume. It represents an attempt to move the discourse on policy practice beyond the limited confines that have characterised it until now and, for the first time, to undertake a cross-national study of the engagement of social workers in social policy. This should enable us to understand better the nature of involvement of social workers in policy practice and the differences between nations in the types and levels of this involvement.

As such, the aims of the book are to better clarify the notion of policy practice and the role of social workers in formulating and implementing social policy, to describe the role of social workers in social policy formulation and implementation in various countries, to compare the degree to which social workers engage in policy practice and the nature of this type of practice across nations, to explain differences in the engagement of social workers in policy practice across nations and to identify the implications of a cross-national comparison of engagement in policy practice for research and practice. The goal of this volume is to examine the role that social workers play in social policy formulation in different liberal democracies, and the forms and directions that social workers' interventions in social policy take. In doing so, it seeks not only to understand policy practice in social work better but also to move the issue of policy practice to the forefront of social work discourse and practice.

Given that it is impractical to discuss in a single volume the engagement of social workers in policy practice across the globe, this book adopts a middle way between most-similar and most-different comparative analysis approaches. It seeks to focus on countries that share certain similarities. More specifically, all the countries are high-income developed nations with democratic political systems. One major difference between the countries is the nature of the social work profession and its historical development. The assumption here is that the level of engagement in policy practice and its nature is linked to the form that the profession takes in a specific national setting and the way in which it has developed over time. Another obvious difference is the nature of the welfare regimes in the various countries. While this limited number of national case studies clearly cannot do justice to the richness of the profession and does not claim to be representative of the profession globally, it is hoped that the cases described in the following chapters are indicative of distinctive and relevant trends in social work with regard to policy practice. The cases studied in this volume are those of Australia, England, Israel, Italy, Russia, Spain, Sweden and the US.

In each of the chapters that follow, leading experts on social work and the policy engagement of social workers have undertaken country case studies. In each country study, the authors seek to reflect on the following questions: what is the importance of policy practice in the contemporary social work discourse in the country? To what degree, and how, do social workers engage in policy practice in order to influence social policy? Does social work education prepare social work graduates to engage in policy practice, and, if so, in what way? What are the factors that influence social workers' involvement in policy practice, and what are the implications of this? A concluding chapter will offer a synthesis of the findings of the country chapters and their contribution to a cross-national perspective on policy practice.

References

Alavikko, M. (2008) 'Community, identity and "civil society from above": The arrival of individual responsibility and local social policy', in V. Fortunato, G.J. Friesenhaln and E. Kantowicz (eds) *Social Work in Restructured European Welfare Systems*, Rome: Carocci.

Banks, S. (2006) *Ethics and Values in Social Work* (3rd edn), Basingstoke: Palgrave Macmillan.

Barker, R.L.(2003) *The Social Work Dictionary* (5th edn), Washington, DC: NASW Press.

BASW (British Association of Social Workers) (2012) 'Code of Ethics', www.basw.co.uk/codeofethics.

Bateman, N. (2000) *Advocacy Skills for Health and Social Care Professionals*, London: Jessica Kingsley Publishers.

Bode, I. (2006) 'Disorganized welfare mixes: Voluntary agencies and new governance regimes in Western Europe', *Journal of European Social Policy*, vol 16, no 4, pp 346–59.

Butcher, H., Banks, S., Henderson, P. with Robertson, J. (2007) *Critical Community Practice*. Bristol: The Policy Press.

Campanini, A. and Fortunato, V. (2008) 'The role of professional social work in the light of the Italian welfare reform', in V. Fortunato, G.J. Friesenhaln and E. Kantowicz (eds) *Social Work in Restructured European Welfare Systems*, Rome: Carocci.

Chandler, S.K. (2009) 'Working hard, living poor: Social workers and the movement for livable wages', *Journal of Community Practice,* vol 17, pp 170–83.

Colby, I.C. (2008) 'Social welfare policy as a form of social justice', in K.M. Sowers and Dulmus, C.N. (eds) *Comprehensive Handbook of Social Work and Social Welfare*, Hoboken, NJ: Wiley.

Craig, G. (2002) 'Poverty, social work and social justice', *British Journal of Social Work*, vol 32, pp 669–682.

CSWE (Council on Social Work Education) (2010) 'Educational Policy and Accreditation Standards', March, www.cswe.org/File. aspx?id=43974.

Dominelli, L. (2004) *Social Work: Theory and Practice for a Changing Profession*, Cambridge: Polity Press.

Doron, A. (1989) 'The social image of social work', *Society and Welfare*, vol 10, pp 170–78 (in Hebrew).

Ellis, R.A. (2008) 'Policy practice', in K.M. Sowers and C.N. Dulmus (eds) *Comprehensive Handbook of Social Work and Social Welfare, Volume 4: Social Policy and Policy Practice* (volume ed. I.C. Colby), Hoboken, NJ: Wiley.

Ezell, M. (1994) 'Advocacy practice of social workers', *Families in Society*, vol 75, no 1, pp 36–55.

Ezell, M. (2001) *Advocacy in the Human Services*, Belmont, CA: Brooks/ Cole.

Farrell, C. and Morris, J. (2003) 'The "neo-bureaucratic" state: Professionals, managers and professional managers in schools, general practices and social work', *Organisation*, vol 10, no 1, pp 129–56.

Figueira-McDonough, J. (1993) 'Policy practice: The neglected side of social work intervention', *Social Work*, vol 38, pp 179–88.

Figueira-McDonough, J. (2007) *The Welfare State and Social Work*, Thousand Oaks, CA: Sage.

Forder, J., Knapp, M., Hardy, B., Kendall J., Matosevic, T. and Ware, P. (2004) 'Prices, contracts and motivations: Institutional arrangements in domiciliary care', *Policy and Politics*, vol 32, no 2, pp 207–22.

Fraser, N. (1995) 'From redistribution to recognition? Dilemmas of justice in a "post-socialist" age', *New Left Review*, vol 212, pp 68–93.

Gibbons, J. and Gray, M. (2005) 'Teaching social work students about social policy', *Australian Social Work*, vol 58, pp 58–75.

Grimshaw, D., Vincent, S. and Willmott, H. (2002) 'Going privately: Partnerships and outsourcing in UK public services', *Public Administration*, vol 80, no 3, pp 475–502.

Hare, I. (2004) 'Defining social work for the 21st century', *International Social Work*, vol 47, pp 407–24.

Haynes, K.S. and Mickelson, J.S. (2003) *Affecting Change: Social Workers in the Political Arena* (5th edn), Boston, MA: Allyn & Bacon.

Hepworth, D.H. and Larsen, J.A. (1993) *Direct Social Work Practice: Theory and Skills*, Pacific Grove, CA: Brooks/Cole.

Herbert, M.D. and Mould, J.W. (1992) 'The advocacy role in public child welfare', *Child Welfare*, vol 71, pp 114–30.

Hoefer, R. (2005) 'Altering state policy: Interest group effectiveness among state-level advocacy groups', *Social Work*, vol 50, no 3, pp 219–27.

Hoefer, R. (2006) *Advocacy Practice for Social Justice*, Chicago: Lyceum.

Holosko, M.J. and Au, E. (1996) 'Social and public policy analysis: A niche for social work practice', *Journal of Health and Social Policy*, vol 7, no 3, pp 65–73.

Hugman, R. (1998) *Social Welfare and Social Values*, Houndmills: Macmillan.

ISASW (Israeli Association of Social Workers) (1995) *Code of Ethics*, Tel-Aviv: ISASW (in Hebrew).

Jansson, B.S. (1984) *Social Welfare Policy: Analysis, Process, and Current Issues*, Belmont, CA: Wadsworth.

Jansson, B.S. (2008) *Becoming an Effective Policy Advocate: From Policy Practice to Social Justice* (5th edn), Belmont, CA: Thomson, Brooks/Cole Pub.

Jansson, B.S., Dempsey, D., McCroskey, J. and Schneider, R. (2005) 'Four models of policy practice: Local, state, and national arenas', in M. Weil (ed) *Handbook of Community Practice*, Thousand Oaks, CA: Sage, pp 319–38.

Johnson, L.C., and Yanca, S.J. (2001) *Social Work Practice: A Generalist Approach*, Boston, MA: Allyn and Bacon.

Jordan, B. (1990) *Social Work in an Unjust Society*, New York: Harvester Wheatsheaf.

Keller, T.E., Whittaker, J.K. and Burke, T.K. (2001) 'Student debates in policy courses: Promoting policy practice skills and knowledge through active learning', *Journal of Social Work Education*, vol 37, pp 343–55.

Koeske, G.F., Lichtenwalter, S. and Koeske, R.D. (2005) 'Social workers' current and desired involvement in various practice activities: Explorations and implications', *Administration in Social Work*, vol 29, no 2, pp 63–83.

Kondrat, M.E. (2002) 'Actor-centered social work: Re-visioning "person-in-environment" through a critical theory lens', *Social Work*, vol 47, pp 435–48.

Korazim, J. (1985) 'Preparing social workers for advocacy and social warning in an era of resource decline', *Social Security*, vol 27, pp 128–36 (in Hebrew).

Litzelfelner, P. and Petr, C.G. (1997) 'Case advocacy in child welfare', *Social Work*, vol 42, pp 392–402.

Lymbery, M. (2000) 'The retreat from professionalism: From social worker to care manager', in N. Malin (ed) *Professionalism, Boundaries and the Workplace*, London: Routledge.

Lyons, K. (2003) 'Dame Eileen Younghusband (Jan. 1902–May 1981), United Kingdom', *Social Work and Society*, vol 1, no 1, www.socwork. net/sws/article/view/264

McGowan, B.G. (1978) 'The case advocacy function in social work', *Child Welfare*, vol 57, pp 275–84.

McInnis-Dittrich, K. (1994) *Integrating Social Welfare Policy and Social Work Practice*, Pacific Grove, CA: Brooks/Cole.

Malin, N. (2000) 'Professionalism and boundaries of the formal sector: The example of social and community care', in N. Malin (ed) *Professionalism, Boundaries and the Workplace*, London: Routledge.

Marsh, J.C. (2005) 'Social justice: Social work's organizing value', *Social Work*, vol 50, no 4, pp 293–4.

May T. and Buck, M. (2000) 'Social work, professionalism and the rationality of organisational change', in N. Malin (ed) *Professionalism, Boundaries and the Workplace*, London: Routledge.

Mazibuko, F.N.M. (1996) 'Social workers and social policy', *Social Work/ Maatskaplike Werk*, vol 32, pp 148–61.

Mendes, P. (2003) 'Social workers and social action: A case study of the Australian Association of Social Workers Victorian Branch', *Australian Social Work*, vol 56, pp 6–27.

Mendes, P. (2006) 'Welfare lobby groups responding to globalization: A case study of the Australian Council of Social Service (ACSS)', *International Social Work*, vol 49, no 6, pp 693–704.

NASW (National Association of Social Workers) (2008) *Code of Ethics*, Washington, DC: NASW.

Noordegraaf, M. (2007) 'From "pure" to "hybrid" professionalism', *Administration & Society*, vol 39, no 6, pp 761–85.

OECD (2009) *How Expensive is the Welfare State? Gross and Net Indicators in the OECD Social Expenditure Database (SOCX)*, Paris: OECD.

Pearlmutter, S. (2002) 'Achieving political practice: Intergrating individual need and social action', *Journal of Progressive Human Services*, vol 13, pp 31–51.

Pierce, D. (2000). 'Policy practice', in J. Midgley, M.B. Tracy and M. Livermore (eds) *The Handbook of Social Policy*, Thousand Oaks, CA: Sage

Potting, M. (2009) 'Changing social responsibilities: The role of advocacy organisations in the construction of the Social Support Act in the Netherlands', *European Journal of Social Work*, vol 12, no 2, pp 169–83.

Reamer, F.G. (1993) 'From the editor: Near and farsightedness in social work education', *Journal of Social Work Education*, vol 29, pp 3–5.

Reisch, M. (2002) 'Defining social justice in a socially unjust world', *Families in Society*, vol 83, pp 343–54.

Reisch, M. and Andrews, J. (2001) *The Road not Taken. A History of Radical Social Work in the United States*, Philadelphia: Brunner-Routledge.

Rocha, C.J. and Johnson, A.K. (1997) 'Teaching family policy through a policy practice framework', *Journal of Social Work Education*, vol 33, pp 433–44.

Rothman, J. (2001) 'Approaches to community intervention', in J. Rothman, J.L. Erlich and J.E. Tropman (eds) *Strategies of Community Intervention* (6th edn), Belmont, CA: Thompson.

Rothman, J. and Tropman, J.E. (1987) 'Models of community organization and macro practice perspectives: Their mixing and phasing', in F.M Cox, J.L. Erlich, J. Rothman and J.E. Tropman (eds) *Macro Practice: Strategies of Community Organization* (4th edn), Itasca, IL: F.E. Peacock Publishers.

Saulnier, C.F. (2000) 'Policy practice: Training direct service social workers to get involved', *Journal of Teaching in Social Work*, vol 20, pp 121–44.

Schmid, H., Bar, M. and Nirel, N. (2008) 'Advocacy roles of nonprofit human service organizations: Implications for policy', *Nonprofit and Voluntary Sector Quarterly*, vol 37, no 4, pp 581–602.

Schneider, R.L. and Lester, L. (2001) *Social Work Advocacy: A New Framework for Action*, Belmont, CA: Brooks/Cole.

Stuart, P.H. (1999) 'Linking clients and policy: Social work's distinctive contribution', *Social Work*, vol 44, pp 335–47.

Trattner, W.I. (1984) *From Poor Law to Welfare State: A History of Social Welfare in America* (3rd edn), New York: The Free Press.

Webb, S.A. (2006) *Social Work in a Risk Society*, Houndmills: Palgrave Macmillan.

Weiss-Gal, I. (2006) 'Policy practice in social work: A conceptual framework for action', *Society & Welfare*, vol 26, pp 445–78 (in Hebrew).

Weiss-Gal, I. (2008) 'The person-in-environment approach: Professional ideology and practice of social workers in Israel', *Social Work*, vol 53, pp 65–75.

Weiss-Gal, I. and Gal, J. (2009) 'Realizing rights in social work', *Social Service Review*, vol 83, pp 267–92.

Weiss-Gal, I. and Gal, J. (2011) *Policy Practice in Social Work*, Jerusalem: Magnes (in Hebrew).

Wyers, N.L. (1991) 'Policy practice in social work: Models and issues', *Journal of Social Work Education*, vol 27, pp 241–50.

Zubrzycki, J. and McArthur, M. (2004) 'Preparing social work students for policy practice: An Australian example', *Social Work Education*, vol 23, pp 451–64.

TWO

Social workers affecting social policy in Australia[1]

Philip Mendes

The Australian welfare state

The Australian welfare state has always been largely a 'residual' welfare state based on the targeted direction of means-tested payments to the poor and disadvantaged. Welfare programmes have generally involved a combination of public funding and private provision. This mixed economy of welfare includes Commonwealth, state and local governments; private employers providing wages and superannuation; the market or private sector that is involved in the commercial provision of services such as health, education and housing; voluntary agencies; and the informal sector where care is provided by families and individuals. In practice, voluntary agencies, including church groups and other private charities, have historically played a central role in the provision of health services and other social programmes (McDonald, 2000; Bryson and Verity, 2009).

The Commonwealth government takes responsibility for all income security, but the state and territory governments retain responsibility for indigenous peoples and most forms of social welfare service delivery including education, health, and housing and community services (Bryson and Verity, 2009). There is considerable regional variation in these welfare frameworks, as is reflected in the case of child and youth welfare especially.

At the national level, Australia developed a unique welfare state model which concerned itself primarily with the protection of wage levels (at least for white male breadwinners), rather than the provision of supplementary welfare benefits. Castles (1985) called this model a 'wage earners' welfare state and contrasted it with both a residual model of welfare (because Australia had a relatively generous minimum living wage) and the institutional model of welfare (because full inclusion in the system depended on one's status as a wage earner rather than one's status as a citizen).

Australia spent $90 billion on welfare payments and services in 2005–6, which is the equivalent of 66.49 billion euros. This figure included expenditure by governments, non-government community services organisations and households. Of the total, $61 billion was social security benefits and other cash payments while the other $29 billion was expenditure on the provision of welfare services. The largest overall share of spending went to older people ($34 billion), followed by families and children ($27 billion) and people with disabilities ($17 billion) (AIHW, 2007).

Australia possesses one of the most selective income support systems in the Western industrialised world. Financial assistance is provided on a flat-rate basis, funded from general revenue rather than via insurance schemes. Welfare programmes are mostly means tested, targeted to the poor, and are low in monetary value, at about 25% of average weekly earnings (Mendes, 2008a). Consequently, international commentators such as Gøsta Esping-Andersen (1990) have often described the Australian welfare state as a residual or liberal welfare state typified by low levels of welfare spending and minimum interference with the free market or decommodification.

However, some writers have contested this assumed link between greater social expenditure and income redistribution. They argue that the Australian model is both effective and egalitarian. It is effective because its careful targeting of benefits to particular needy groups maximises the reduction in poverty attained by any given expenditure. Australia appears to be more successful than any other OECD country in redistributing income to the poorest 20% of the population. For example, the poorest group receives more than 12 times as much in income security benefits as the wealthiest group. It is egalitarian because its historical focus on the rights of wage earners and full employment has ensured a relatively low level of 'working poor' people (Castles and Mitchell, 1992; Castles, 2010; Whiteford, 2006, 2010).

Nevertheless, the conservative Liberal–National coalition government, which governed Australia from 1996 to 2007, constructed a new public debate about the welfare system and welfare recipients, based on narrow notions of individualism and self-reliance. There was no longer any serious discussion about the collective obligation of the state and community to defend the rights of poor and disadvantaged people, or about the specific role of the welfare system in promoting greater equity. Rather, income security payments were increasingly viewed as a means of social control designed to integrate recipients within the frameworks and values of the free market. Cuts to wages and welfare were synchronised, with the aim of producing more work and less welfare (Mendes, 2009a).

The centre-Left Australian Labor Party (ALP), which has held power since late 2007, has only partly reversed this free market trend. Certainly, the ALP has pursued a social inclusion agenda aimed at promoting the participation of particularly disadvantaged groups. This holistic agenda recognises that disadvantage is caused by a complex interaction of structural, local community and individual factors, and differs from the former coalition government's primary emphasis on individual responsibility. The government has significantly increased the level of social investment in a number of key areas such as homelessness and Indigenous affairs.

However, the ALP government's application of social inclusion principles still appears to be inconsistent and unduly limited by political and budgetary considerations. While it has rightly recognised that older pensioners and carers need additional resources to participate in society, it has failed to apply the same assumptions to sole parents and unemployed people. The government has also retained and even extended the compulsory income management scheme introduced by the former government in a number of disadvantaged communities (Mendes, 2009b).

The social work profession and its education structure

The Australian social work profession first emerged in the late 1920s and early 1930s as a by-product of state welfare service expansion. Hospital social work was initially predominant, followed by the employment of some non-medical social workers in non-government agencies. The professional association – the Australian Association of Social Workers (AASW) – was established on a national basis in 1946 (Lawrence, 1965).

Early Australian social work was strongly influenced by the psychoanalytic tradition emanating from Great Britain and the US. There was a particular emphasis on casework at the expense of alternative methods such as social and community development. Some critical views emerged in local social work education in the late 1950s and early 1960s involving the identification of structural causes of social problems and the use of sociological techniques in research. These ideas were quickly suppressed by the popular *Bulletin* magazine's McCarthyist attack on alleged communist influence in the Melbourne University

Social Studies Department. The attack also discouraged social work involvement in broader social reform activities (Mendes, 2009c).

Australian social workers were later influenced in part by the radical (often Marxist) critiques of social work that emerged in the mid-1970s. But it took until the 1980s for a growing feminist consciousness to develop among Australian female social workers concerning their own career opportunities and broader patriarchal influences on social welfare policies and social work practice. This consciousness resulted in the formation of a national caucus of the Australian Association for Social Work and Welfare Education, called Women in Welfare Education, which addressed issues of specific concern to women (Weeks, 2000).

Over time, Australian social workers, influenced by socialist and feminist assumptions, developed a number of practice-based approaches to critical social work theory and practice. The critical perspective was characterised by two major themes: the structural basis of personal and social problems and an awareness that problems are not amenable to individual, family or subcultural solutions; and the need to work at both personal (through individual consciousness raising that connects private troubles with structural sources) and political levels to challenge oppressive and inequitable structures. In recent years, critical social work approaches have integrated older modernist forms of structural analysis and newer postmodern ideas which emphasise more diverse sources of power and emancipation (Mendes, 2009c).

Australian authors appear to have made a significant contribution to the history and development of critical social work theory and practice. However, the specific contribution of critical social work approaches to Australian social work practice is less evident, and it appears that most Australian social workers favour conventional rather than critical practice models (Payne, 2005; Mendes, 2009c).

Social work is not a numerically significant profession in Australia. Over 1,800 social workers graduate every year from the 28 university schools of social work, either via the Bachelor of Social Work which involves four years of full-time study, or the relatively new Master of Social Work qualifying programmes, which require five years of study. However, there are only 17,000 Australians working in specific social work positions, although a significant minority of the 53,000 Australians employed in welfare, community work or counsellor positions may have social work training. They constitute only a small proportion of the nearly 300,000 Australians who work in the community services sector (AIHW, 2007, 2010; Healy and Lonne, 2010).

Social workers are employed in virtually all fields of welfare practice, including child and youth welfare, care for older people, housing, criminal justice, immigration and refugee support, mental health, drug and alcohol and disability. Only two organisations continue to use social workers exclusively to provide front line welfare services: public hospitals and Centrelink, the Commonwealth agency that provides all income security payments (Fitzgibbon, 2000). In addition, somewhere between 5% and 10% of social workers work in private practice. Most social workers are employed in generic positions such as child protection and support for disabled people, and are not specifically identified as social workers. It is often difficult to segregate the practice activities of these social workers from other workers employed under similar job titles.

Social work in Australia is not a registered profession with legal professional boundaries, in contrast to both the mandatory registration of social work in most English-speaking countries and the registration of most other allied health professions in Australia. All social work graduates are eligible to join the AASW, but many elect not to join because membership is not a requirement for professional practice. Consequently, the AASW has only about 6,500 members, which is estimated to be about 30% of eligible social workers. This relatively small membership appears to have negative implications in terms of the social work profession's profile and influence (Lonne and Duke, 2009; Cintio, 2010; Lonne, 2010).

The AASW has formed a National Registration Committee to pursue registration, and has argued that registration and protection of the title of social workers is necessary to protect the interests, physical safety and wellbeing of service users. But the AASW has acknowledged that gaining registration is likely to be a lengthy, complex and difficult process in the current political environment. In the interim, the AASW has introduced a Continuing Professional Education (CPE) policy, which enables members to attain professional accreditation if they choose to do so. As we shall see later, this CPE policy has been influential in assisting mental health social workers to gain recognition by government health bodies (Cumming, 2010; Kent, 2010).

Australian attitudes towards social work tend to be ambivalent, with the profession having a low profile and sometimes evoking considerable public hostility (Friedewald, 2009). In earlier years, most censure came from the Marxist Left, which constructed social workers as social control agents involved in intrusive and moralising investigations of low-income and working-class people. In recent years, conservative attacks have been more influential. Social workers have been accused of undermining traditional social values and morality, and of promoting subversive theories and gay and lesbian rights. Social workers employed in child protection are particular targets of public criticism. They are labelled as bungling and incompetent fools or wimps when they do not act decisively enough to protect children from abusive caregivers, and alternatively as zealots or child-stealing bullies when they remove children too hastily (Mendes, 2001, 2008b).

Professional social work discourse on social policy

All the official statements of the AASW endorse the involvement of social workers in policy practice and define policy advocacy as a core professional requirement. The AASW Practice Standards define social policy as one of the six core areas of social work practice. Practitioners are required to analyse, challenge and develop social policies in order to promote a fairer and more socially just society. Policy practice includes participation in policy debates concerning social work services and bodies, government and non-government service providers and in broader public policy discourse about social justice and human rights (AASW, 2003).

The Practice Standards also inform the AASW Education and Accreditation Standards that identify 'policy development, implementation and change' as one of the six required areas of practice. Graduates are expected to be able to 'apply social work knowledge and skills to identify inappropriate or inequitable policy goals and outcomes, and to promote and implement policy which achieves equity and effective distribution of social resources' (AASW, 2010a, pp 8, 10).

Similarly, the AASW Code of Ethics affirms one of the key aims of social work as being the promotion of human rights and social justice through social and systemic change and advocacy. This is to be achieved by 'promoting policies and practices that achieve a fair allocation of social resources' (AASW, 2010b, p 8). The AASW CPE policy also recommends the involvement of social workers in policy practice to promote social justice and human rights (AASW, 2002).

In addition, the AASW National Social Policy Committee (NSPC), formed originally in 1998 and revamped in 2006, has been active in promoting an activist social policy agenda within the social work profession. The NSPC is involved in making submissions to government inquiries, issuing media releases, developing position statements in areas such as child protection, housing, mental health and Indigenous affairs, establishing partnerships with other stakeholders such as peak welfare advocacy groups and schools of social work, motivating social workers to get involved in policy debates and advancing the capacity of the AASW to provide an informed and effective voice on social policy (Cheron-Sauer, 2008).

The question here is whether the practice matches the rhetoric. There is no doubt that some Australian social workers are involved in social and political activism both within the formal structures of political parties or professional associations, and as everyday practice in local agencies, neighbourhoods and communities. We will detail some specific examples later in this chapter.

Equally, though, many (perhaps most) social workers do not participate in policy activities and appear to believe that policy activism is incompatible with professional practice (Mendes, 2008a). For example, most of the leading Australian social work texts contain few if any specific chapters on policy practice. It is also noticeable that the last two CPE calendars for the largest AASW branch – that of Victoria – do not offer any training on social policy issues (Kent, 2010).

Education and training in policy practice

The AASW is responsible for accrediting all social work degrees in Australia. The AASW Education and Accreditation Standards (2010a) identify social policy analysis and development as a core component of social work practice. As a result, all 28 schools of social work are obliged to include policy practice as a mandatory subject. For example, at Monash University, the Bachelor of Social Work requires all students to complete both the Social Policy and Social Justice I and Social Policy and Social Justice II subjects.

The objectives of the first subject are:

• to enable students to understand the meaning and nature of social policy, and describe the ways it can be understood from different theoretical and practical points of view;
• to introduce students to the way political parties deal with policy issues, and to enable them to describe the key trends and philosophies underlying the positions of major political parties;
• to enable students to describe key theories and ideological perspectives in social policy, to apply these to selected fields and to learn how understanding different policy perspectives helps both to explain the nature of current policies and to increase the options for policy development and change;
• to enable students to understand the link between social policy and the goals and values of social work;

- to provide students with an understanding of the impact of social structure and social policy on welfare service users;
- to enable students to implement social policy interventions in their everyday social work practice. In particular, to adhere to the AASW Practice Standards for Social Workers, which require social workers to 'promote and implement policies and practices which would achieve a fair, equitable and effective allocation of social resources; and identify inappropriate or inequitable policy goals and outcomes'.

The objectives of the second subject are:

- to enable students to develop an informed understanding of Marxist, feminist, neo-liberal and other ideological critiques of the welfare state and their implications for particular policy areas;
- to develop student understanding of the role, strategies and effectiveness of a range of lobby groups in social policy debates;
- to enable students to understand the link between local and global welfare trends;
- to provide students with an understanding of social work's specific role in policy practice and advocacy. Students should be able to meet the standards outlined in the AASW Practice Standards for Social Workers, particularly including the capacity to analyse and critique existing policies drawing on social work practice, knowledge, experience, values, ethics and principles.

The topics covered in the first subject include political ideologies and the welfare state, the historical and political development of the Australian welfare state, frameworks for analysing social policy – including a case study of young people transitioning from out-of-home care – Indigenous social policy, case study of homelessness policy, the social policy of the Liberal Party, and the social policy of the Labor Party and Greens. The topics covered in the second subject include Marxist and other progressive critiques of the welfare state, the neo-liberal critique of the welfare state, globalisation and welfare states, the welfare lobby via a case study of the peak advocacy group, the Australian Council of Social Service, the churches and social justice, and the AASW and social action (For an earlier summary of Monash subjects, see Mendes, 2003a).

However, the form and extent of social policy education appear to vary considerably across the schools of social work. A study by Pawar (2004) surveyed the social policy subject objectives, topics, common themes, textbooks and learning and assessment methods of 15 Australian social work schools. He found that a number of factors, either positive or limiting, influenced whether schools offered what he called an 'effective' or 'ineffective' social policy curriculum.

Specific positive factors identified were: applying social work's core mission and objectives; adding new textbooks and reading material; consulting with interest groups or seeking peer advice; linking social policy with other forms of social work practice; and adopting active learner-centred teaching and assessment methods. Conversely, the limiting factors identified were: the uncritical adoption of prior curriculum; learning by trial and error; failing to integrate the subject with other social work subjects; and using passive teaching and assessment methods not linked to actual practice. Pawar concluded that the greater or lesser influence of positive or limiting factors was linked to whether or not the subject coordinators had an informed background, their level of interest and motivation concerning the subject, their ability to present a range of ideologies and philosophies to students and the coordinators' capacity for creative thinking.

A couple of other practical reasons have been advanced to explain why social policy may sit on the periphery of some (or perhaps even most) social work courses in Australia. Firstly, most social policy subjects are taught separately from social work theory and practice subjects. This distinction appears to leave social work students with the impression that social policy is simply about theoretical knowledge, without any need for practical application. Few students, for example, complete their fieldwork practicums in social policy agencies, although this decision probably also reflects the popular view that social work employment is to be found in direct practice rather than in broader policy work.

Secondly, the AASW does not require social policy to be taught by qualified social workers, or even by lecturers with some direct practice experience in social policy activities. This leaves open the possibility of social policy subjects being taught in a highly dry and theoretical manner by armchair theorists with little practice-based application (Ife, 1997; Mendes, 2003a). While many social policy lecturers obviously do not fit this generalisation, some graduates have described social policy subjects as boring and irrelevant (Dellidis and Hanlon, 1991).

Two particular initiatives appear necessary to address these deficits in social policy skill development. Firstly, there needs to be greater integration between social policy and the social work theory and practice subjects. At the very least, interpersonal practice subjects should incorporate examples of social policy interventions in small group skills sessions. In addition, there needs to be greater emphasis in social policy subjects on the utilisation of social policy skills within traditional direct practice settings. Secondly, there needs to be a greater opportunity for students to implement their social policy skills in the real world. This could particularly occur via greater access to field practicums in the social policy field (Mendes, 2003a).

Involvement of social workers in policy practice

There has been no systematic analysis of involvement by Australian social workers in policy practice similar to that conducted in other jurisdictions (Ramon, 2008; O'Brien, 2010). However, two discrete studies have examined the specific role of the AASW in policy activism. These studies suggest that the AASW has consistently espoused a rhetorical commitment to promoting more equitable social policy outcomes, but that its actions have often failed to live up to the rhetoric.

Mendes (2003b) explored the social action history of the Victoria branch of the AASW from 1932 to 2000. He argued that historically the AASW had a strong commitment (at least in principle) to social action, but that in practice the branch had often failed to meet its stated objectives. Social activism was minimal until 1965, but reached a high point over the next decade, including significant involvement in a successful campaign for improved health insurance and a number of other policy initiatives. However, the formation in 1975 of the Australian Social Welfare Union as a trade union for all social welfare workers, rather than just social workers, split the AASW and precipitated a gradual decline in activism. From 1985 onwards there was – with minor exceptions – little organised branch commitment to social action or reform.

Similarly, Gillingham (2007) analysed the social policy initiatives of the national AASW and some of the state and territory branches from approximately 2002 to 2006. He found evidence of numerous activities, including submissions to government inquiries, letters to ministers, networking and partnerships with other welfare bodies and the development of position papers. Policy areas covered included income security and welfare reform, poverty, mental health, anti-terrorism legislation and child custody arrangements in the event of family separation. However, it was apparent that a number of factors – among them the AASW's relatively small membership – limited the efficacy of these activities, and that social policy was not a high priority for the association.

A report by the AASW National Social Policy Committee convenor (Cheron-Sauer, 2008) provided a good summary of AASW policy activities from 2006 to 2008. She cited a number of activities, including:

submissions to government inquiries on drugs, mental health, child protection, domestic violence, housing, healthcare and Indigenous issues; participation in policy forums on housing and climate change; collaborative work with state and territory branches on Indigenous, child protection and domestic violence policy; co-hosting a welfare to work round table and collecting case studies from social work practice on the limitations of welfare reform; and the development of position statements in a range of areas. She admitted that the committee had commenced from a low base and suggested that it was still developing the processes, procedures and expertise (both in terms of utilising experts within the membership and employing experienced paid staff) required to have an effective impact on policy debates.

An informal overview of the AASW *National Bulletin* for the last two years by the author suggests a growing and more influential engagement by the association with social policy debates. Examples of activities included the formation of an AASW Aboriginal and Torres Strait Islander Working Group to promote Indigenous voices and perspectives within the AASW, opposition to the introduction of compulsory income management for some income security recipients, advocacy for improved support services for homeless people, support for the Australian Services Union campaign for better wages/equal pay for non-government community services workers, commentary on child protection policies – including workforce issues in particular – and the preparation of position papers on domestic and family violence and disability. Strategies implemented included issuing media releases and interviews, writing letters to ministers, participating in the Equal Pay public rally, providing evidence to a Queensland wage hearing for non-government workers, and making submissions to government inquiries into rural and remote Indigenous communities, disability, child protection and human rights (AASW, 2009–10).

There is also evidence of involvement by rank-and-file Australian social workers in social and political activism. Some of this has occurred within the formal structure of political parties, but much activism has also taken place as an everyday practice within local agencies, neighbourhoods and communities. Examples include advocacy on behalf of groups of clients within certain agencies, research projects designed to demonstrate the unmet needs of disadvantaged groups, the resourcing and facilitating of community groups and campaigns, local activities to support Indigenous Australians and asylum seekers, participation in peak welfare lobby groups such as the Australian Council of Social Service and the associated State and Territory Councils of Social Service, and involvement in broader social change activities such as local and national electoral politics and global campaigns for human rights (Ife, 1997; Weeks and Quinn, 2000; Gray et al, 2002; Fraser and Briskman, 2005; Mendes, 2005; Harms et al, 2008).

However, much of the existing literature focuses on the details of the social activism rather than links with social work per se. One small-scale purposive study of 10 activist social workers attempted to address this gap in knowledge by examining the extent to which social work education, values, skills and identity were utilised in the subjects' social activism. All were experienced social workers working in senior or management positions based in the inner-city suburbs of Melbourne and were employed by non-government or semi-independent agencies.

The study provided examples of social work activism in areas such as opposing racism, empowering sole mothers raising boys, refugee advocacy, opposing physical discipline of children, adoption law reform, gun control, women's refuges, supporting adequate funding of foster care and family support services, ethnic mental health services and dental health services. The strategies employed included submissions to government and legal advocacy, involvement in a federal election campaign, participation in a government committee, research, public and media advocacy, community development regarding the social inclusion of disadvantaged groups in the local neighbourhood and the formation of a support group for sole mothers.

The study's findings suggested that personal background, experiences and beliefs play a key role in promoting the involvement of social workers in social justice activism. For most of the interviewees, their social work education primarily reinforced their existing beliefs and values. Equally, social work values, skills and identity tended to complement rather than shape their activist commitment.

Other key factors that enhanced their social activism appeared to include working in senior or management positions that permitted considerable practice autonomy, provision of support from the employing agency, a belief that social action is a core requirement of social work practice, a commitment to a broad social justice agenda that transcends social work practice per se, and a greater engagement with broader social and political movements than with specific professional social work structures and networks. Unfortunately, this study did not investigate the policy practice of social workers based in rural or regional locations, those who work in less senior or less high-profile positions, or those who work for statutory government agencies (Mendes, 2007).

Case studies of social workers in policy practice and its contribution to social policy development

This section presents two specific examples of Australian social workers influencing social policy. The first example involved a campaign by the Australian Council of Heads of Schools of Social Work (ACHSSW) assisted by a number of rank-and-file social work practitioners and students to contest Australian government policies concerning the rights of refugees seeking asylum. Australia's policy of mandatory detention for on-shore asylum seekers has been widely criticised, particularly for the way in which it was universally applied to children. It was only in June 2005 that Australian legislation changed, and unaccompanied children and young people are no longer being automatically detained, but the option is still available as a matter of last resort.

The campaign was motivated by the social work commitment to social justice and human rights as reflected in both national and international Codes of Ethics (Briskman et al, 2009; Briskman and Fiske, 2009). The ACHSSW initiated a citizen-driven People's Inquiry into Detention in order to expose the abuses of long-term detention and place the stories (and suffering) of those in detention on the public record. The terms of reference included the question of the accountability of detention policies and practices to government and the community, concerns about the wellbeing and mental health of detainees, deportation methods and outcomes, and consideration of the efficacy of alternative policies and methods. Volunteers from a wide range of backgrounds, including social work, law, media and mental health, assisted with the inquiry. Assistance was also provided by a large number of students from social work and other disciplines who undertook field placements or internships. Funding was provided by a number of organisations, among them the AASW.

The inquiry consisted of public hearings and of written submissions. The hearings took place in 10 different cities and towns, and over 200 people testified, including asylum seekers and refugees, lawyers, a range of health professionals, migration agents and refugee advocates and activists. In addition, about 200 people contributed written submissions. The first report of the inquiry, *We've Boundless Plains to Share* (ACHSSW, 2006), was released at a national social work conference in Perth. This report analysed the evidence given to the inquiry about boat journeys to Australia and the detention experience, and presented terrible stories concerning assaults in detention facilities, poor levels of healthcare and a number of deaths (Briskman and Goddard, 2007).

The final report was released as a book in early 2008 with a preface from Professor Margaret Alston, head of the ACHSSW (Briskman et al, 2008). Launches were held in four cities, and the book received the prestigious Australian Human Rights Commission literature award (Briskman et al, 2009).

The second example involved the campaign led by the AASW that included rank-and-file social workers to restore the government Medicare rebate for accredited mental health social workers under the Better Access to Mental Health care programme. This rebate had been available to approximately 1,100 mental health social workers in private practice and their clients since 2006 (plus occupational therapists and psychologists) as a means of encouraging the provision of preventive healthcare to those with high-prevalence mental health disorders such as anxiety, depression and post-traumatic stress disorders. Of the users of mental health social work services 37% live in rural and regional areas, and at least half of the total appear to be living on low incomes and would not be able to afford services without Medicare funding (Charikar, 2010; Lonne and Allen-Kelly, 2010).

However, in May 2010, the AASW was suddenly informed by the Commonwealth Department of Health and Ageing – without any prior consultation – that the rebate would be withdrawn from social workers and occupational therapists in the July 2010 budget. The only explanation given was a concern to reduce costs, and to divert resources to people with the most severe mental health disorders via flexible care packages. This was despite the fact that social work mental health services had cost less than $9 million in 2008–9 out of a total budget of a $666 million, and the proposed savings would involve only 4% of the Better Access programme budget (AIHW, 2009).

The announcement of this decision provoked considerable shock and anger among many AASW members since its implementation would have meant a severe reduction in the income of accredited mental health social workers (AASW, 2010c). The AASW immediately launched a public campaign to have this decision reversed. The campaign involved a number of different strategies, including: attaining the public support of prominent mental health experts such as Professor Pat McGorry, the Australian of the Year, and various general practitioners, psychologists, psychiatrists and non-government mental health and community services groups; issuing media releases and briefing journalists; having meetings with prominent members of parliament including ministers, shadow ministers and Greens senators and their advisers, plus sending letters to every single member of parliament; empowering large numbers of mental health social workers and some service users to share their stories of effective and accessible practice interventions; and informing the general public of the potentially detrimental impact on service users who were low earners and/or living in rural and remote areas and who would otherwise be unable to afford or access services due to the absence of alternative service providers or the higher fees charged by psychologists (Allen-Kelly and Charikar, 2010; Evans, 2010).

The AASW was able to use new social networking methods, including a regular e-bulletin to provide all 6,500 members with information and resources such as briefing fact sheets and draft letters to initiate their own advocacy activities. The campaign produced a number of positive outputs: there were over 1,000 individual letters by AASW members to the minister providing numerous case studies, a petition was launched by a general practitioner which gained several thousand signatures, supportive speeches were made by 10 members of parliament and there were extensive print and broadcast media reports (AASW, 2010c; Allen-Kelly, 2010a)

The campaign had an initial success in May 2010 when the minister apologised for the poor treatment of social workers, and promised a full and transparent consultation process. She offered the AASW a seat on both the steering committee for the ongoing evaluation of the Better Access programme and the expert advisory committee for the Access to Allied Psychological Services (ATAPS) programmes that assist people with chronic mental health conditions, and agreed to defer the proposed budget measure until April 2011.

The minister also organised a full-day meeting by the Department of Health and Ageing with 35 social workers chosen by the AASW, consisting of accredited mental health social workers, members working in ATAPS, social work mental health researchers and 15 occupational therapists. Social workers used this meeting to share information about the particular skills, intervention strategies, knowledge and experience they contribute to the Better Access programme, and the potential negative impact of the proposed changes on their clients and local communities (AASW, 2010d; Addinsall, 2010; Allen-Kelly, 2010b; 2010c; Creswell, 2010; Sommerville, 2010).

The ultimate success came in November 2010 when the government announced a complete reversal of the original decision, and committed to working with the AASW to deliver high quality mental healthcare services (Allen-Kelly, 2010d; Roxon and Butler, 2010).

Factors which enhance or impede social work involvement in policy practice

There are a number of institutional factors that may encourage Australian social workers to engage in policy debates. The first is the AASW's formal recognition of policy action as a core practice requirement which sends a clear message that policy practice is a legitimate and expected component of a professional social work career. The second factor is the compulsory social policy education that is provided in all Australian social work courses. This education should provide graduates with the necessary skills and knowledge to participate in policy action effectively.

It is evident from our small study of activist social workers that these factors do assist social workers to participate in policy action. A number of the interviewees argued that their activism had been positively influenced by their social work education and values. They referred to the person-in-environment approach of social workers, which enabled them to link private problems with a broader social context, and also the detailed training they had received in social change strategies (Mendes, 2007). It is also evident from the two case studies detailed earlier concerning refugees and mental health rebates that social workers can be very effective leaders of social policy debates and campaigns.

A third positive factor is that the AASW has recently invested serious resources in developing quality staff and technological infrastructure support that will enhance the potential for effective policy action. The success of the mental health rebate campaign suggests that the AASW is now able to lead policy action initiatives and actively facilitate the involvement of ordinary social workers, including their practice experiences and case studies in these activities.

However, many (perhaps most) Australian social workers do not participate in policy activism. There are a number of factors which appear to pose barriers to social work activism. One inhibiting factor may be public sector and other workplace constraints. Many social workers are employed by government departments or government-funded agencies, and may be restricted from speaking out against government policies (Gillingham, 2007). This problem has in the past extended to the AASW, which has often selected leaders at a state and national level that were employed by public sector agencies, and hence unable to express critical views in the public sphere. The AASW is currently headed by an academic who is a forceful public commentator on social policy issues, but is willing on most occasions to delegate public representation to the AASW CEO. It is important that the AASW continues to select spokespersons – either elected presidents or paid officers – who are able to speak freely and effectively to a wider audience as well as to mobilise the AASW membership (Mendes, 2003b).

Another negative factor – as previously noted – can be social work education. Although all Australian social work courses offer social policy units, many do not appear to prepare graduates effectively to implement social action objectives within their everyday practice. It is important that social policy teachers be required to have direct practice experience in social policy activities and are able to offer practice-based as well as theoretical content (Mendes, 2003b).

Similarly, narrow definitions of professionalism that emphasise the development of clinical therapeutic interventions with individuals at the expense of broader systemic approaches may inhibit involvement in policy practice. The AASW should highlight the need for more of its CPE policy training providers to address social policy issues specifically.

A further problematic factor is the ambiguous language contained in the professional Code of Ethics. The Australian code (AASW, 2010b) professes a formal commitment to the promotion of social justice and suggests that social workers have a responsibility to advocate on behalf of service users and to oppose structural inequity and injustice. But the code provides no concrete case examples to illuminate the meaning of social justice or injustice in policy issues commonly experienced by social workers, nor does it recommend any specific strategies that social workers should use to promote social justice in various policy areas. In addition, the code provides little or no guidance to activist social workers confronting tensions between legislative or organisational directives and broader moral and ethical questions. The code is silent on the legitimacy of direct action interventions such as civil disobedience (Briskman and Noble, 1999).

Policy practice in the future

The evidence presented here suggests that Australian social workers are also following the global trend of greater engagement with policy practice. However, the two case studies cited suggest that policy activism is principally apparent in two areas.

The first area is issues which tend to hold national and indeed international political symbolism and happen to integrate closely with social work values. These issues include, most notably, defending the rights of refugees and asylum seekers, closing the gap for Indigenous Australians and addressing the impact of climate change (McKinnon,

2008). I would expect to see increasing social work involvement in these policy debates. Conversely, it remains surprising that so few social workers have been active in other social policy debates such as the introduction of compulsory income management for some income security recipients and the ongoing failure of the Australian child protection systems to enhance outcomes for children and young people in out-of-home care.

To some extent this relative silence may reflect the fact that many of the social workers involved in these systems work for government agencies, which precludes individual public comment. They may also hold a professional identity linked more closely to their agency (Centrelink or state and territory government child protection services) rather than to social work per se. The challenge for the AASW and the profession as a whole is to identify a suitable professional framework for engaging with these social workers and for utilising their enormous first-hand knowledge of these problems in policy initiatives.

The second area is that of professional self-interest as reflected in the mental health rebate campaign. It is unusual for such large numbers of social workers to get involved in a public campaign, and there is no doubt that the potential loss of income drove much of this passion. Nevertheless, social work interventions do disproportionately assist disadvantaged groups, and the collaborative nature of the campaign suggests that narrower professional social work identity and broader social justice advocacy can be reconciled. However, such campaigns will arguably be even more effective if social workers can form more active partnerships with service users to promote common concerns.

Note
[1] Thanks to Kate Incerti of the AASW National Social Policy Committee for her comments on an initial draft.

References

AASW (Australian Association of Social Workers) (2002) *Continuing Professional Education Policy Planner Logbook*, Canberra: AASW.

AASW (2003) *Practice Standards for Social Workers*, Canberra: AASW.

AASW (2009–10) *National Bulletin*, vols 19–20.

AASW (2010a) *Australian Social Work Education and Accreditation Standards*, Canberra: AASW.

AASW (2010b) *Code of Ethics*, Canberra: AASW.

AASW (2010c) *National E-bulletins*, May–November.

AASW (2010d) *Social Work and Focused Psychological Strategies: AASW Mental Health Continuing Professional Development Project May–June 2010*, Canberra: AASW.

ACHSSW (Australian Council of Heads of Schools of Social Work) (2006) *We've Boundless Plains to Share: The First Report of the People's Inquiry into Detention*, Melbourne: ACHSSW.

Addinsall, A. (2010) 'Better outcome for mental health care? Get your hand off it', www.crikey.com, 25 May.

AIHW (Australian Institute of Health and Welfare) (2007) *Welfare Expenditure Australia 2005–06*, Canberra: AIHW.

AIHW (2009) *Mental Health Services in Australia 2007–08*, Canberra: AIHW.

AIHW (2010) *Australia's Health 2010*, Canberra: AIHW.

Allen-Kelly, K. (2010a) 'The journey: AASW Better Access campaign', *AASW National Bulletin*, vol 20, no 2, pp 13–15.

Allen-Kelly, K. (2010b) 'Editorial: Out of the wilderness – Australian social workers embrace their campaigning roots', *Australian Social Work*, vol 63, no 3, pp 245–9.

Allen-Kelly, K. (2010c) 'Supporting social workers across Australia', *AASW National Bulletin*, vol 20, no 4, pp 7–8.

Allen-Kelly, K. (2010d) 'A time to reflect', *AASW National Bulletin*, vol 20, no 5, pp 7–8.

Allen-Kelly, K. and Charikar, K. (2010) 'Social workers and occupational therapists shut out of Medicare', *ACOSS Impact*, no 2, pp 17–19.

Briskman, L. and Fiske, L. (2009) 'Working with refugees', in M. Connolly and L. Harms (eds) *Social Work Contexts and Practice*, Melbourne: Oxford University Press, pp 135–48.

Briskman, L. and Goddard, C. (2007) 'Not in my name: The People's Inquiry into Detention', in D. Lusher and N. Haslam (eds) *Yearning to Breathe Free: Seeking Asylum in Australia*, Annandale: Federation Press, pp 90–9.

Briskman, L. and Noble, C. (1999) 'Social work ethics: Embracing diversity?', in B. Pease and J. Fook (eds) *Transforming Social Work Practice*, Sydney: Allen & Unwin, pp 57–69.

Briskman, L., Latham, S. and Goddard, C. (2008) *Human Rights Overboard: Seeking Asylum in Australia*, Melbourne: Scribe.

Briskman, L., Latham, S. and, Goddard, C. (2009) 'Social work exposes human rights abuses', *AASW National Bulletin*, vol 19, no 1, pp 30

Bryson, L. and Verity, F. (2009) 'Australia: From wage-earners to neo-liberal welfare state', in P. Alcock and G. Craig (eds) *International Social Policy*, Houndmills: Palgrave Macmillan, pp 66–87.

Castles, F. (1985) *The Working Class and Welfare*, Sydney: Allen and Unwin.

Castles, F. (2010) 'The English-speaking countries', in F. Castles, S. Leibfried, J. Lewis, H. Obinger and, C. Pierson (eds) *The Oxford Handbook of the Welfare State*, Oxford: Oxford University Press, pp 630–42.

Castles, F. and Mitchell, D. (1992) 'Identifying welfare state regimes: The links between politics, instruments and outcomes', *Governance*, vol 5, no 1, pp 1–26.

Charikar, K. (2010) 'Social workers unconvinced by responses to Senate estimates on mental health', media release by the AASW, 3 June.

Cheron-Sauer, M.C. (2008) 'Why does social policy matter to social work? A case study in developing policy leadership', address to Strength in Unity Conference, Sydney, 9 November.

Cintio, V. (2010) 'Is the professional project dead or just sleeping? Some reflections on the pathways proposal', *AASW National Bulletin*, vol 20, no 5, pp 14–15.

Creswell, A. (2010) 'PM yields on rebate cut', *The Australian*, 20 May.

Cumming, S. (2010) 'Registration update', *AASW National Bulletin*, vol 20, no 2, pp 17–19.

Dellidis, H. and Hanlon, R. (1991) 'Re-claiming the social: The importance of social policy development', *Australian Association of Social Workers Victorian Branch Newsletter*, vol 4, no 6, pp 12–13.

Esping-Andersen, G. (1990) *The Three Worlds of Welfare Capitalism*, Princeton, NJ: Princeton University Press.

Evans, K. (2010) 'Social workers angry with mental health cuts', *ABC News*, 17 May.

Fitzgibbon, P. (2000) 'Social work and the human services in a corporatized environment: The case of Centrelink', in I. O'Connor, P. Smyth and J. Warburton (eds) *Contemporary Perspectives on Social Work and the Human Services*, Sydney: Longman, pp 176–89.

Fraser, H. and Briskman, L. (2005) 'Through the eye of a needle: The challenge of getting justice in Australia if you're indigenous or seeking asylum', in I. Ferguson, M. Lavalette and E. Whitmore (eds) *Globalisation, Global Justice and Social Work*, London: Routledge, pp 109–23.

Friedewald, J. (2009) 'The profile of social work', *AASW National Bulletin*, vol 19, no 1, pp 19–20.

Gillingham, P. (2007) 'The Australian Association of Social Workers and social policy debates: A strategy for the future?', *Australian Social Work*, vol 60, no 2, pp 166–80.

Gray, M., Collett van Rooyen, C., Rennnie, G. and Gaha, J. (2002) 'The political participation of social workers: A comparative study', *International Journal of Social Welfare*, no 11, pp 99–110.

Harms, L., Clarke, A. and Douglass Whyte, J. (2008) 'Preparing social work students to work with Indigenous Australian communities', in B. Littlechild, K. Lyons and H. Parada (eds), *Social Work in the Context of Political Conflict*, Birmingham: British Association of Social Workers, pp 245–70.

Healy, K. and Lonne, B. (2010) *The Social Work and Human Services Workforce: Report from a National Study of Education, Training and Workforce Needs*, Strawberry Hills: Australian Learning and Teaching Council.

Ife, J. (1997) *Rethinking Social Work*, Melbourne: Longman.

Kent, H. (2010) 'The Australian Association of Social Workers Continuing Professional Education Program: Strengths and Weaknesses in achieving its aims', *Doctor of Philosophy Thesis*, Melbourne: Monash University Department of Social Work.

Lawrence, J. (1965) *Professional Social Work in Australia*, Canberra: Australian National University.

Lonne, B. (2010) 'Change, social work and the AASW', *AASW National Bulletin*, vol 20, no 4, pp 5–6.

Lonne, B. and Allen-Kelly, K. (2010) 'Removal of mental health services to low income and vulnerable Australians', letter to Minister for Health Nicola Roxon, 12 May.

Lonne, B. and Duke, J. (2009) 'The registration of social workers', in M. Connolly and L. Harms (eds) *Social Work Contexts and Practice*, Melbourne: Oxford University Press, pp 378–92.

McDonald, C. (2000) 'The third sector in the human services: Rethinking its role', in I. O'Connor, O. Smyth and, J. Warburton (eds) *Contemporary Perspectives on Social Work and the Human Services*, Melbourne: Longman, pp 84–99.

McKinnon, J. (2008) 'Exploring the nexus between social work and the environment', *Australian Social Work*, vol 61, no 3, pp 256–68.

Mendes, P. (2001) 'Blaming the messenger: The media, social workers and child abuse', *Australian Social Work*, vol 54, no 2, pp 27–36.

Mendes, P. (2003a) 'Teaching social policy to social work students: A critical reflection', *Australian Social Work*, vol 56, no 3, pp 220–33.

Mendes, P. (2003b) 'Social workers and social action: A case study of the Australian Association of Social Workers Victorian Branch', *Australian Social Work*, vol 56, no 1, pp 16–27.

Mendes, P. (2005) 'The history of social work in Australia: A critical literature review', *Australian Social Work*, vol 58, no 2, pp 121–31.

Mendes, P. (2007) 'Social workers and social activism in Victoria, Australia', *Journal of Progressive Human Services*, vol 18, no 1, pp 25–44.

Mendes, P. (2008a) *Australia's Welfare Wars Revisited*, Sydney: UNSW Press.

Mendes, P. (2008b) 'Public criticisms of social work', *AASW National Bulletin*, vol 18, no 2, pp 15–16.

Mendes, P. (2009a) 'Retrenching or renovating the Australian welfare state: The paradox of the Howard government's neo-liberalism', *International Journal of Social Welfare*, vol 18, no 1, pp 102–10.

Mendes, P. (2009b) 'Is social inclusion just a new buzzword? A half time report card on the social welfare policies of the Rudd government', *Practice Reflexions*, vol 4, no 1, pp 27–39.

Mendes, P. (2009c) 'Tracing the origins of critical social work practice', in J. Allan, L. Briskman and, B. Pease (eds) *Critical Social Work*, Crows Nest: Allen & Unwin, pp 17–29.

O'Brien, M. (2010) 'Social justice: Alive and well (partly) in social work practice?', *International Social Work*, vol 54, no 2, pp 174–90.

Pawar, M. (2004) 'Social policy curricula for training social workers: Towards a model', *Australian Social Work*, vol 57, no 1, pp 3–18.

Payne, M. (2005) *Modern Social Work Practice* (3rd edn), Houndmills: Palgrave Macmillan.

Ramon, S. (2008) (ed) *Social Work in the Context of Political Conflict*, Birmingham: British Association of Social Workers.

Roxon, N. and Butler, M. (2010) 'Better access to continue for social workers and occupational therapists', ministerial press release, 12 November.

Sommerville, E. (2010) 'Canberra consultation: Social workers and occupational therapists meet with the Department of Health and Ageing and the minister for health', *AASW National Bulletin*, vol 20, no 4, pp 11–12.

Weeks, W. (2000) 'Reflections on social work and human service theory and practice with families and communities', in W. Weeks and M. Quinn (eds) *Issues Facing Australian Families* (3rd edn), Frenchs Forest: Longman, pp 119–36.

Weeks, W. and Quinn, M. (eds) (2000) *Issues Facing Australian Families*, Frenchs Forest: Longman.

Whiteford, P. (2006) 'The welfare expenditure debate: Economic myths of the Left and the Right revisited', *Economic and Labor Relations Review*, vol 17, no 1, pp 33–77.

Whiteford, P. (2010) 'The Australian tax-transfer system: Architecture and outcomes', *Economic Record*, vol 86, no 275, pp 528–44.

THREE

Social workers affecting social policy in England

Graeme Simpson

Introduction

The United Kingdom of Great Britain and Northern Ireland comprises four separate nations: England, Scotland (the two 'kingdoms', joined by the Act of Union 1703), Wales (a principality since the 14th century) and Northern Ireland (a province since the creation of the Irish Republic). Scotland and Northern Ireland have separate legislatures which have incorporated social work, and, since the Acts of devolution, Wales has attained increasing powers over its own legislature and now has responsibility for the development and regulation of social work. Thus, all four countries of the United Kingdom (UK) have separate systems for social work and social care, which will be referred to as 'social welfare'. In writing about social work there has been a tendency for the term 'UK' to be used until relatively recently, even though it has been, strictly speaking, a term which does not reflect the diversity within it. Latterly it has become more commonplace to refer to the specific country, especially within the social work and social policy literature, as this is a developing field, notably in Scotland (Mooney and Law, 2007) and Wales (Drakeford, 2005). Unless specified, the legislation and policy referred to in this chapter will be English, reflecting the writer's place of residence and work.

A more complex question arises however, when 'social work' is defined. In England, and indeed in the UK in general, social work has come to refer to those activities carried out by qualified social workers, now a protected title. This has resulted in a range of other professional and even non-professional activities being seen as something other than 'social work'. For example, the work undertaken in residential and supported living settings is seen as 'social care'; work in community settings would be regarded as 'community work' or, depending on the service user group, 'youth work' or even 'family support' if located primarily around family or 'Sure Start' centres. It therefore becomes clear that when compared with the international breadth of 'social work', English social work (as defined earlier) is relatively narrow. This creates a difficulty, not always acknowledged, for those who write about social work, especially in an international context.

Within the context of this chapter, this difficulty is compounded since many of these 'local' distinctions are rather recent. A few simple examples will suffice: social workers in the 1970s and even 1980s who worked in residential settings – whatever their qualification – would be called residential social workers. Social workers, even those employed by the local authority would often engage in local community-based campaigns, in activities which would today be seen as the preserve of 'community workers'. Finally, in a historical context, Heaseman (1962), when reviewing 19th-century social work, covered ground from child protection to housing provision – in short any 'work' (paid or usually unpaid) which was 'social'.

It is therefore apparent that in different contexts social work takes on different meanings and forms. Historically, this has shifted away from a broad to a narrower conception: from a wider 'social' focus to a narrower 'individual' focus. It will be argued that this shift has diminished the scope for policy practice, and that recent attempts to 'reclaim' social work with calls for engaged practice (Ferguson, 2008; Simpson and Connor, 2011) stand in the tradition of policy practice.

Historical background

As the introduction indicates, there is a substantial heritage to the involvement of social work professionals in the policy process to give the activity a sense of legitimacy. It is perhaps worth considering, however, the definition of policy practice and its potential difficulties, especially when applied to the historical English and British context. Were a strict definition applied, one which locates it almost exclusively within the specified arena of 'practice', then there might be debates as to whether or not a certain activity was or is 'policy practice' or whether it should be seen as part of 'civic engagement' or 'political participation'. For example, much of the 'social work' of the Victorian era was unpaid activity, largely by middle-class women, often of independent means. Thus, their 'social work' was part of their 'civic engagement' and so equally their attempts to change policy could also be regarded as 'civic engagement' rather than policy practice, although such a distinction in this context remains less clear cut than in a liberal welfare democracy (Esping-Andersen et al, 2002). Many examples of this can be drawn on. One is Mary Carpenter's engagement with what we would now term youth justice, where she proposed a number of policy changes, including many that were eventually implemented long after her death – for example, putting an end to the incarceration of juvenile offenders in adult prisons and the abolition of corporal punishment (Carpenter, 1968 [1851]; Muncie, 1999; Price and Simpson, 2007). Octavia Hill's engagement with social housing is another well-documented aspect of how civic social work was linked inextricably with a policy engagement, even though her aims were questionable (Owen, 1964). Indeed, the Charity Organisation Society (COS), of which Hill was a leading figure, combined such 'civic' duty with its (for them at least) logical extension of 'civic' and policy engagement.

The COS was underpinned by the philosophical claims of 'idealism' (Vincent, 1984), which shaped the practice of its volunteers. Essentially, this was a form of social theory which argued that all actions should promote the common good through individual and collective 'virtues'. Not all members supported the principles of casework which were designed to identify those who could benefit and those who would not – often reduced to a distinction between the deserving and non-deserving, although the original distinction was more subtle. Canon Barnett split with the movement and founded his 'settlements', initially in London. Rather than the middle classes visiting the poor and dispensing 'welfare', he argued that there needed to be a greater amount of social contact between rich and poor, to ensure that 'those who possess the means [to a higher life] ... should pass them on' (Barnett and Barnett, 1972 [1888]). Accordingly, he developed settlements which sought to educate the poor, by inviting the educated middle class to live in the community alongside those who were both materially poor and also (as a consequence) lacking in education. The settlements had some success, and one of their members was William Beveridge, who went on to write the report which set the foundations of the post-war welfare state (Bradley, 2009). This is hardly an example of 'policy practice', but is clearly an example of where a social work experience has substantially influenced 'policy'. As Ferguson (2008) has pointed out, there is a further example of this dynamic at work in the life of the Labour politician and prime minister, Clement Attlee. Attlee published a book in 1920 entitled *The Social Worker*, drawing on his experiences of being a social worker in London's East End, where he argued that social workers need to engage in 'agitation' to improve policy as part of their role.

A new generation: in and against the state

In the years immediately after the Second World War the Labour government established the welfare state, implementing some (though crucially not all) of Beveridge's (1942) proposals. Sapsford (1993) suggested that the boom years of the 1950s led to a somewhat punitive form of social work, operating largely under the belief that the welfare state had achieved its aim of abolishing poverty, and so any set of difficulties that people encountered were regarded as individual as opposed to structural.

The 1960s, however, saw the well-documented 'rediscovery of poverty' (Page, 2007) and the return of a Labour government, and possibly the high tide of post-war social liberalism. Many of the then prime minister, Harold Wilson's reforms were inspired by, and some directly crafted by, people with a social work background (see Younghusband, 1981, for example). The Children and Young People Act 1969, which was a fine example of this, extended not just to how social work was to be undertaken. Although it was later subjected to sustained criticism (see, for example Millham et al, 1975), it established a range of childcare principles within a largely reformist piece of legislation. The Seebohm Report (1968) enabled the establishment of local authorities, and in 1970 the first national social work qualification was established (the Certificate of Qualification in Social Work under the auspices of the Central Council for Education and Training in Social Work). Social work education had previously been localised, albeit often within major universities (Davis, 2008).

Loney (1983), in his review of the Community Development Projects (CPDs), pointed to this timing: radicalised young people from the 1960s – notably the generation that the French refer to as *les soixante-huitards* (the 'sixty-eighters') – entered social work as a profession, seeing it as a potential vehicle for social change. The oil crisis and subsequent austerity programmes created an economic backdrop that inspired the radical social work movement, which borrowed the term from the CPDs of 'in and against the state'. The influence of this group of first-generation state-trained and employed social workers is often overstated; it has to be recognised that while the so-called 'radical' literature had a substantial impact on social work, much social work remained largely traditional and individual focused. The radicals, however, legitimised a type of practice which has much in common with 'policy practice' and 'class advocacy'. It was not uncommon for social workers in the 1970s and even 1980s to enjoy sufficient autonomy to engage in policy formulation and action at local levels, even if the passage of time has often resulted in a somewhat nostalgic and romanticised view of earlier practice among social workers of a certain age (Langan, 2002). The literature, though, stands as a testimony to what was achieved. Bruce Hugman's (1977) account of probation work in Sheffield demonstrates a commitment to local involvement; the accounts to be found in Bailey and Brake (1975) are all of a type of practice which was directly engaged in the very essence of 'policy practice' as part of everyday social work activity. Margaret Humphreys (2011) was a social worker in inner-city Nottingham in the mid-1980s when she stumbled across people who had been subject to 'enforced migration' as children to Australia, and from there her social work activities resulted in the uncovering of the activities of the state in relation to poor children in the post-war era, which eventually led to in official apologies from the Australian and British prime ministers in 2009 (Child Migrants Trust, 2011).

Much of what was deemed radical in the 1970s and 1980s (including social work's commitment to anti-discriminatory and later anti-oppressive practice) became mainstream, in part in its acceptance into training programmes with the establishing of the Diploma in Social Work in the early 1990s. Webb (1991) was one of the few academics to urge caution in relation to the development of anti-oppressive practice, seeing it as being a concept which would serve to underpin the neo-liberal project. Jones and Novak (1993) were also cautious, refocusing their attention on social work's surveillance function. Nonetheless, the 1990s saw many publications outlining empowerment and anti-oppressive practice, located in structural change as being the way forward for social work (Braye and Preston-Shoot, 1995; Thompson, 1997; Dominelli, 2002). Simultaneously, the clouds of managerialism and market forces were gathering, which were to have a far more decisive impact on the development of social work (Dominelli and Hoogveldt, 1996; Jones, 2001; Jordan, 2001).

The rise of managerialism

Much has been written about the rise of New Public Management (NPM) or managerialism and its target culture within the British and English context (see, for example Clarke, 2004; Garrett, 2009). In summary this refers to methods of 'governance': what Clarke (2004, p 120) describes as the 'shifting conditions and location of what might be called statework'. Simpson and Connor argue that:

> NPM represents a combination of 'technical' and 'consumerist' approaches to quality. NPM shares the

> consumerist objectives of increasing service responsiveness,
> but it is driven by a different underlying dynamic.
> Making services more responsive to consumers' needs and
> preferences is not carried out to secure greater market share,
> but to ensure public resources are used more *efficiently* and
> *effectively*. (Simpson and Connor, 2011, p 78)

The impact on social work has been considerable. Jones (2001) studied state social workers (as distinct from those who work in the independent sector). He suggested that the other forms of social work in the voluntary and independent sectors 'might be in far better shape', although 10 years later this may still not be the case as there is evidence that NPM has moved into other sectors. Baginsky et al's (2010) workforce survey, however, indicated that over 90% of its respondents worked in the state sector. Jones' research was undertaken a couple of years into New Labour's first administration (1997–2001), and he asked whether or not the forward march of neo-liberalism had been halted: his answer was a resounding 'no'. Jones' work is significant to an understanding of policy practice in that he refers to the 1970s, when 'social workers had some possibility of getting to know their clients and when social workers often ended up as advocates on behalf of their clients' (Jones, 2001, p 549). Jones identified a number of organisational factors related to NPM which affected social workers activities. These included increased bureaucracy; lack of support; aggressive managerialism to speed up turnover of cases; significant and constant organisational change; and, finally, budgetary control and restrictions. A decade later there is no question that these factors have continued and worsened, as the stories of colleagues working in the state sector almost daily affirm. A crucial shift was towards office-based social work, and Jones noted the beginning of a clear trend: state social workers rarely engage in direct work with their clients; they commission others to do it for them, and the social workers' focus is on case management and assessment. Jones' analysis shifted towards the lives of service users and the growing inequality in Britain – inequalities which have increased in the subsequent 10 years – rooted in neo-liberalism and the market economy, creating a grim picture of state social work.

Jones' work is one of the few accounts which focus on the daily working experiences of social workers and what they actually do. In the wake of the death of 'Baby P.', some of his findings were finally publicly acknowledged. Perhaps the most significant was the office-based nature of contemporary social work and that state childcare social workers can spend up to 80% of their time 'office based' – a figure which rises for those involved in work with adults (White et al, 2010). Stepney (2010) argues that the neo-liberal modernising agenda (begun under Tony Blair and continued with increased momentum under the Conservative–Liberal Democrat coalition) has been rebranded within a modernised welfare state, consequently becoming compliant. In this context it is perhaps not surprising that little has been written about the actual experiences of social workers, how they experience their work and more importantly how they address some of the key questions raised by policy practice and 'class advocacy'. Jones expressed his concern in 2001 that social work academics were not writing about the actual position and experiences of frontline staff, preferring to focus on other aspects of social work. There has been recent work about the use of time and the focus of interventions (see Baginsky et al, 2010; White et al, 2010) but the lack of published work about the experiences of frontline staff remain limited.

A key feature of managerialist discourse is that it sets the parameters of the debate as it establishes its particular hegemonic structure. Using Hall's (1987) argument it sets the limits of what is, and what is not, 'thinkable'. Much of the social work literature focuses on what can be described as the more technical aspects of practice, of disseminating 'best practice' and supporting this with evidence. There is nothing intrinsically wrong with such an approach, but it is what Mayntz (1976) argued is a 'technician's' approach. The focus here is on the individual practice in what is largely seen as a politically neutral, or inevitable, context. Work that has concentrated on social workers and their practice has identified workplace stress, but then addressed individual resilience factors to improve this (Kinman and Grant, 2011); in a similar vein Graham and Shier (2010) investigated personal factors to enhance subjective wellbeing among social work practitioners. Munro (2010) in analysing the over-proceduralised social work in child protection services restricted her analysis to 'feedback loops' between managers and front line practitioners as a means of creating a better learning environment. Within such a context, where the terms of potential debates are delineated, the most discretion and autonomy that social workers have is to be found in 'street-level bureaucracy' (Evans and Harris, 2004) – interestingly a feature of other economies in the process of marketisation, for example Sweden's transition towards greater marketisation (Dellgran and Hojer, 2005).

In summary, the conditions in which most English social workers operate in the early 21st century are not conducive to policy practice and indeed do not promote it. The terms of reference for state social workers have been restricted and developed within a context of neo-liberalism and managerialist structures, diminishing autonomy at all levels. It is against this background that the final section of this chapter will identify moves to reclaim social work's heritage and to promote a social work of engagement.

Policy practice in context

It is in the context of the drive towards neo-liberalism and heightened managerialist control that policy practice in England has to be understood. Writing in 2001, Jones described the picture for state social work as 'grim' (p 590); he also suggested that few academics were actually writing about these developments in a critical fashion – both aspects of this analysis can be endorsed 10 years on. In 2011, however, social workers and more crucially their service users were facing a sustained attack from a government which appeared committed not just to 'reforming' public service provision, but also to privatising services and relying on voluntarism and the private sector to fill the gaps. While this is continuing, social work is undergoing yet another period of reform, both in relation to its curriculum and organisation. Social workers are involved in aspects of the SWRB's work and have been able to engage in consultation about the future of the profession. This consultation, however, does not extend to the future of the very services that they provide and their service users rely on. There is, though, increasing evidence that a profession which has largely remained silent is beginning to find a voice (see Price and Simpson, 2007; Ferguson, 2008; SWAN, 2011). While in the English context 'policy practice' as a concept is barely discussed, there exist other features which make it a possibility. The British Association of Social Workers' Code of Ethics (2012) defines social work interventions as ranging from 'primarily person focused psychosocial processes to involvement in social policy, planning and development'. It continues by suggesting that 'Interventions also include agency administration, community organisation and engaging in social and political action to impact social policy and economic development' are legitimate social work roles (BASW, 2012, p 7). The code states that social workers have a responsibility to promote social justice, and it identifies five fields where this occurs, including the challenging of unjust practices: 'Social workers have a duty to bring to the attention of their employers, policy makers, politicians and the general public situations where resources are inadequate or where distribution of resources, policies and practice are oppressive, unfair, harmful or illegal' (ibid, p 9).

Drawing on work by Weiss et al (2006), there is perhaps little explicitly within England's educational framework for social workers to promote policy practice through a study of 'social policy' – indeed, there is a view that students only need to know about policy. There remain aspects of teaching which would create a framework for policy engagement (anti-oppressive practice being the most obvious).

Social work education still emphasises the role of sociology, ethics and human rights, and the review of the curriculum has seemingly confirmed this, albeit with a less critical position on social policy. Nevertheless, there are indications that key areas for potential policy-oriented practice will remain. A key area which has entered the Professional Capability Framework (PCF, 2012) for social workers, from their qualifying courses through to principal social worker level is that of 'rights, justice and economic well-being: advance human rights, and promote social justice and economic well-being'. Even though some of the detail remains under discussion, there can be little doubt that such a set of capabilities could provide the framework for a more directly policy-oriented practice – at the very least it should legitimise social workers engaging in action.

Without any direct commitment to policy practice or even policy engagement in a revised curriculum, it therefore becomes apparent that, for the majority of social workers, policy practice is, regrettably, hardly likely to become a mainstream activity. In this regard it is questionable whether policy practice in a pure form as defined in the introduction to this book exists as a social work activity. That is not to say that social workers are not engaged in helping shape policy at a local level through various working groups and committees – yet, as will be demonstrated later, this is an activity which is often tokenistic, although some real gains can be made. There is also evidence that social work practitioners are involved in shaping the future of social work in relation to the work of the SWRB. Many academics with a social work background are often consulted either formally or informally by government ministers or civil servants, and, of course, senior officers in local government, many of whom are social workers, frequently contribute to policy development at the national level. At a different level there is the work of Bob Holman, a former academic and latterly community social worker in Glasgow's Easterhouse Estate (*The Guardian*, 2011). Yet such activities remain largely beyond the scope of mainstream state social workers, that is, the majority of social workers in England.

Does this mean that policy practice does not exist in an English context? The following sections will examine this question.

Policy practice and social work reform

Perhaps one of the clearest examples of social workers and social work academics engaging in policy practice is in the national 'reform' of social work in England following the inquiry into the death of 'Baby P.', which was made public after the trial of his mother and two other adults charged with causing his death. The SWRB was established, led by Moira Gibb, a social worker with a lengthy management career. The SWRB sought to encompass a range of social workers at all levels as it sought to address many of the difficulties brought about by NPM and the so-called 'target culture' it generated. Crucial to this was the research of Sue White and colleagues (see, for example White et al, 2010) into the amount of time social workers spent engaged with bureaucratic tasks, as opposed to service users. Alongside the SWRB, Professor Eileen Munro undertook a systematic review of child protection and safeguarding in England (see p 45). Although at the time of writing the government had yet to adopt all of the review's recommendations, some of them were already being adopted by local authorities in 2012. This process has engaged social workers, and in the West Midlands several have sought to become involved, particularly in moves towards a more responsive community-oriented practice. The experience of social workers engaged in such developments varies according to their role and level of involvement, and much remains anecdotal at this stage. Certainly for some it has been an empowering process; others have suggested that their presence is merely tokenistic; possibly for most it lies somewhere in between. These developments stand firmly in one of the traditions of policy development and engagement in England and it needs to be acknowledged that this has always occurred. The more recent examples, with their focus on the workings of social work, have certainly led to a number of practitioners and academics having direct contact with government ministers, civil servants and, at the local level, local councillors and senior managers. There is a sense, however, that engagement in this arena, while significant, poses few challenges to a government whose other policies have had a damaging impact on the very people social work is engaged with.

This section has been concerned with promoting a particular practice-based initiative. The next will explore attempts to promote social justice in the increasingly hostile environment of the European-wide 'austerity measures' of 2010 onwards.

Policy practice in a hostile environment

The previous sections have shown that there is a clear tradition of those involved in social work becoming involved in policy processes as a result of their social work activities. The move towards increased regulation and control of social workers with the introduction of new public management has created a hostile environment for such an engagement. Although the National Occupation Standards for Social Work (NOS) referred to engagement in policy (Topps UK Partnership, 2004, unit 21.1), this was through 'contributions to policy review and development', which remained largely undefined – there were also references to social justice and anti-oppressive practice. The PCF not only includes sections relating not only to anti-oppressive practice and social justice, but also to engagement with the contexts which shape practice – though the extent to which these will become embedded activities, rather than a 'knowledge base' is questionable. Nevertheless, while there is, I would suggest, little to promote policy practice explicitly within the English framework, there is – and there is likely to continue to be – sufficient room to ensure that it remains on the agenda. More significantly, there is evidence that recent policies which have resulted in cuts in services have encouraged social workers to become more explicitly engaged as a consequence.

The chapter will now focus on some distinct areas of engagement which show that social work retains its voice in promoting social justice and, while many of the activities outlined below are primarily concerned with the defensive response of 'defeating policy initiatives', this should not diminish their importance. Jones et al's manifesto for social work starts from the position that many people entered social work 'out of a commitment to social justice or, at the very least, to bring about positive change in people's lives' (2004, p. 1). Subsequently, the Social Work Action Network (SWAN) was formed as a loose coalition of members who share the aim of practice seeking to recapture the essence of a campaigning social work, committed to social justice. Its essence and aim is summed up as

> a network of social work practitioners, academics, students and social welfare service users united in their concern that social work activity is being undermined by managerialism and marketisation, by the stigmatisation of service users and by welfare cuts and restrictions. SWAN promotes a model of social work and social care practice, which is rooted in the value of social justice. (SWAN, 2011)

Its organisation is national and regional and it aims to 'strengthen the radical voice within social work practice [and] education' (SWAN, 2011). The West Midlands network has been at the forefront of campaigns against current policies, notably the attempts by Birmingham City Council to save in excess of £30 million by increasing the thresholds for a service – a move which would remove support and services from many disabled people. Many of those involved are social workers and, even though most of the activity is outside working hours, it is an example of policy practice, in that it is emerging out of the social workers' own experiences and knowledge and is being run in conjunction with service user groups and trades unions. In May 2011 the council lost a court case brought against it by service user groups, in what was possibly the 'first round' of legal action against its proposals (BBC News, 2011).

Another significant site of engagement is in relation to the possible development of social enterprises – effectively the privatisation of social work. These are often primed with start-up grants and cream off the services they seek to provide, which they would then do on a contracted-out basis. They are being piloted with language promising reduced bureaucracy and greater control for workers, masking the drive towards neo-liberalism and marketisation (Garrett, 2009). Simon Cardy (2010, p. 437), a social worker from the West Midlands, identified the potential uncritical nature of some aspects of English social work in relation to the emerging 'independent social work practices' in that they have attracted 'significant support from social work organizations and yet there has been little discussion as to their quasi-market origins and even less interrogation of the official documentation'. Local authorities will make a saving, and while short-term improvements may ensue, the long-term cost is likely to be borne by both social workers and service users alike. In one authority, no social workers joined the proposed 'co-operative', as a result of a sustained campaign by social workers in the authority supported by a wider network (Cardy, 2010, p 437).

A third piece of action undertaken by social workers relates to the activities of the UK Border Agency and children seeking asylum. As a consequence of cuts to the Home Office-funded grants, some authorities (including Solihull in the West Midlands) were left in a position where they could not continue to provide the same level of service to asylum-seeking children and potentially could only provide them with an inferior service (Pemberton, 2011).

There is also evidence that some social workers have developed a wider international stance. In the mainstream there is the continuing activity to internationalise the curriculum (Lawrence et al, 2009) and to develop an outward-looking, rather than inward-looking practice. This is the case in situations where social workers have tried to incorporate and develop practices more rooted in social pedagogy at the local level – a good example of policy practice which is not driven by English policy. Others have linked to campaigns and practice in relation to asylum seekers. Finally, there are those who have engaged in social work *in extremis* (Lavalette and Ioakimidis, 2011) with a specific focus on social work in the West Bank and Greece, along with other countries facing internal upheaval and conflict.

On a more local, agency level, social workers have taken up offers to engage in developmental groups seeking to implement services in the West Midlands, and the following are some of their experiences. One recalled how they were initially welcomed with open arms as the practitioners' voice, only to be asked to leave when it became apparent that they were not wholeheartedly embracing the proposals. Notwithstanding this response, taking local opportunities to engage in localised developments remains one way in which current social workers can engage in a policy process, within their working hours. As such this is, perhaps, the closest English workers will come to a work-based engagement. Social workers are involved in developing processes to implement aspects of the Munro Review in several local authorities and through this can bring a front line practice experience to bear on the potential policies developed. In some local authorities social workers are active in specific workplace groups to focus on matters of equality – for example, black workers groups. Many of these social workers report that their views and opinions have not always been dismissed, which in itself induces a level of surprise from those workers, who expected their perspectives to be dismissed. Indeed, some have reported positive outcomes from their engagement in the local process, indicating that this is often a worthwhile activity.

Social workers have engaged in attempts to oppose new patterns of service provision, where the first contact is with an unqualified telephone operative – essentially a 'call-centre' operation, although social workers are clearly warned by their managers against suggesting that this is the model. This again reflects the move towards business-oriented approaches to social work delivery with the 'scripted interview' (Harris, 2003, p 3). Social workers' activities in this arena have been less successful, predictably so, since this relates to structural and organisational factors at a senior management and political level. In the current economic climate many local authorities are seeking to make substantial budgetary cuts, and social work reorganisation is one way to develop a more 'efficient' workforce. The intention is to 'free up' social work time by employing unqualified staff to deal with front line enquiries. In some teams social workers have argued that this is not beneficial either to them or to service users, and that often this results in social workers having to re-evaluate the initial information: as one social worker intimated, it is a case of false economy.

Thus, at a local level there is significant evidence of social workers engaging in policy-oriented practice. Where this is part of a management-directed strategy (that is, national policy implementation), there is evidence of some success. Where it presents a counter-argument to an economically driven 'strategic' policy it is less likely to succeed.

These are some examples in five areas; there are doubtless many more. One of the challenges facing the development of policy practice, however, is that of potential isolation. In short, individual acts (or even group acts) are not aggregated, and as such those engaging in them struggle to sustain them and to maintain their engagement. The social work press has reported pieces of action and is increasingly doing so: the British Association of Social Workers has a list of news reports and releases, but generally the social work voice remains at best sidelined; SWAN engages in more public displays of engagement and attempts to develop common cause with other more radical campaigning groups. All of them arguably have a part to play, but unless policy practice and engagement are features of social work education, it is likely to remain an activity which gains little professional recognition.

Educating for engagement and policy practice

In a briefing paper relating to independent social work practice, Cardy (2010, p 4) argues that 'social workers have a responsibility to examine things critically and to look below the surface'. If social workers are to develop these skills, they need to be nurtured and taught in relation to social work practice. Ferguson (2008) argues that social work needs to reclaim its own traditions and identifies a number of key areas for reclamation in this project: the ethical; relationships and process; the social; and the structural – all of which should result in social work reclaiming a political voice. Weiss et al's work (2006), which produced an outline for a comprehensive approach to social policy teaching, began from the assumption that an ethical commitment to social justice is a given. That in an English context there is a need to stress that the ethical considerations of social work need to be reclaimed suggests the extent to which these have diminished. It is not that social work has abandoned its ethical principles, but rather that these have become primarily focused on aspects of individual choice or an aspect of personal empowerment. As Ferguson (2008, p 69) argues, in itself choice is no bad thing, but when it moves away from the structural factors which shape people's lives it becomes reduced to lifestyle choice through which the poor are essentially held to account for structural problems. The need to rediscover the ethics of social, as opposed to personal, morality becomes of prime importance.

There needs to be a renewed emphasis not merely on the teaching of social policy, which can all too easily become learning about existing policy, but of developing the skills needed for a critical analysis and engagement (Simpson and Connor, 2011). Ferguson (2008) supports Price and Simpson's (2007) view that it is essential for social workers to reclaim the structural, and an essential key to this is a sociological critique.

Simpson and Connor (2011) go further to suggest key analytical skills which are needed for social workers to develop a sense of political engagement, with a view to developing the critically aware social workers Cardy (2010) calls for. Agency – the ability to engage and act – is essential, and they eschew a crude dichotomy, arguing that agency cannot be understood without a grasp of structure, and that structure is understood in the context of human actions, something which is particularly relevant for social workers, who, as Simpson and Connor go on to suggest, are subject to daily dialectical pressures. Being aware of and then understanding how these daily pressures are created and sustained is essential, whether it be in relation to how the economy is spoken about or how vulnerable groups are presented in the media – usually in a negative fashion. With this basis, social workers can then move towards policy practice and social engagement.

Conclusions

With English social work in a state of change, the future for policy practice in England is uncertain. Conditions in which English social workers practice remain highly regulated and the autonomous practitioner, though an ambition, is perhaps some way distant. In addition, cuts in public expenditure have led to fewer social work positions being available, and there is the rather contradictory nature of a profession being buoyed by the outcomes of the SWRB, and yet at the same time being squeezed by the government's fiscal policies. Recent developments in the SWRB have led to a number of social workers becoming involved in local and even national developments, and this type of policy practice is a useful starting place for many and may well develop greater levels of confidence for wider and continued engagement. Responses to welfare cuts are a starting point and while for some this may appear to be radical and outside the notion of policy practice as a mainstream activity, it reflects the current conditions of practice in England at the time of writing. It is apposite to recall that 'Men make their own history, but they do not make it as they please; they do not make it under self-selected circumstances, but under circumstances existing already' (Marx, 1852). Those who engage in policy practice do so not in circumstances of their own choosing: they need to start from where they are and build; the evidence, albeit fleeting, of local engagement suggests that there are those who are actively engaging in the process. That this is, for the most part, seen as a radical activity speaks more about the state of English social work than it does about the nature of these social workers.

References

Attlee, C. (1920) *The Social Worker*, London: Heinemann.

Baginsky, M., Moriarty, J., Manthorpe, J., Stevens, M., MacInnes, T and Nagendran, T. (2010) *Social Workers' Workload Survey: Messages from the Frontline. Findings from the 2009 Survey and Interviews with Senior Managers*, www.education.gov.uk/publications/eOrderingDownload/social%20workers%20workload%20survey%202009.pdf.

Bailey, R. and Brake, M. (1975) 'Social work and the welfare state', in R. Bailey and M. Brake (eds) *Radical Social Work*, London: Edward Arnold.

Barnett, S.A. and Barnett, H. (1972 [1888]) *Practicable Socialism: Essays on Social Reform*. Freeport, NY: Books for Libraries Press.

BASW (British Association of Social Workers) (2012) 'Code of Ethics', www.basw.co.uk/codeofethics.

BBC News (2011) Birmingham City Council disabled care limits 'unlawful', 20 April, www.bbc.co.uk/news/uk-england-birmingham-13147675.

Beveridge, Sir W. (1942) *Report on Social Insurance and Allied Services*, Cmd 6404, London, HMSO.

Bradley, K. (2009) *Poverty, Philanthropy and the State: The University Settlements and the Urban Working Classes, 1918–1979*, Manchester: Manchester University Press.

Braye, S. and Preston-Shoot, M. (1995) *Empowering Practice in Social Care*, Buckingham: Open University Press.

Cardy, S. (2010) "Care matters" and the privatization of looked after children's services in England and Wales: Developing a critique of independent social work practices', *Critical Social Policy*, vol 30, no 3, pp 430–42.

Carpenter, M. (1968) [1851] *Reformatory Schools: For the Children of the Perishing and Dangerous Classes and for Juvenile Offenders*, London: Woburn Press.

Child Migrants Trust (2011) www.childmigrantstrust.com.

Clarke, J. (2004) *Changing Welfare, Changing States: New Directions in Social Policy*, London: Sage.

Davis, A. (2008) 'Celebrating 100 years of social work, University of Birmingham, www.birmingham.ac.uk/Documents/college-social-sciences/social-policy/IASS/100-years-of-social-work.pdf.

Dellgran, P. and Hojer, S. (2005) 'Privatisation as professionalisation? Attitudes, motives and achievements among Swedish social workers', *European Journal of Social Work*, vol 8, no 1, pp 39–62.

Dominelli, L. (2002) *Anti-oppressive Social Work Theory and Practice*, Basingstoke: Palgrave Macmillan.

Dominelli, L. and Hoogvelt, A. (1996) 'Globalisation and the technocratization of social work', *Critical Social Policy*, vol 16, no 2, pp 45–62.

Drakeford, M. (2005) 'Wales and a third term of New Labour: Devolution and the development of difference', *Critical Social Policy*, vol 25, no 4, pp 497–506.

Esping-Andersen, G. with Gallie, D. Hemerijck, A. and Myles, J. (2002) *Why We Need a New Welfare State*, Oxford: Oxford University Press.

Evans, T. and Harris, J. (2004) 'Street-level bureaucracy and the (exaggerated) death of discretion', *British Journal of Social Work*, vol 34, no 6, pp 871–96.

Ferguson, I. (2008) *Reclaiming Social Work: Challenging Neo-liberalism and Promoting Social Justice*, London: Sage.

Garrett, P.M. (2009) *Transforming Children's Services: Social Work, Neo-liberalism and the 'Modern World'*, Buckingham: Open University Press.

The Guardian (2011) 'Profile: Bob Holman', www.guardian.co.uk/profile/bob-holman.

Graham, J.R. and Shier, M.L. (2010) 'Social work practitioners and subjective well-being: Personal factors that contribute to high levels of subjective well-being', *International Social Work*, vol 53, no 6, pp 757–72.

Hall, S. (1987) 'Gramsci and us', *Marxism Today*, June, www.hegemonics.co.uk/docs/Gramsci-and-us.pdf.

Harris, J. (2003) *The Social Work Business*, London: Routledge.

Heaseman, K. (1962) *Evangelicals in Action: An Appraisal of their Social Work*, Letchworth: Garden City Press.

Hugman, B. (1977) *Act Natural: A New Sensibility for the Professional Helper*, London: Bedford Square Press.

Humphreys, M. (2011) *Empty Cradles*, London: Transworld Publishing.

Jones, C. (2001) 'Voices from the front line: State social work and New Labour', *British Journal of Social Work*, vol 31, no 4, pp 547–62.

Jones, C. and Novak, T. (1993) *Poverty, Welfare and the Disciplinary State*, London: Routledge.

Jones, C., Ferguson, I., Lavalette, M. and Penketh, L. (2004) *Social Work and Social Justice: a Manifesto for a New Engaged Practice,* University of Liverpool.

Jordan, B. (2001) 'Tough love: Social work, social exclusion and the Third Way', *British Journal of Social Work,* vol 43, no 4, pp 527–46.

Kinman, G. and Grant, L. (2011) 'Predicting stress resilience in trainee social workers: The role of emotional competencies', *British Journal of Social Work*, vol 41, no 2, pp 261–75.

Langan, M. (2002) *The Legacy of Radical Social Work*, London: Macmillan.

Lavalette, M. and Ioakimidis, V. (2011) *Social Work in Extremis*, Bristol: The Policy Press.

Lawrence, S., Lyons, K., Simpson, G. and Hügler, N. (2009) *Introducing International Social Work*, Exeter: Learning Matters.

Loney, M. (1983) *Community Against Government: The British Community Development Project 1968–78*, London: Heinemann.

Marx, K. (1852) *The Eighteenth Brumaire of Louis Bonaparte*, www.gutenberg.org/files/1346/1346-h/1346-h.htm.

Mayntz, R. (1976) 'Conceptual models of organizational decision making and their application to the policy process', in G. Hofstede and M.S. Kassem (eds) *European Contributions to Organization Theory*, Amsterdam: Van Gorcum.

Millham, S., Bullock, R. and Cherrett, P. (1975) *After Grace, Teeth: A Comparative Study of the Residential Experiences of Boys in Approved Schools*, London: Human Context Books.

Mooney, G. and Law, A. (eds) (2007) *New Labour/Hard Labour? Restructuring and Resistance in the Welfare Industry*, Bristol: The Policy Press.

Muncie, J. (1999) *Youth and Crime: A Critical Introduction*, London: Sage.

Munro, E. (2010) *The Munro Review of Child Protection – Final Report: A Child Centred System*, Cm 8062, London: HMSO, www.education.gov.uk/munroreview/downloads/8875_DfE_Munro_Report_TAGGED.pdf.

Owen, D.E. (1964) *English Philanthropy: 1660–1960*, Cambridge, MA: Belknap Press of Harvard University Press.

Page, R. (2007) *Revisiting the Welfare State,* New York/Maidenhead McGraw-Hill/Open University Press.

Pemberton, C. (2011) 'Protests against cuts to services for child asylum seekers', CommunityCare, www.communitycare.co.uk/Articles/08/04/2011/116644/protests-against-cuts-to-services-for-child-asylum-seekers.htm.

PCF (Professional Capabilities Framework) (2012) www.collegeof socialwork.org/pcf.aspx.

Price, V. and Simpson, G. (2007) *Transforming Society? Social Work and Sociology*, Bristol: The Policy Press.

Sapsford, R. (1993) 'The growth of an expertise', in J. Clark (ed) *A Crisis in Care? Challenges to Social Work*, London: Sage Publications/ Open University.

Seebohm, F. (1968) *Report of the Committee on Local Authority and Allied Personal Social Services (the Seebohm Report)*, London: HMSO.

Simpson, G. and Connor, S. (2011) *Social Policy for Social Welfare Professionals: Tools for Understanding, Analysis and Engagement,* Bristol: The Policy Press.

Stepney, P. (2010) 'Social welfare at the crossroads: Evidence-based practice or critical practice?', *International Journal of Interdisciplinary Social Sciences*, vol 5, no 5, pp 105–20.

SWAN (Social Work Action Network) (2011) www.socialworkfuture. org.

Thompson, N. (1997) *Anti-Discriminatory Practice* (2nd edn), Basingstoke: Macmillan.

Topps UK Partnership (2004) *The National Occupational Standards for Social Work*, Leeds: Topps England.

Vincent, A.W. (1984) 'The Poor Law Reports of 1909 and the social theory of the Charitable Organisation Society', in D. Gladstone (ed) *Before Beveridge: Welfare Before the Welfare State*, London: Institute of Economic Affairs.

Webb, D. (1991) 'Puritans and paradigms: A speculation on the form of new moralities in social work', *Social Work and Social Sciences Review*, vol 2, no 2, pp 146–59.

Weiss, I., Gal, J. and Katan, J. (2006) 'Social policy for social work: A teaching agenda', *British Journal of Social Work*, vol 36, pp 789–806.

White, S., Wastell, D., Broadhurst, K. and Hall, C. (2010) 'When policy o'erleaps itself: The "tragic tale" of the Integrated Children's System', *Critical Social Policy*, vol 30, no 3, pp 405–29.

Younghusband, E. (1981) *Newest Profession: A Short History of Social Work*, London: Community/Care/IPC Business Press.

FOUR

Social workers affecting social policy in Israel

Idit Weiss-Gal

The central claim of this chapter is that policy practice is an emergent form of social work practice in Israel, yet, to a large extent, it remains relatively marginalised in the field. Following a brief description of the context in which social workers operate, the Israeli welfare state and the social work profession in Israel, the place that policy practice plays in contemporary social work discourse, education and practice will be examined and explained. The chapter will conclude with a brief summary of the trends identified.

The Israeli welfare state

Israel is a welfare state in the sense that among both decision makers and the public as a whole there is acknowledgement of the fact that the state has a responsibility to ensure the social rights of individuals in society. In other words, there is explicit recognition of the role of the state in providing an acceptable standard of living for all and furthering redistribution of societal resources. This recognition is, of course, tempered by diverse views on both the actual standard of living that should be ensured and the manner and degree to which resources should be distributed. Nevertheless there is a large body of legislation and diverse institutions in Israel through which welfare state goals are furthered and the benefits and services that constitute it are provided. In expenditure terms, half of the state budget is devoted to social services, though this makes up only 15.6% of the country's gross domestic product, an expenditure level that is significantly lower than that in most welfare states (Bendelac, 2010).

Initial efforts to establish social protection institutions in Israel were undertaken immediately after independence in 1948. Despite the need to deal with an ongoing military conflict and mass immigration during much of its short history, Israel managed to establish a welfare state in the early 1970s. To a large degree the Beveridge model, with its emphasis on universal social insurance based benefits, served as the fundamental basis for structuring major social security programmes (Doron, 1994). In addition, categorical non-contributory universal benefits have traditionally played a major role in the Israeli welfare state, these serving as a means of compensating victims of the Arab–Israeli conflict and of dealing with immigrants' needs and their integration into society (Gal, 2008). Finally, a nationally administered social assistance programme was introduced in the early 1980s. Universal health and education, housing assistance and social care complement the social security system. The Israeli welfare state appeared to be moving towards a more social-democratic model during its formative period in the mid-1970s, with the introduction of more universal services, greater state involvement in welfare, wider coverage of needs and the introduction of more wage-related and better indexed benefits. However, from the 1980s onwards efforts to privatise social services, to target benefits, to move benefit recipients into work and to cut social spending have been common. These efforts peaked during a period of recession and neo-liberal political dominance in the initial years of the new millennium.

Seen as a whole, the Israeli welfare state is a relatively comprehensive system that offers benefits and services which provide support and resources to deal with a wide range of needs and contingencies. However, the generosity of the benefits, the quality of the services and access to them are often limited. As is the case in other Mediterranean welfare states, the family remains a major source of welfare provision in Israel, and clientelism still plays a significant role in the social welfare system (Gal, 2010).

Despite its comprehensiveness, the Israeli welfare state has been relatively unsuccessful in overcoming income inequalities created within an ever more polarised labour market, in reducing differential access to social services which have undergone a rapid process of privatisation and commercialisation, and in dealing with poverty. These are exacerbated by the relatively low levels of social protection and specific demographic and ethnic characteristics of Israeli society (Hemmings, 2010). In particular, the trend for large families in the Arab and the orthodox Jewish communities and the low level of labour market participation among members of these communities create large pockets of social exclusion. Existing discrimination in the labour market of Arabs and an unequal distribution of state resources intensify this social problem. As a result, poverty levels in Israel remain high, with nearly a fifth of all families and a third of all children living below the poverty line. Clearly the Israeli welfare state has not managed to deal effectively with poverty nor to offer sufficient protection to diverse segments of the population.

Social work in Israel: an overview

Social work has existed in Israel for more than eight decades and its development is closely linked to that of the Israeli welfare state. Social work was formally established in 1931, when the National Committee, the governing body of the Jewish community prior to the establishment of the state, established a Social Work Department (Loewenberg, 1993). Headed by Henrietta Szold, this department sought to transform voluntary social work activity into a paid occupation that required formal and systematic professional training. The department initiated the development of local social assistance departments in various cities and towns, which rapidly became the main employers of social workers. Formal social work education began in 1934 with the establishment of the first school of social work, under the auspices of the Social Work Department, which offered a one-year training programme (Deutsch, 1970).

Ever since, the social work profession in Israel has undergone a substantial process of professionalisation (Weiss, Spiro, Sherer, and Korin-Langer, 2004). The academicisation of social work was a prime manifestation of this process. The social work education system developed from two small non-university social work schools in the 1930s, through the establishment of the first university-based social work school at the Hebrew University in 1958, to five university-based schools of social work in the following two decades (Spiro, 2001). With the establishment of these schools, licensing for social work practice was now fully dependent on undergraduate training within academic institutions (Spiro et al, 1997). An additional development in this process during the 1990s and 2000s was a substantial increase in the supply of social work education with the opening of five college-based schools of social work. During the 1970s and the 1980s Masters in Social Work (MSW) and PhD programmes were established at the university-based schools. These programmes offer a growing number of social workers advanced training, specialisation and research opportunities. During the last decade, MSW programmes were also introduced in two public colleges (Levin and Weiss-Gal, 2011).

This academicisation process has also been reflected in the production of knowledge within social work. This has taken the form of an impressive volume of research undertaken within social work academia and its publication in Israel and outside the country. One outlet for this knowledge is a peer- reviewed quarterly social work journal, *Society & Welfare*, established in 1978 on the basis of a Ministry of Welfare journal, initially published during the late 1950s (Bargal, 2008).

A second aspect of the professionalisation of social work in Israel is related to the public recognition of social work in Israeli society (Spiro et al, 1997; Weiss, Spiro, Sherer, and Korin-Langer, 2004). This recognition is manifested in the role of legislation in the definition of social work's task. Pieces of legislation adopted over the years have identified a number of statutory functions in the fields of protection of at-risk population groups, probation and long-term care that can be filled solely by licensed social workers.

The professional status of social work is also based on the 1996 Social Workers Law. This stipulates that a licence to engage in social work will be granted only to individuals holding a Bachelor of Social Work degree granted by an institution of higher education, and prohibits the employment of anyone lacking these credentials in positions earmarked for social workers. The law grants formal status to the Social Work Council, a body comprising representatives of the profession, social work schools and the social services, which recognises levels of professional competence and expertise. Finally, the law authorises the minister of welfare and social affairs to issue regulations that identify positions which are intended exclusively for social workers. These include a large number of managerial and supervisor positions in social care, hospitals, probation and other services.

A third aspect of the professionalisation process that has characterised Israeli social work relates to its professional organisation (Spiro et al, 1997; Weiss, Spiro, Sherer, and Korin-Langer, 2004). The Israeli Association of Social Workers (ISASW) was established in 1937, at a very early stage in the development of the profession (Deutsch, 1970). In contrast to many other countries (Weiss and Welbourne, 2007), this organisation serves as both a professional association and a trade union. Membership of the ISASW is relatively high, with approximately 75% of all active or retired social workers being members. The association has played a major role in efforts to further the licensing legislation and those laws that determine a social work monopoly over fields of practice. It also developed a Code of Ethics in 1978 that was reformulated in 1995 (ISASW, 1995), and established mechanisms for dealing with complaints. Parts of the code were recognised in regulations incorporated in the 1996 Social Workers Law.

Despite these advanced processes of professionalisation, as is the case in other countries, the remuneration of social workers in Israel remains relatively low, and working conditions are often difficult. These issues have been the subject of growing dissatisfaction among social workers and indeed led to a bitter labour dispute in 2011.

Social work in Israel is a very diverse profession in terms of the welfare sectors and social services in which social workers are employed, the populations they serve, the problems they address and the methods they adopt (Spiro et al, 1997). Most social workers are employed by local government in social care services and by the state in probation services, adoption services, hospitals and mental health medical centres. The outsourcing of social care in the last three decades has also led to a dramatic increase in the numbers of social workers employed by non-state organisations in the for-profit and non-profit sectors. A growing number are employed by non-profit service providers and advocacy organisations, and to a lesser degree by for-profit organisations, mostly in the long-term care field (Bar-Zuri, 2004). In terms of problems and populations, the social work profession deals with people living in poverty and social exclusion, children and women at risk, families in distress, older people, adult and juvenile offenders people with disabilities, immigrants and asylum seekers.

Social workers in Israel engage in a wide range of methods: clinical social work, counselling, group work, social casework, case management, childcare and protection, community work and policy practice. However, studies undertaken in recent decades indicate that social work in Israel tends to emphasise direct practice with individual and families. This reflects the fact that the Israeli profession is still based, to a large degree, on an individualistic model of social work, with macro forms of practice still on the sidelines (Weiss, 2001; Buchbinder et al, 2004; Weiss-Gal, 2008).

Policy practice: discourse, education and practice

Discourse

A review of the social work discourse in Israel, as it is reflected in the professional literature, conferences and documents such as the Code of Ethics, as well as formal government documents drawn up by social workers, shows that the place of policy practice in this discourse has undergone major changes over time. These include increasing calls for greater involvement and changes in the perception of who can, and should, be involved in policy practice. Moreover, the focus of the discourse has widened and moved beyond calls for involvement in policy practice to the conceptualisation and study of this type of practice, which enhances the knowledge base of policy practice in Israel.

Though a small minority of social workers, most of whom served as high-level government officials in the Ministry of Welfare and the social security system, had been involved in the social policy formulation process previously, the demand for greater social work involvement in the policy process was initially raised by social work academics and community social workers in the late 1960s and early 1970s (Rosenfeld, 1975; Korazim, 1978). In a watershed address to a congress of the Association of Social Workers that convened in 1975, a leading social work professor called on the association to play a more active role in furthering social reform (Rosenfeld, 1975). The demand that social workers engage in social policy formulation grew stronger during a period of welfare state retrenchment in the 1980s (Korazim, 1985; Doron, 1989).

Calls for greater social work engagement in the policy process intensified significantly in the first decade of the new millennium (*Meidaos*, 2003; Kaufman, 2005; Weiss-Gal, 2006; Eytan et al, 2009; Weiss-Gal and Ben-Arieh, 2009). These calls stressed the need for the involvement of diverse types of social workers in policy formulation, including caseworkers. This trend probably stemmed from major processes in the Israeli welfare state and the social work profession. First, while the Israeli welfare state has grown over time, during this period the retrenchment of the welfare state intensified and the ongoing process of privatisation of social care accelerated. Not surprisingly, wider social work involvement in the policy process can be linked to professional frustration over major cuts in social spending during an extended economic crisis at the time. Notably, these developments in the welfare state were accompanied by a widening economic gap and increase in poverty levels among social work's client groups and a consequent increase in demand for services provided by social workers.

Apart from being confronted with the harsh realities of an ever more unequal society, Israeli social work was influenced by ideas prevalent in the more general social work discourse, particularly that in North America, Europe and Australia. This is especially true of the growing development of critical perspectives in social work in Israel (Mansbach, 2005; Weiss, 2005; Weiss-Gal, 2009), which greatly emphasised the role of social workers as agents of social change, social justice and human rights.

The actual usage of the term 'policy practice' in the Israeli social work discourse first emerged in an article entitled 'Policy practice in social work: A conceptual framework for action', (Weiss-Gal, 2006). Drawing on conceptualisations and definitions of policy practice as developed in the US from the 1990s (Jansson, 1990; Wyers, 1991; Figueira-McDonough, 1993; McInnis-Dittrich, 1994; Iatridis, 1995; Hoefer, 1999; Schneider and Netting, 1999; Fauri et al, 2000; Haynes and Mickelson, 2003) and on Israeli case studies, this work sought to introduce the notion of policy practice to Israeli social workers. In particular, the article underscored the idea that policy practice is a practice that can and should be employed by all social workers as an integral part of their practice and as an important vehicle through which they can fulfil social work's unique mission.

In the years since, policy practice has enjoyed growing attention in the social work literature in Israel. One focus of this literature has been on an ongoing effort to conceptualise this practice and its strategies better, to analysze its underlying rationale and describe and examine case studies in which social workers (including caseworkers) were involved in policy practice, and to employ theoretical developments in public and social policy in order to understand its relevance to the policy formulation process better (Weiss-Gal and Gal, 2011; Weiss-Gal and Filosof, 2012). Another component of this burgeoning scholarship consists of initial efforts to construct an integrative explanatory model that can identify the factors that contribute to the involvement of Israeli social workers in policy practice (Weiss-Gal and Gal, 2008, 2011).

Growing attention has also been devoted to policy practice training and its evaluation. Here the focus has been on undergraduate- and graduate-level programmes in addition to advanced training courses for practising social workers (Kaufman, 2005; Eytan et al, 2009; Weiss-Gal and Savaya, 2012). Additionally the literature has sought to examine the degree to which social workers are engaged in policy practice. In this case, quantitative tools have been developed in order to determine the level of involvement of social workers in policy practice (Weiss-Gal, 2008), and the degree to which engagement in policy practice is incorporated in social work job descriptions (Weiss-Gal and Levin, 2010).

Evidence of the growing recognition of policy practice in the social work discourse can be discerned in professional and official publications. Formal recognition of the role of social workers in social policy formulation is to be found in the revised Israeli social work Code of Ethics published in 1995. In the first *Code of Ethics of the Israeli Association of Social Workers*, published in 1978, the sole mention of policy goals was a preamble that determined that social work seeks to develop resources in the community and awareness of the need for social change (ISASW, 1978). By contrast, the revised and much enlarged version of the Code of Ethics (ISASW, 1995) reflects a much clearer understanding that social workers have a responsibility to further wider social goals and that policy involvement is a means by which these can be attained. One of the chapters of the code

(ISASW, 1995, ch. 2.A) is devoted to the social role of social workers, and states that the social work is required to further social welfare. The chapter contains both explicit and implicit demands for engagement in policy practice on the part of Israeli social workers. Social workers are called on 'to support policy and legislation aimed at improving social services and furthering social justice' and to encourage service users and the public at large to participate in policy formulation. Alongside these more explicit calls for policy involvement, the code identifies a number of social goals that imply that their achievement requires, among other things, social worker participation in the policy process. These social goals include ensuring enhanced access to public goods and opportunities, particularly by vulnerable social groups. Similarly, the code identifies dismantling discriminatory structures and practices as a desired goal that social workers should seek. In another chapter of the Code of Ethics that focuses on the relationship between social workers and their employees, social workers are required to improve the policies of the organisation (ISASW, 1995, ch.4.A).

Indications of the acknowledgement that the policy practice function of social workers has become better integrated into the way in which the profession is defined in Israel can be found in a more recent report of the State Commission on Reform of Local Social Care Services (State of Israel, The Ministry of Welfare and Social Services, 2010). This commission, which primarily comprised of social workers, was established by the minister of welfare and social services in order to identify changes required in the structuring and in the functioning of local social care services and of the social workers employed in them. Discussing the various goals and intervention strategies of local social care services, the report notes that the goals of social care can be best served if social workers adopt diverse intervention methods. Policy practice is identified specifically as one of these. The report goes on to state that social workers 'should engage in the formulation of social policy of other social services, local authorities, and the state' (State of Israel, The Ministry of Welfare and Social Services, 2010, p 36).

Education

Changes in the perceived role of policy practice can also be found in social work education in Israel. Here again policy practice is enjoying growing attention. Unlike some other nations (such as Australia, Spain, the United Kingdom and the US), in Israel there is no official body that sets required parameters of social work education or the content of curricula. As such, schools of social work have a large degree of discretion over their training agenda.

Prior to the early 2000s, training in policy practice, as distinct from social policy, was absent from social work education in Israel. In a study of the social policy content of courses in the five university-based schools of social work operating in Israel during the late 1990s (Gal and Weiss, 2000), it emerged that no explicit policy practice courses were offered. Rather, the programmes included social policy courses that sought to elucidate the context in which social workers and service users lived and worked, the impact of social policy, and policies in specific fields, such as social care and social security, that were identified as being of particular relevance to the social work profession. These courses offered theoretical and conceptual knowledge on social policy but did not provide the tools actually to engage in policy practice. Given that the accepted wisdom of the time was that generic social workers did not need to engage in policy practice, the courses that did focus on engagement in policy formulation were offered primarily in community social work specialisations.

The marginal role of policy practice in social work education may be one of the factors that shaped the professional preferences and attitudes of social work students during this period. The findings of longitudinal studies on the professional ideologies and preferences of Israeli social work students at two universities undertaken in the 1990s and the first half of the 2000s indicated that, although they identified with welfare state goals and universal services, the students' willingness to engage in policy practice was only moderate and far weaker than their willingness to engage in direct practice. This was the case both at the beginning (Weiss et al, 2002) and completion of their studies (Weiss, Gal & Cnaan, 2004). An additional analysis of 136 graduating students at one university in Israel identified three distinctive clusters of students based on their willingness to engage in six modes of social work practice (direct work, family therapy, group work, community organisation, social policy formulation, social service management) (Weiss, 2006). The study revealed that only 7% of the students could be identified as belonging to a macro practice cluster. Those in the macro practice cluster were students who preferred social policy formulation and social service management over the other modes of social work intervention.

By contrast, over the last decade, policy practice has begun to be better integrated into social work education. Following calls in the literature within Israel (Weiss et al, 2006) and in the wider social work world (Pierce, 2000) to adapt social work training so that it conveys the understanding, knowledge and skills that will encourage students to engage in policy practice, it is possible to discern a movement towards the introduction of more applied policy practice courses in most social work schools in Israel on both the bachelor (Kaufman, 2005) and the masters levels (Weiss-Gal and Savaya, in press). In addition, policy practice is now incorporated, to a certain degree, in in-service training for social workers (Eytan et al, 2009). The following table shows the results of a survey undertaken by the author of the curricula of the bachelor-level (BSW) and master-level (MSW) programmes at all 10 schools of social work in Israel in the 2010–11 academic year.

As can be seen from Table 4.1, over a third of all schools of social work in Israel offer a compulsory course on policy practice to all BSW-level students. Of these, three also offer policy practice content in other courses. An additional school offers a single elective course. In three schools, there are no compulsory or elective courses on policy practice but policy practice components are included in policy courses. Two of the BSW programmes do not include any policy practice content.

Table 4.1: Policy practice in schools of social work in Israel (by number of schools)

Schools of social work that	BSW	MSW
• offer a compulsory course for all students and policy courses that include policy practice content	3	1
• offer a compulsory course and elective courses	1	
• include policy practice content in policy courses only	3	3
• offer elective courses and include policy practice content in policy courses	1	1
• offer no courses	2	2
Total	**10**	**7**

Although advanced social policy courses are included in the curricula in all seven schools that offer master-level degrees, these courses tend to be theoretical in nature. Nevertheless, in three of the schools policy practice is a substantial component of these courses. In one of the schools there is a compulsory policy practice course and elective courses, and in an another school there are elective courses in addition to the inclusion of policy practice content in social policy courses. In two schools, there is no policy practice content in the MSW programme.

In short, there is clearly a tendency to integrate training in policy practice in social work education in Israel. However, in marked contrast to the growing place of policy practice in the social work discourse in Israel, the extent of this training on the BSW and MSW levels still remains limited.

Practice

An examination of Israeli social workers` involvement in policy practice over the last six decades reveals both an increase in involvement and a greater diversity with regard to the characteristics of the social workers engaged in policy practice and to the strategies they have adopted. As noted earlier, social workers were involved in the social policy formulation process ever since the establishment of a social welfare department in 1931 by the Jewish community in pre-state Palestine. A small number of social workers, most of whom were immigrants from the US and Germany and who held lead roles in this department, played a major role in the formulation of social welfare institutions during this period. With the establishment of the state in 1948, responsibility for social welfare services was transferred to the newly formed Ministry of Welfare. But, to a large degree, the same small group of social workers remained the prime source of professional knowledge in the ministry and they continued to play a major role in the policy formulation process, primarily with regard to local social welfare provision (Doron, 2004).

By contrast, the social work impact on wider issues of social policy was very limited. This was partly due to the extremely centralised nature of decision making in Israel at the time and the sharp differentiation between narrowly defined social welfare issues – which were the domain of the Ministry of Welfare and hence of the social worker leadership of that ministry – and wider issues of social security, work and disability, which were dealt with by the more powerful Ministry of Labour, in which the social work presence was limited.

Moreover, during this period social workers were an integral part of a social welfare system engaged in a rapid process of nation building that focused especially on the absorption of immigrants and the development of a social welfare infrastructure throughout the country. The dominant professional ethos during the initial decades after statehood viewed social work as a profession that dealt with the social distress of individuals, families and communities in a newly emerging immigrant society that lacked sufficient social services. This ethos was also linked to an effort on the part of social work to achieve greater legitimisation and to consolidate the professional status of social work among decision makers and the public at large. As such, social workers tended to regard themselves as faithful agents of the state engaged in these tasks and as caseworkers far removed from the policy formulation process. Not surprisingly, engagement in policy practice was limited to a very small number of social workers who held high-level positions within the Ministry of Social Welfare and the National Insurance Institute, while critical challenges to existing policies and the consequences of these were virtually non-existent. Reflecting this approach, the ISASW focused exclusively on occupational rights and refrained from taking stands on policy issues. The absence of any reference to policy involvement in the first version of the social work Code of Ethics, as noted above, was indicative of this perception.

Change in the pattern of social work involvement in social policy formulation began during the 1960s and 1970s. Within the Ministry of Welfare, a new generation of social workers with PhDs from universities in the US began to play a growing role in the decision-making process within the state bureaucracy. At the same time, academics from the Hebrew University school of social work (until the end of the 1960s the only school operating) were integrated into the policy-making process, often as the heads of state commissions that set social welfare policy. Finally, community social workers influenced by activist trends in the US and elsewhere, sought to have an effect on social policy. This was particularly the case during the early 1970s, when public attention to issues of poverty and inequality grew following a wave of unrest and protests by poorer people (Itzhaky and York, 1998).

Despite the rise in policy involvement on the part of academics and community workers, there was growing criticism within the ISASW of the limited engagement of the association, and of social workers in general, in social policy. This pressure, along with change in the ISASW leadership and a period of welfare state retrenchment and economic crisis during the 1980s led to a more activist stance by the association and to greater involvement of social workers in the policy process, particularly at the local level and as part of advocacy organisations (Kadman, 1988).

Since the 1980s, social workers in Israel have diversified and extended their involvement in policy practice. This reflects not only the evolving policy practice discourse and an emphasis on policy practice in social work training but also the transformation in the structure of the social welfare labour market and in its social welfare governance. In particular, the growth of employment in non-state agencies and the widening of the social policy formulation process beyond its traditionally narrow boundaries have facilitated the participation of social workers employed within the state bureaucracy, of those working in advocacy organisations and of social workers employed by local social care services and other social services in this process (Gal and Weiss-Gal, 2011; Weiss-Gal and Filosof, 2012). Policy practice in Israeli social work takes diverse forms, among them policy analysis, legislative advocacy, social action with both internal and external (the use of the mass media, active involvement in diverse protest activities) foci and reform through litigation at multiple policy levels (organisational, local and national) (*Meidaos*, 2003; Kaufman, 2005; Maymon et al, 2008; Weiss-Gal and Filosof, 2012).

The changing nature of policy practice among Israeli social workers is reflected in a recent study of the involvement of social workers in the deliberations of parliamentary committees in the Knesset, Israel's parliament (Gal and Weiss-Gal, 2011). The findings indicated that, during the period studied (1999–2006), social workers participated in 14% of relevant parliamentary committee meetings. Significantly, social workers were party to between a third and a half of the meetings of six different parliamentary committees, such as committees dealing with the status of women, the rights of children and immigration issues. A content analysis reveals that their participation centred on social problems and policy issues. The input of the social workers showed that these generally took the form of agenda setting, the provision of information, expressions of opinions and explanations. The organisational affiliation of the social workers that participated in the parliamentary committee meetings reflects the breadth of social worker involvement in policy practice in Israel. Although a significant proportion (30%) of the social worker participants in the parliamentary committee discussions were civil servants, a large proportion were affiliated with organisations and agencies outside the traditional social policy formulation realm: 28% of these were employed by local authorities and 31% represented diverse non-profit organisations.

Alongside the more formal policy formulation process, social workers in Israel have also sought to adopt additional paths to influence social policy. One example of this was the struggle against food insecurity in Israel during the early years of the 2000s. In this case, a coalition of social work academics and students from the school of social work at Ben Gurion University and social workers from both state and non-profit agencies were involved in a struggle to raise awareness to the problem of food insecurity caused by cuts in the level of the safety net cash benefit programme. The campaign began with a survey, undertaken by social work students, of food insecurity among the poor residents of towns in the south of the country. The findings of the study served as the basis for a campaign that included demonstrations and conferences to raise awareness to the issue of food insecurity in Israel. Working with advocacy organisations and members of parliament, the campaigners then demanded the reintroduction of school lunches as a response to the findings the study. The public struggle eventually resulted in the passage of legislation in the Israeli parliament that led to the establishment of a school lunch programme in schools throughout the country in 2004 (Kaufman, 2005).

An example of policy practice involvement by a caseworker in a local government social welfare agency is that of Ronit Filosof. Working with families of infants with physical disabilities, she identified major limitations in the eligibility criteria for access to rehabilitation centres for infants. These limitations prevented a large number of infants from receiving services from these centres. Filosof joined a coalition of advocacy organisations that sought to bring about a change in legislation that would enable greater access to these centres on the part of families with infants with disabilities. Drawing on her extensive experience in this field, she contributed to the formulation of proposed changes in the eligibility criteria, in particular those that related to income levels. The struggle to bring about changes in the legislation, which included testimonies in parliamentary committees and media coverage, lasted for over five years and culminated in the adoption of changes in the legislation in 2008 (Weiss-Gal and Filosof, 2012).

However, despite these trends, policy practice involvement still remains a relatively marginal aspect of the professional activity of most social workers in Israel. A recent study of 400 social workers from different social work organisations revealed that social workers attributed the greatest importance to professional aims that seek to protect groups at risk and enhance individual inner resources and give less importance to social justice (Weiss-Gal, 2008). The respondents reported engaging most in direct practice with individual and families, followed by activities protecting at-risk groups. Social and community development and policy practice were at a considerable distance from those two. When questioned as to the degree to which they engaged in different levels of social work practice (individual, family, couple, group, community, organisational and social policy formation), social policy formation was ranked last with an average of 1.52 (on a scale of 1 to 5).

The marginality of policy practice in social work in Israel can be traced to trends in the social work profession. Operating in a strongly neo-liberal context, the social work profession in Israel is still dominated by an individualistic ideology that understands distress, be it that of individuals, families or communities, primarily through intra-psychic and psychological processes (Buchbinder et al, 2004; Weiss-Gal, 2008). This reflects both the ongoing impact of the therapeutic model dominant in US social work and alongside it the intensive professionalisation process (Weiss, Spiro, Sherer, & Korin-Langer, 2004) that has sought to link Israeli social work to more prestigious clinical professions such as psychology and psychiatry. One consequence of this is a growing demand among social workers to specialise in clinical aspects of social work rather than in social change and community action.

This marginality would also appear to be influenced by the nature of the workplace environment of many social workers. Local social care services are underfunded and understaffed and, as a result, social workers are overwhelmed by large case loads (Lavee, 2008; Ofek, 2009). Moreover, due to the adoption of protective legislation, they are often occupied by statutory activities that leave little time for them to move beyond casework. As policy practice has neither been identified as an integral part of the tasks of most social workers employed in social care (Levin and Weiss-Gal, 2010), nor has it been encouraged by management, motivation to engage in this type of practice has been limited.

Conclusions

During the initial decades after Israeli independence in 1948, social worker involvement in the policy process was limited primarily to a small group of social workers who held high-level positions in the government and later to a handful of social work academics. This began to change in the 1970s. The impact of ideas and concepts from abroad, coupled with frustration with the rise of inequality and poverty, contributed to a growing readiness on the part of Israeli social workers to engage in policy practice. This involvement intensified during the early 2000s due to a growing incorporation of the notion of policy practice in the social work discourse and in training, and as a consequence of changes in the labour market structure and governance of social welfare in Israel.

However, this chapter has indicated that although policy practice in Israel has been a growing area of practice, education and knowledge development over recent decades – in particular during the 2000s – it still remains, to a certain extent, on the margins of the social work profession. In other words, despite its enhanced profile in the social work discourse and in training, social workers generally devote most of their efforts to casework, focusing on individual change.

Enjoying growing legitimacy, policy practice in Israel is now at a critical juncture. Its future development and wider integration into social work practice depend on ongoing efforts to continue the expansion of its place in education, research and in-service training, in order to influence social workers' perceptions about their roles in policy processes.

References

Bargal, D. (2008) 'From the editor', *Society & Welfare*, vol 28, pp 363–381 (in Hebrew).

Bar-Zuri, R. (2004) *Social Workers in Israel: Review of the Developments 1990–2002*, Jerusalem: Ministry of Industry, Trade and Employment (in Hebrew).

Bendelac, J. (2010) *The Social Protection system in an International Perspective: Israel and the OECD Countries*, Jerusalem: National Insurance Institute.

Buchbinder, E., Eisikovits, Z. and Karnieli-Miller, O. (2004) 'Social workers' perceptions of the balance between the psychological and the social', *Social Service Review*, vol 78, pp 531–52.

Deutsch, A. (1970) 'The Development of Social Work as a Profession in the Jewish Community in the Land of Israel', unpublished doctoral dissertation, Jerusalem: Hebrew University (in Hebrew).

Doron, A. (1989) 'The social image of social work', *Society & Welfare*, vol 10, pp 170–8.

Doron, A. (1994) 'The effectiveness of the Beveridge model at different stages of social-economic development', in J. Hills, J. Ditch and H. Glennerster (eds) *Beveridge and Social Security*, Oxford: Oxford University Press, pp 189–202.

Doron, A. (2004) 'The system of personal social services in Israel: Changes in leadership', *Social Security*, vol 65, pp 11–33 (in Hebrew).

Eytan, S., Aran, L., Khamra, K., and Obed, W. (2009) 'Training for enlarging the role of social workers in formulating policy processes', *Social Security*, vol 81, pp 135–66 (in Hebrew).

Fauri, D.P., Wernet, S.P. and Netting, F.E. (2000) *Cases in Macro Social Work Practice*, Boston, MA: Allyn & Bacon.

Figueira-McDonough, J. (1993) 'Policy practice: The neglected side of social work intervention', *Social Work*, vol 38, pp 179–88.

Gal, J. (2008) 'Immigration and the categorical welfare state in Israel', *Social Service Review*, vol 82, no 4, pp 639–61.

Gal, J. (2010) 'Is there an extended family of Mediterranean welfare states?', *Journal of European Social Policy*, vol 20, no 4, pp 283–300.

Gal, J. and Weiss, I. (2000) 'Policy practice in social work and social work education in Israel', *Social Work Education*, vol 19, no 5, pp 485–500.

Gal, J. and Weiss-Gal, I. (2011) 'Social policy formulation and the role of professionals: The involvement of social workers in parliamentary committees in Israel', *Health and Social Care in the Community*, vol 19, no 2, pp 158–67.

Haynes, K.S. and Mickelson, J.S. (2003) *Affecting Change: Social Workers in the Political Arena* (5th edn), Boston, MA: Allyn and Bacon.

Hemmings, P. (2010) *Policy Options for Reducing Poverty and Raising Employment Rates in Israel*, Paris: OECD.

Hoefer, R. (1999) 'The social work and politics initiative: A model for increasing political content in social work education', *Journal of Community Practice*, vol 6, pp 71–87.

Iatridis, D.S. (1995) 'Policy Practice', in R.L. Edwards (ed in chief), *Encyclopedia of Social Work* (19th edn), Washington, DC: NASW Press, pp 1855–66.

ISASW (Israeli Association of Social Workers) (1978) *Code of Ethics*, Tel-Aviv: ISASW.

ISASW (Israeli Association of Social Workers) (1995) *Code of Ethics*, Tel-Aviv: ISASW.

Itzhaky, H. and York, A.S. (1998) 'Social work practice in the community', in F. Lowenberg (ed) *Meeting the Challenge of a Changing Society: Fifty Years of Social Work in Israel*, Jerusalem: Magnes, pp 179–95.

Jansson, B.S. (1990) *Social Welfare Policy: From Theory to Practice*, Belmont, CA: Wadsworth.

Kadman, Y. (1988) 'Social work and social action', in I. Ben Shahak, R. Berger and Y. Kadman (eds) *Social Work in Israel*, Tel Aviv: Israel Association of Social Workers, pp 31–46.

Kaufman, R. (2005) 'Involvement of faculty and students in promoting the rights to food security: Lessons from a social change project', *Society & Welfare,* vol 25, pp 511–32 (in Hebrew).

Korazim, J. (1978) 'The Israeli social worker as a social warner', *Social Security*, vol 16, pp 124–31 (in Hebrew).

Korazim, J. (1985) 'Preparing social workers for advocacy and social warning in an era of resource decline', *Social Security*, vol 27, pp 128–36 (in Hebrew).

Lavee, Y. (2008) *The Report of the Commission on Family Welfare Policy in Israel*, Jerusalem: Ministry of Welfare and Social Services.

Levin, L. and Weiss-Gal, I. (2011) 'Social work education in Israel at the dawn of the 21st century', in S. Stanley (ed), *Social Work Education in Countries of the East: Issues and Challenges,* Nova Science Publishers, pp 191- 207.

Loewenberg, F.M. (1993) 'Preparing for the welfare state? A reexamination of the decision to establish the social service department of the Vaad Leumi', *Journal of Social Work and Social Policy in Israel*, vol 7/8, pp 21–30.

McInnis-Dittrich, K. (1994) *Integrating Social Welfare Policy and Social Work Practice*, Pacific Grove, CA: Brooks/Cole.

Mansbach, A. (2005) 'Criticism without fear: A critical view of social work as espoused by Karl Marx and Michel Foucault', *Society & Welfare*, vol 25, pp 167–84 (in Hebrew).

Maymon, A., Amzalek, N., Epstein, B., Gross, T. and Rei, G. (2008) *Monitoring as a Tool for Social Change,* Jerusalem: Jerusalem Foundation and the New Israel Fund.

Meidaos (2003) 'A social struggle for a policy that ensures the welfare of the population', *Meidaos*, vol 34, pp 5–6 (in Hebrew).

Ofek, A. (2009) *A Research Report: Preparing for the Reform of Local Social Welfare Services,* Jerusalem: Ministry of Welfare and Social Services (in Hebrew).

Pierce, D. (2000) 'Policy practice', in J. Midgley, M.B. Tracy and M. Livermore (eds) *The Handbook of Social Policy,* Thousand Oaks, CA: Sage, pp 53–63.

Rosenfeld, J.M. (1975). 'Social work: The profession to where?', *Saad*, vol 19, pp 3–7 (in Hebrew).

Schneider, R.L. and Netting, F.E. (1999) 'Influencing social policy in a time of devolution: Upholding social work's great tradition', *Social Work*, vol 44, pp 349–57.

Spiro, S.E. (2001) 'Social work education in Israel: Trends and issues', *Social Work Education*, vol 20, pp 89–99.

Spiro, S.E., Sherer, M., Korin-Langer, N. and Weiss, I. (1997) 'Israel', in N.S. Mayadas, T.D. Watts and D. Elliot (eds) *International Handbook on Social Work Theory and Practice,* Westport, CT: Greenwood, pp 223–44.

State of Israel, the Ministry of Welfare and Social Services (2010) *The Report of the State Commission on Reform of Local Social Care Service*, Jerusalem: Ministry of Welfare and Social Services.

Weiss, I. (2001) 'The ideology, policy and practice of adult probation service in Israel', *British Journal of Social Work*, vol 31, pp 775–89.

Weiss, I. (2005) 'Critical perspectives on social work', *Society & Welfare*, vol 25, pp 249–81 (in Hebrew).

Weiss, I. (2006) 'Modes of practice and the dual mission of social work: A cross-national study of social work students' preferences', *Journal of Social Service Research*, vol 32, pp 135–51.

Weiss, I. and Welbourne, P. (eds) (2007) *Social work as a Profession: A Comparative Cross-National Perspective*, Birmingham: Venture Press.

Weiss, I., Gal, J., Cnaan, R.A., and, Maglejlic R. (2002) 'Where does it begin? A comparative perspective on the professional preferences of first year social work students', *British Journal of Social Work,* vol 32, pp 589-608.

Weiss, I., Gal, J. and Cnaan, R.A. (2004)'Social work education as professional socialization: A study of the impact of social work education upon students' professional preferences', *Journal of Social Service Research*, vol 31, pp 13–31.

Weiss, I., Spiro, S., Sherer, S. and Korin-Langer, N. (2004) 'Social work in Israel: Professional characteristics in an international comparative perspective', *International Journal of Social Welfare*, vol 13, no 4, pp 287–96.

Weiss, I., Gal, J. and Katan, J. (2006) 'Social policy for social work: A teaching agenda', *British Journal of Social Work*, vol 36, pp 789–806.

Weiss-Gal, I. (2006) 'Policy practice in social work: A conceptual framework for action', *Society & Welfare*, vol 26, pp 445–502 (in Hebrew).

Weiss-Gal, I. (2008) 'The person-in-environment approach: Professional ideology and practice of social workers in Israel', *Social Work*, vol 53, pp 65–75.

Weiss-Gal, I. (2009) 'Teaching critical perspectives: Analyses of professional practice in the film "Ladybird, Ladybird"', *Social Work Education*, vol 28, pp 873–86.

Weiss- Gal, I. and Ben-Arieh, A. (2009) 'Social workers and social policy in Israel', *Social Security*, vol 81, pp 5–11 (in Hebrew).

Weiss-Gal, I. and Filosof, R. (2012) 'Policy practice in social work', in H. Hovav, E. Lawental and Y. Katan (eds) *Introduction to Israeli Social Work*, Tel Aviv: Hakibbutz Hameuchad (in Hebrew).

Weiss-Gal, I. and Gal, J. (2008) 'Social workers and policy-practice: The role of social and professional values', *Journal of Social Service Research*, vol 34, pp 15–27.

Weiss-Gal, I. and Gal, J. (2011) *Policy Practice in Social Work*, Jerusalem: Magnes (in Hebrew).

Weiss- Gal, I. and Levin, L. (2010) 'Social workers and policy-practice: An analysis of job descriptions in Israel', *Journal of Policy Practice*, vol 9, pp 183–200.

Weiss- Gal, I. and Savaya, R. (2012)'A hands-on policy practice seminar for social workers in Israel: Description and evaluation', *Journal of Policy Practice*, vol 11, no 3, pp 139–57.

Wyers, N.L. (1991) 'Policy-practice in social work: Models and issues', *Journal of Social Work Education*, vol 27, pp 241–50.

FIVE

Social workers affecting social policy in Italy

Annamaria Campanini and Carla Facchini[1]

Social work and the welfare state in Italy

Social work developed in Italy immediately after the Second World War with an orientation towards values of democracy and solidarity and seeking to address the material and moral damage that civil society was facing. At the Tremezzo convention, which can be regarded as the founding moment of Italian social work (*servizio sociale*), the political foundations of social assistance were explicitly recognised (Dellavalle, 2008). Indeed, an animated debate ensued on the different interpretations proposed by representatives of the two principal tendencies present: one Catholic oriented and the other lay oriented. An historical analysis of the professional commitment of some of the first social workers reveals an interesting correlation between their involvement in the anti-fascist movement and an awareness that work in social assistance should be based on knowledge of the social causes underlying social problems.

In this context, it is interesting to note that the term used in Italy is *assistente sociale* (social assistant). It is a term that highlights the aspect of 'personal' readiness to help others and not, as suggested instead by the English term 'social worker', the dimension of work, the competences required, and of negotiability. It should be remembered that conditions in Italy at the end of the Second World War were marked by a considerable lack of economic and social development. Almost half of the labour force was employed in agriculture and over three quarters of the adult population had a primary school diploma only (Ginsborg, 1989). The social services were national institutions founded on a categorical basis and characterised by a high level of bureaucracy (Campanini, 2007), so that it was very difficult to introduce changes from within. Consequently, the impact of modernity, coming after the phenomena of industrialisation, urbanisation and the growth in mass education in the decades after the end of the war, was particularly strong and gave rise, at the end of the 1960s, to radical social movements that continued for over a decade. Social workers, together with other professionals, played a role in these movements and they had a marked effect on the social services.

As was the case in the US (Jansson et al, 2005) and elsewhere, the debate within the profession was between micro practice focused on the individual and organisational and reform-focused macro practice. In Italy students and professionals criticised the dominance of casework in social work, and advocated a move away from a functional logic of a Parsonian type (Toren, 1974), which was more oriented to adapting individuals to society than to making the social context more suitable for people's lives. The emphasis during this period was on the need to develop intervention that centred on the collective dimension.

Similarly, in this period the demand was to encourage the participation of citizens in social change at the structural level. This resulted in the closure of many institutions such as hospitals for mental health service users (Donnelly, 1992), institutions for children and special schools for disabled people (Begeny and Martens, 2007). The social services moved from a central national structure to a community-based one, from services tailored for people with additional needs and conditions to universal services open to all (Fasol, 2000).

This period of change led to original contributions on the part of the social services in the organisation of new solutions and new services. Legislation in the social field reflected a deep cultural change in the ways of dealing with social problems, while experimental intervention by social workers in some areas became the point of reference for structuring new guidelines for social policy. These changes mostly took place in the northern regions of Italy but also led to national legislation that was valid for the entire country.

Among other things, the social work profession contributed to the adoption of laws on the social integration of poorer people (law 118/71), the establishment of family planning centres (law 405/75), the treatment of addiction and alcoholism (law 685/75), and psychiatry (law 180/78). Similarly, health reform (law 833/78), which offered universal healthcare and emphasised the need for healthcare and social care to be integrated, was introduced. Moreover, from the early 1970s onwards, home assistance for older people and services for not self-sufficient people and for minors in difficulty began to spread as a result of specific regional legislation.

The 1980s saw an initial phase of consolidation of social services, organised on a territorial basis with a strong commitment to attaining the integration of social and health services. The transformation process of local health units (decree 502/92)[2] into managerial organisations and the reform of local power (decree 517/93) that led to the progressive withdrawal of powers from the local authorities produced transitions in the social services and difficulties in reorganising the activities of social workers, who had previously been employed by both the local authorities and the National Health Service (Campanini and Fortunato, 2008). Despite major developments in social services and the contribution of social workers to these, Italian social work did not manage to assume the form of a coherent professional group, capable of formulating proposals at a political level; instead social workers tended to focus on activities mainly carried out within the services in which they were employed.

In the 1990s new challenges emerged. These included poverty and an ageing society, an increase in the number of sick and dependent older people, and of adults with chronic diseases (such as disabilities and HIV), an increase in unemployment and a growth in immigration from non-European and east European countries. At the same time, Italian society faced an economic crisis that led to cuts in the public sector and the outsourcing of social services (Bifulco and Vitale, 2006; Campanini and Fortunato, 2008).

This was the background to a wide-ranging reform of social services. This reform (law 328/2000), which was adopted in 2000, had been eagerly awaited for decades by social workers and took into account long-standing debates in society as a whole and in the world of social services in particular. The legislation's title, 'A framework law for the realisation of an integrated system of social service interventions', reflects the intended scope of the reform. It was perceived as contributing to 'preventing disadvantage, opposing poverty, helping whoever is in difficulty, improving the quality of life for everyone: finally fully implementing the Italian Constitution' (Turco, 2000, p 1).

The role of social workers was seen to be of primary importance in this reform. Professional social workers were considered a key element at a basic level of intervention in the organisation of social services. As well as developing personalised projects for people in need, social workers were asked to play an active role in the community, to facilitate the participation of citizens, to activate social platforms to discuss the needs of the population and to create plans to enhance wellbeing and to support families, networking with all social actors involved in the community (Facchini, 2010).

However, a change in the political climate, the approval of fiscal federalism and a worsening economic crisis, leading to a process of privatisation of social services, had a marked impact on the law throughout Italy (Gori, 2005). In contrast to other European countries (Kazepov, 2008), the economic crisis resulted not in the market assuming a more important role but in the greater involvement of non-profit organisations (for example, charity groups, social cooperatives, foundations, self-help groups and social associations) in the social services (Ascoli and Ranci, 2003). The resulting model has been defined as the 'negotiation model' (Pavolini, 2003) or a social market of services, 'based on a reduced financial effort by the state and on its ability to identify families' needs for services in order to orient them towards a private offer coming from accredited organisations, increasingly structured and formalised, in competition with each other' (Paci, 2005, p 140). In practice this implies a move from the traditional top-down logic of government to a bottom-up approach to governance (Mayntz, 2003) where different autonomous actors (public, private and non-profit) can contribute with their own resources to solving problems in a collaborative and horizontal process. In this way, social partners working at local or community level can tackle the challenge of co-designing the system of social policies and of evaluating the results in delivering social services.

The specific nature of the Italian welfare mix is probably due to both social and economic reasons. First, the emphasis on social solidarity in Italy, along with the key role played by families – which in Italy represent the main care givers (Saraceno, 2002) – led to a definition of a family/kinship solidarity model (Naldini, 2003). Secondly, social services are characterised by low productivity and are labour intensive, making them unattractive to private entrepreneurs. Finally, as Ferrera (2005) has argued, the spread of particularism also played a central role in the transformation process, contributing to the peculiarity of the Italian case.

In this widespread and deeply culturally rooted model, combined with the change in the political climate and the halt in resources destined for social policies, social workers have not been able to become a group capable of entering the political decision-making arena nor have they been able to integrate the individual caring dimension with an awareness of the political aspects of their own actions.

An overview of social work education

Social work education in Italy was introduced at the end of the Second World War and was undertaken initially by a variety of private institutions (both secular and religious), but it lacked any state regulation of the study programmes (Tonon Giraldo, 2005). Not until the second half of the 1980s did social work education attain legitimacy and formal state recognition. During this period, universities were acknowledged as the only institutions in which social work education could be undertaken, a Professional Register was established, and a Code of Ethics drawn up (Campanini, 2004).

Since 2000, in accordance with the principles of the Bologna Declaration,[3] Italy has introduced a national reform of higher education which establishes three levels of degree in all university faculties. There is a bachelor's degree, 'Sciences of social work' (180 credits), and a master's degree in 'Planning and management of politics and social services' (120 credits). In the 2010–11 academic year, there were 39 BA programmes, 35 MA programmes and only five doctoral programmes with special paths for social work (in Trieste, Rome, Milano Bicocca, Sassari and Trento).[4] In all, in 2009–10 there were 3,332 enrolments in the first year of the BA course and 1,616 in the first year of the MA course. In the same year there were 2,530 and 904 graduates respectively.

While these developments can be seen as an important step in the process of recognising social work in Italy, there are still many difficulties. The structure of the curriculum in social work has been defined at national level, as is the case for other disciplines, but it has been strongly influenced by academic lobbies. Despite the recommendations of the Professional Register and the Association of Italian Teachers of Social Work, and intervention by the European Association of Schools of Social Work (EASSW), the resulting social work curriculum has been very unsatisfactory. Out of 180 credits for the BA degree, ministerial regulations require a minimum of 15 credits for social work disciplines and 18 credits for placement in fieldwork. However, due to a shortage of social work faculties, most universities offer the minimum number of social work courses. Moreover, social work has not been recognised as an independent discipline in Italy, but is included in general sociology, and during the transition of education in social work from the private schools to the universities the ministry failed to adopt measures to protect chairs in social work, as was the case in Spain (Martinez, 2004).

For this reason, and because of the severe economic crisis in higher education, there have been very few appointments of lecturers or professors in social work. As a result, the majority of social work courses are taught by professionals working in the social services and not tenured faculty. Moreover, as social work has not been recognised as an autonomous discipline, this has created a situation in which a sociologist with a university chair can teach social work courses (such as principles of social work or methods of social work) even if he or she has no specific knowledge or experience in the field.

Also problematic is the fact that the change in structure was not followed by a change in the philosophy and methodology of social work education. The courses are not sufficiently focused on competences, the teaching methods are more teacher-centred than student-centred and the number of students accepted is high, which limits the possibility of organising groups and following their progress in a more individualised learning process. The general structure of the curriculum is thus inadequate for a process of professional training. There are general courses on the principles and history of social work and on methods, social policies and the organisation of social services, but none that deals with specific methods or clients' problems, nor are there modules specifically on human rights, social justice, advocacy or policy practice.

Clearly the form that social work education has taken in Italy may have had a negative effect on the development of a sense of collective identity for the profession. In its two decades of existence, teaching in the schools of social work has been based on knowledge and models imported from other contexts (the US in particular). Added to this, the strong ideological current in the 1970s led to a failure to recognise the profession's specific methods and techniques. Finally, with the shift to university training there has been a lack of adequate social work academic faculties able to develop an empirically based body of knowledge and to participate in the training process.

The social work profession

The development of social services that took place in Italy from the 1960s onwards led to legislation that gradually normalised the role of the social services. This legislation conferred on social workers the task of dealing with demands for support from people suffering from socioeconomic disadvantage, as well as responsibility for specific sectors of the population in need and the case management of a range of interventions and services. Thus, by the end of the 1970s, social services were already present in municipalities, family consultancy centres and psychiatric services, and in those dealing with addiction. They were also active in important sectors such as healthcare and prisons, due to the awareness that social intervention needed to be accompanied by specific treatment or rehabilitation (Diomede Canevini, 2005). As an indicator of this development, it is sufficient to note that the number of social workers has grown tenfold from the early 1960s to the present (from approximately 3,500 to over 35,000).

The wide range of different operational contexts affects not only the types of users that social workers deal with, but also the social workers' roles and functions. In the municipalities, particularly small and medium-sized ones, or in social health structures, the role and function of social workers are primarily to cope with the demands of those who require intervention or support. In services dealing with young people, mental health, addiction and prisons, the role is one of identifying and monitoring strategies aiming at prevention and social reintegration. In other cases, such as in the Uffici di Piano (planning offices), social workers coordinate complex interventions and engage in preventive or rehabilitative work to support the sectors of the population with additional needs. Finally, in the ASLs (the local public health centres) or in the provinces, it is rather more a case of verifying the adequacy of the services offered by providers who are in direct contact with service users, and formally accrediting them. The result of this range of operational contexts, user sectors, problems and functions carried out is that social workers are a crucial 'hub' of the welfare system and are professional figures of considerable importance in the Italian welfare system.

There are no officials surveys of the number of social workers employed in the various services, however we do have data on the number of those enrolled in the Order of Social Workers.[5] In order to delineate the operational contexts and roles actually undertaken by social workers, we can also take advantage of data emerging from a national research project[6] carried out in 2008 on a sample of 1,000 social workers,[7] drawn at random from the lists of those enrolled in the various regional orders (4% from each region). The findings of the study indicate that social workers are most frequently placed in municipalities (45% of the interviewees), followed by local public health centres (24.4%). Smaller numbers worked for the Ministry of Law and Justice, engaged in private practice or worked in hospitals. Still less frequent were positions with the provincial or regional authorities, associations, public social security offices or residential homes for older people (less than 10% in all).

In the past few years there have been many changes in the social services and the division of labour between the different bodies within this system. On the one hand, social services have become more deeply rooted in the municipalities, partly due to law 328/2000, and the restructuring of the local public health centres. On the other hand, private social services have become more widespread as a consequence of outsourcing in the service sector and the growing importance of the third sector, particularly in some regions.

The service user sectors with whom social workers come into contact most frequently are families and children (26.6%) and older people (19.3%), while a mix of service users (15.2%), those with addiction and mental illness (11.4%), people with disabilities (9.2%) and those involved in legal proceedings (6.7%) are less frequently encountered. There are very few cases in which there is no direct contact with any sort of service user (3.6%). Overall, when considering the main user categories, it is evident that these social workers deal with a broad mixture of problems (socioeconomic, family and health related) that require complex interventions.

A breakdown of the working hours of the social workers in the survey revealed the tasks that they engage in. The tasks included intake, working directly with and for service users, administrative work and documentation, networking and community work, coordination and planning, research and training (Facchini and Tonon Giraldo, 2010). The findings revealed that most of the social workers' time is devoted to working directly with and for service users (40% of total working hours). Less time is devoted to the community, to planning and documenting the work done (around 15%) and even less to training and research (less than 5%).

Lastly, the interest that social workers attribute to the various activities that constitute their job was examined. The results reveal that social workers attribute a particularly high degree of interest in working directly with clients (8.5 points on a scale of 1 to 10), in activities linked to training and research, networking, planning and coordination (8.2, 8.1 and 8 respectively). There is decidedly less interest in intake (6.2) and in administrative duties and documentation (5.6).

In general, the results highlight the central interest – not only in operational terms but also in terms of identity – in relationships with service users, which objectively, as well as subjectively, constitute the nucleus of the profession. This is even more pertinent when we take into account that the degree of interest shown in the various activities does not change according to the social worker's role in the organisation. Thus, while a certain role has a considerable effect on the structural aspects of a job, it affects basic attitudes far less. These are apparently a consequence of shared expectations and cultural models. The social work profession tends to assume a markedly relational dimension (Fargion, 2008), presumably corresponding to the actual expectations of those who undergo training in the profession (Facchini and Tonon Giraldo, 2010). However, this overshadows other aspects regarding the organisation, research and evaluation of the overall impact of work carried out, or reflections and theoretical elaboration. These are issues to which the Italian and international literature on social services attributes great value (Dominelli, 2004; Lorenz, 2006a; Kessl, 2009) and, above all, themes that are increasingly important in the logic of governance that seems to preside over the complex reorganisation underway in the social services (Bifulco and Centemeri, 2008; Campanini and Fortunato, 2008). Themes connected to citizens' rights (Colby, 2008), advocacy (Ezell, 2001; Hoefer, 2006) and the political dimension of professional intervention (Haynes and Mickelson, 2003; Ellis, 2008) seem to be afforded just as little importance.

Social workers' involvement in social policy: the professional discourse

An analysis of the professional literature, in the form of both texts and articles, indicates that debate on the involvement of social workers in social policy is not particularly keen in Italy today. This is despite the fact that when the profession was constituted, and during the 'radical' 1970s, this dimension of sociopolitical commitment was at the forefront, at least among some of those who contributed to the establishment of the social services (Dellavalle, 2008). The term 'advocacy' is not commonly used in professional discourse and related practice and is not widespread in Italy. Nevertheless, we can find some important statements in the Code of Ethics and in some positions adopted by the Professional Register in relation to phenomena challenging social work and governmental decisions that go against the principles and values of social work (www.cnoas.it). Although the Italian National Association of Social Workers proposed a deontological code for social workers in Italy in 1992, it was not until the process of professionalisation had progressed and a Professional Order of Social Workers was established that, on 18 April 1998, the first Code of Ethics (Campanini, 2004) was formally issued. This was revised in 2009. If we compare the official documents, such as the definition of social work as stated in the Professional Register or in the Code of Ethics, with those issued, for example, by the US National Association of Social Workers (NASW, 2008) or by the British Association of Social Workers (2008), the Italian documents contain very general indications regarding policy practice. No competences are specifically defined, although the clear responsibility of professional social workers in relation to society is acknowledged in Title IV of the Italian Code of Ethics. In the documents it is possible to find statements that support and promote participation in defending citizens' rights and realising social welfare through various form of intervention at different levels. Thus in the

Code of Ethics the social worker is required to help clients to become aware of their rights and responsibilities within and to the community. The professional code emphasises aspects of action oriented towards; client relationships; to respect the rights of all and in particular the rights of the family, whatever its form or structure; to help clients to become aware of their rights and responsibilities within and to the community, and contribute to, and encourage, a culture of solidarity and subsidiarity in the community. At a more general level, social workers are expected to play an active role in the promotion, development and advancement of integrated social policies aimed at fostering social and civic advancement, emancipation and responsibility within the community and minority groups; promote programmes designed to improve the quality of life of both citizens and the community; develop activities that encourage dialogue and integration; alert the authorities and the general public to any situations where poverty, extreme hardship, oppression and inequality are not being adequately addressed (www. cnoas.it/_download/codice_comparato.pdf).

Until now the Professional Register has not made any efforts to define more precisely the competences related to the social work profession. Moreover, although it has tried to create a dialogue with the ministry and with the heads of the degree courses, it has no statutory control or power to define specific competences that have to be attained by students by the end of their education, nor is it recognised as a body with the authority to accredit study programmes.

Concerning the social policy arena, the Professional Register of Social Workers has repeatedly made its voice heard in relation to situations that require a political statement. These include observations on government documents in relation to social policy in 2008 and observations on the white paper on the future of the Italian model of welfare. In the document produced by the Professional Register,[8] the inconsistencies between the declarations of principle, which stress human values and the values of family and community, and promise a system of services capable of protecting citizens from birth to death, and the actual policies that are adopted is emphasised.

The register has also criticised the major cuts in the welfare budget and the marked differences between regions, which can be linked to tax federalism. Similarly, it has highlighted the lack of services capable of supporting and implementing the exercise of the citizen's individual freedom of choice in the face of increasing outsourcing of services and the underestimation of the role and presence of the public in the construction of an effective network of services. There is also an interesting contribution by the Professional Register to the technical groups of the Welfare Ministry, aimed at building up synergy between professionals involved in the protection of children and families and the sharing of protocols, procedures and effective practices aimed at improving relations between families, social services and the judiciary sector. Of particular importance is the position taken by the Professional Register of Social Workers, together with the Juvenile Judges Association, against the so-called 'security package' (Act 15 July 2009, n. 94), which provided, inter alia, the obligation for public officers or public servants to report the crime of illegal immigration.

A further document[9] was issued at the Conference on the Family held by the Italian government in 2010, which noted the complete lack of policy support for families or promotion of the family as an institution that comes under great pressure, partly because of the lack of services to support it in providing care for its weaker members. More recently (26 April 2011) the Professional Register also took a stance on Libyan immigration (linked to the political crisis in that country), which underlines the commitment of social work to help enable protection for the universal rights of people exposed to conditions of extreme disadvantage, with particular attention to children and unaccompanied adolescents who are at risk of being taken advantage of by criminal networks. It has to be said that these positions, while forcefully taken at a national level, have failed to implement change at a local level and are unlikely to involve social workers in professional policy-oriented action.

Despite these national declarations, there are no significant signs that regional and local representatives of the profession are aware of some of the consequences deriving from the application of recent trends in social policy, or that they have been capable of developing a critical attitude or of offering possible alternatives. In terms of conferences, there have been some rare examples of clear and firm positions and proposals for practical intervention. Worth noting are the conferences proposed by the journal *Animazione Sociale*, the seminars organised by the Fondazione Zancan, and the initiatives of the Bottega del Possibile in which some social workers are involved.

Social workers and policy practice

There is no research on the engagement of Italian social workers in policy practice. We can, however, employ results that emerge from the research previously quoted as indicative of the ways social workers relate to the political sphere. Initially we use the data emerging from telephone interviews with social workers and then complete this picture with accounts from 50 in-depth interviews with directors of the social services[10] carried out during the same research project. With regard to the telephone interviews, we analysed the answers given to two sets of questions: the former concern who the interviewees feel they should answer to for their work; the latter concern how far they agree with certain statements about the implications of their work and their relationship with the political decision makers in their services.

Interviewees were asked to rank the importance of a series of figures that might be points of reference for their work. These figures were identified according to two dimensions. The 'outside' consisted of those who benefit from the work of the interviewees, and the 'inside' consisted of the organisation they belong to. The latter distinguishes an overall macro dimension and a micro dimension relating to individuals. Where these two dimensions intersect, four typologies arise: the community (outside-macro); the clients with whom work is carried out (outside-micro); the organisation belonged to (inside-macro); and the workgroup (inside-micro). Interviewees were asked to rank these in first, second, third and fourth places.

Table 5.1 shows that the great majority of the interviewees (71.8%) ranked the users of their own service in first place, while the numbers of those who believe they should answer mainly to the organisation they belong to (11.9%) or to the community (11.3%), or those who identify the team they work with as their main point of reference (5%) are far lower. These results are mirrored by those relating to the figures ranked in fourth or last place: those most frequently quoted are the community (38.5%), followed by the organisation belonged to (30.4%) and the workgroup (24.7%), while there are obviously very few who place their own clients in the lowest position (6.4%).

Table 5.1: Who do you think you should be answering to (by order of importance, %)?

Ranking	Community	Individual citizen/ user	Workgroup	Organisation belonged to
I	11.3	71.8	5.0	11.9
II	28.3	15.7	25.7	30.3
III	21.9	6.1	44.6	27.4
IV	38.5	6.4	24.7	30.4
Total	100.0%	100.0%	100.0%	100.0%

These results demonstrate that social workers perceive themselves as a profession whose goal is to address the problems of service users and not as a profession whose work should be accounted for to a workgroup or organisation (Trivellato and Lorenz, 2010). At the same time, the data confirm the central role that social workers attributed to relationships with their clients and the individual dimension of care, in contrast to the lower importance attributed to the more 'collective' dimension. Indeed, this does not vary much according to the role the interviewees hold in their organisation nor the area in which they work. Nevertheless, the importance attributed to the organisation belonged to increased among managers and those who work in the ministry or in private social services.

A second set of results relates to the respondents' agreement with statements regarding the perception they have of their own work and their relationships with the political sphere. They were asked if they agreed with the following statements:

- The social worker deals with specific practical problems rather than with general ones.
- A social worker 'mainly' has to find practical/technical solutions.
- The solutions the social worker has to find are 'also' of a political nature.
- A social worker often has to cope with politicians and their interests.

As emerges from Table 5.2, all the statements met with agreement from most of the interviewees, but the range of agreement differs. While there is widespread agreement with the first statement (72.2%), and even greater with the last (79.6%), it is limited for the other two. Around half the interviewees agreed with the statement that solutions are mainly technical (56.5%) or with that they are also of a political nature (59.4%).

Table 5.2: Degree of agreement

	Total
A social worker deals with specific practical problems rather than with general ones	72.2%
A social worker 'mainly' has to find practical/technical solutions	56.5%
The solutions the social worker has to find are 'also' of a political nature	59.4%
A social worker often has to cope with politicians and their interests	79.6%

As they are formulated, the second and third statements are not contradictory, since one foresees the solutions being 'mainly' technical and the other that they 'also' have political significance. The distribution of the data suggests that, instead, the two statements were at least partly seen as alternatives. In fact, in a cross-comparison of the replies to the two questions, it can be seen that only one third of respondents agree with both, while around 25% agree with one only and the remaining 10% do not agree with either. This means that, while a considerable proportion of interviewees are aware of the links between the technical aspect of their work and its political dimension, the majority tend to highlight only one of the two dimensions. Lastly, the fact that the statement on having to cope with politicians and their interests meets with most agreement suggests that in many cases the political sphere is seen more as an intrusion than as a point of reference.

In all, the results indicate that social workers identify themselves as members of a helping profession (Roth and Briar-Lawson, 2011) in which the relational dimensions with individual clients are of central importance, while the awareness of a link between individual work and the community they are members of is less widespread, and where there is clearly a critical element in the more strictly political sphere.

Expected developments in the engagement of social workers in policy practice

In their constitutive phase, social services in Italy had strong political and social connotations which diminished gradually over the following decades, with social workers being placed in autonomous organisations offering social services. In the 1970s, the workers' and students' movements redirected the attention of social workers to the socioeconomic roots of issues related to their work. This emerges in several indepth interviews with long-standing managers of social services. The atmosphere and political commitment of social workers during the 1970s is well documented in this passage from an interview with a social worker responsible for the social sector in a public health centre in Rome:

> 'At the beginning of my professional career [in the 1970s] there was commitment and a political vision ... I chose this profession because I thought there should be political commitment, in my profession and as a citizen ... We wanted to change things, make people's lives better, with more opportunities. This idealistic drive was shared in the political area, too. In this sense, it was an age of reform, change, transformation of the social services, coming closer to the citizens, giving more space to citizens ... things that have been lost over time together with the ideology.'

From the 1990s onwards, we have witnessed a period of 'reflux' characterised by the collapse of the great ideologies, with social workers focusing more on their relationship with the person in need. These cross-national changes had a greater impact in Italy, both because of the weight of the radical ideologies that foundered in the 1990s and because of the social services' lack of roots or a strong collective professional identity among social workers. Added to all this was the specific nature of the Italian right-wing parties. A testimony to the change in the political climate comes from an interview with a social worker from a big city in the north:

> 'Before, there was a political formation … you could work serenely with them in building up projects, but with the rise of the right-wing, which reigned unchallenged here for 10 years, relationships changed completely. While professionals from the services used to be able to present projects, with the right wing it was impossible to do anything: it was the politicians who decided what to do and we had to put it into practice. These few years took the edge off the desire to create new services.'

This change in the cultural climate also contributed to a diminishing of social workers' ability to recognise the political and collective aspect of social problems, with the social workers focusing more on the dimension of individual relationships in their professional work with clients.

There have, of course, been public stands taken by the Professional Register, and its growing awareness of being a 'political creature' is clear in this interview with the president of a regional register: "The register is a public body and must consequently deal with political decision makers, it must do so because this is necessary and it's a good thing."

Nonetheless, as also emerges from the results presented above, politicians tend to be seen more frequently as a disturbance rather than as an interlocutor with whom a relationship of real collaboration can be established. Some of the interviews underscored the considerable difficulties in relationships with the political sphere. Sometimes this is due to the unwillingness of politicians to enter into relationships with the responsible heads of the services, as described by the coordinator of an important social cooperative in a large northern city: "In the five years of my mandate, I have never met the head of social policy."

In others it is due to a lack of awareness of the complexities attached to social intervention. The head of social services in a large southern city explained: "It doesn't seem to me as though there is much awareness in politics as to what it means to build a territorial welfare system ... there's no real dialogue."

However, there are cases in which relationships are positive and effective collaboration takes place. The head of a service for drug abusers in a southern region said:

> 'In this region there is a very close link and strong synergy between the political sphere and the technical-administrative ... In the last few years there has been a change and the relationship with politics is no longer seen as being with an enemy from whom to defend oneself, but on the contrary as a great resource. In the sense that there's the political sphere which is the engine and then there's the technical administrative which makes sure to get the ideas onto their feet.'

Similarly, here is what the regional manager of social policies in a northern region said:

> 'The guidelines on the area projects [*Piani di Zona*] were drawn up by the region together with a small group representing both the regional and district social services. Work on drawing up these guidelines was integrated, so there were no problems later in interpreting them, because at the outset there had already been agreement between the region and the social workers.'

Finally, a social worker in Rome noted:

> 'Our latest experience in the area of social regulation came with all stages being shared by politicians and the offices ... they make proposals but, thanks to the fact that we highlighted the important aspects, there was a dialogue ... without our input and observations they wouldn't be familiar with the real situation, without their decisions we couldn't get anything done. In this process social assistants are also involved. For example, for the strategic plan, meetings were held with all the social assistants and each of them was asked to point out the problems of the services they direct or are part of.'

These cases underline the variation in the situation in Italy. The variety seems to stem not only from the subjective willingness of politicians to have dialogue with directors and social workers, but also from the real competences the latter possess and how authoritatively they express them.

In our final observations, we should like to refer to what has been emphasised by other scholars (Dominelli, 2004; Payne and Askeland, 2008): a neo-liberal political orientation tends to force the profession in a direction which is totally opposite to the principles and values of social work. Rampant managerialism, fragmentation of services, economic constraints and lack of resources, increased bureaucracy and workloads, the domination of care management approaches by performance indicators and the increasing recourse to use of the private sector are factors that affect the social workers' scope in performing their role (Ferguson and Woodward, 2009). This situation is becoming more and more evident in Italy, too, (Carabelli and Facchini, 2010) where social workers, at an individual level, tend to adjust their behaviour to the requirements of the organisation, and where it is difficult to promote a debate within the professional community.

If social workers want to be active players in the restructuring of welfare systems in Europe, it is imperative that they rediscover the connections between politics, social policy and social services (Richan, 2006; Jansson, 2008). The challenge for social workers in Italy is to understand the political dimensions involved in decision making regarding the provision of social services and the connection between the local and the global in order to provide professional practice with a policy aimed at achieving social justice and human rights (Lundy and van Wormer, 2007, p 737). In the present situation, the suggestions of a 'radical social work' (Ferguson and Woodward, 2009) may be useful to activate a debate and cooperation between the Professional Register and the universities (Lorenz, 2006b), so that they will work together in order not to lose faith in the possibilities for change, to resist unethical demands and, in close collaboration with user participation movements, to find the path to build a better world based on social justice.

Notes

[1] This paper is the outcome of shared reflections. Annamaria Campanini edited the first, second and fourth sections and Carla Facchini the third and fifth sections. The conclusions were written jointly.

[2] See www.parlamento.it.

[3] The Bologna Declaration is a document drawn up by the ministers of education of European countries in 1999 to harmonise structures in higher education.

[4] Nationally there are no specific courses for a professional doctorate in social work. A doctorate is recognised for an academic career only, not as a qualification for social work practice. There are, however, some special routes into social work that have been established in the social sciences area via doctoral research. We should emphasise that in Italy doctoral courses are very few and the small number of students who are admitted have to pass a very difficult exam beforehand.

[5] On 31 December 2010 there were 37,972 social workers registered. In order to practise as a professional social worker, graduates of social work studies must sit for a state examination. The examination is held at the university, a full professor is the head of the examining commission, while three of the four other members of the commission are social workers.

[6] The research was carried out with funding from the Ministry of Education and from universities. The study used telephone interviews (CATI methodology) and addressed various issues, from motivation for the choice of studies to evaluation of the training received, from the job context to salary, from evaluations of the changes taking place in the services to perceptions of the role and causes of stress. The results were published in a volume edited by C. Facchini (2010) which includes a complete account of the methodology used.

[7] Of whom 730 actually worked as social workers. The remaining respondents were employed in other positions or had just graduated.

[8] See the section titled 'Primo piano' at www.cnoas.it/professionisti.php.

[9] See note 7.

[10] In the choice of these 50 interviewees their specific role, how far they could be considered representative of the territory, and their main fields of intervention were taken into account. Even though these managers are not necessarily social workers, we consider that the findings are nonetheless indicative of the complex relationship between the heads of these services and political decision makers.

References

Ascoli, U. and Ranci, C. (eds) (2003) *Dilemmas of the Welfare Mix: The New Structure of Welfare in an Era of Privatisation*, New York: Kluwer/Plenum.

Begeny, J.C. and Martens, B.K., (2007) 'Inclusionary education in Italy: A literature review and call for more empirical research', *Remedial and Special Education*, vol 28, no 2, pp 80–94.

Bifulco, L. and Centemeri, L. (2008) 'Governance and participation in local welfare: The case of the Italian Piani di Zona', *Social Policy and Administration*, vol 42, no 3, pp 211–27.

Bifulco, L. and Vitale, T. (2006) 'Contracting for welfare services in Italy', *Journal of Social Policy*, vol 35, pp 495–513.

British Association of Social Workers (2008) 'Code of Ethics', www.basw.co.uk/Default.aspx?tabid=64.

Campanini, A. (2004) 'Italy', in A. Campanini and E. Frost (eds) *European Social Work: Commonalities and Differencies*, Rome: Carocci.

Campanini, A. (2007) 'Social work in Italy', *European Journal of Social Work*, vol 10, no 1, pp 107–16.

Campanini, A. and Fortunato, V. (2008) 'The role of social work in the light of the Italian welfare reform', in V. Fortunato, G. Frisenhahn and E. Kantowicz (eds) *Social Work in Restructured European Welfare Systems*, Rome: Carocci.

Carabelli, G. and Facchini C. (eds) (2010) *The Lombard Model of Welfare*, Milan: Franco Angeli (in Italian).

Colby, I.C. (2008) 'Social welfare policy as a form of social justice', in K.M. Sowers and C. N. Dulmus (eds) *Comprehensive Handbook of Social Work and Social Welfare*, Hoboken, NJ: Wiley.

Dellavalle, M. (2008) *The Social Work Roots in Italy*, Turin: Celid (in Italian).

Diomede Canevini, M. (2005) 'Social work history', in M. Dal Pra Ponticelli (ed) *Social Work Dictionary*, Rome: Carocci (in Italian).

Dominelli, L. (2004) *Social Work: Theory and Practice for a Changing Profession*, Cambridge: Polity Press

Donnelly, M. (1992) *The Politics of Mental Health in Italy*, London: Routledge.

Ellis, R.A. (2008) 'Policy practice', in K. M. Sowers and C. N. Dulmus (eds) *Comprehensive Handbook of Social Work and Social Welfare*, Hoboken, NJ: Wiley.

Ezell, M. (2001) *Advocacy in the Human Services*, Belmont, CA: Brooks/Cole.

Facchini, C. (ed) (2010) *Between Commitment and Profession: Social Workers as Welfare Subjects*, Bologna, Il Mulino (in Italian).

Facchini, C. and Tonon Giraldo, S. (2010) 'Social workers' education: motivations, paths, assessments', in C. Facchini (ed) *Between Commitment and Profession. Social Workers as Welfare Subjects*, Bologna: Il Mulino (in Italian).

Fargion, S. (2008) 'Reflections on social work's identity: International themes in Italian practitioners' representation of social work', *International Social Work*, vol 2, pp 206–19.

Fasol, R. (2000) 'Social work in Italy', in A. Adams, P. Erath, S. Shardlow (eds) *Fundamentals of Social Work in Selected European Countries*, Lyme Regis: Russell House Publishing.

Ferguson, I. and Woodward, R.R. (2009) *Radical Social Work in Practice: Making a Difference*, Bristol: The Policy Press.

Ferrera, M. (2005) *The Boundaries of Welfare: European Integration and the New Spatial Politics of Social Protection*, New York: Oxford University Press.

Ginsborg, P. (1989) *History of Italy since the War to Date*, Turin: Einaudi (in Italian).

Gori, C. (2005) *The Social Services Reform in Italy: The 328 Implementation and the Future Challenges*, Rome: Carocci (in Italian).

Haynes, K.S., and Mickelson, J.S. (2003) *Affecting Change: Social Workers in the Political Arena* (5th edn), Boston, MA: Allyn and Bacon.

Hoefer, R. (2006) *Advocacy Practice for Social Justice*, Chicago: Lyceum.

Jansson, B.S. (2008) *Becoming an Effective Policy Advocate: From Policy Practice to Social Justice* (5th edn), Belmont, CA: Thomson, Brooks/Cole.

Jansson, B.S., Dempsey, D., McCroskey, J. and Schneider, R. (2005) 'Four models of policy practice: Local, state, and national arenas', in M. Weil (ed) *Handbook of Community Practice*, Thousand Oaks, CA: Sage.

Kazepov, Y. (2008) 'The subsidiarization of social policies: Actors, processes and impacts', *European Societies*, vol 10, no 2, pp 247–73.

Kessl, F. (2009) 'Critical reflexivity, social work and the emerging European post-welfare state', *European Journal of Social Work*, vol 12, no 3, pp 305–18.

Lorenz, W. (2006a) *Perspectives on European Social Work: From the Birth of the Nation State to the Impact of Globalisation*, Opladen: Barbara Budrich/Leverkusen.

Lorenz, W. (2006b) 'Education for the social profession', in K. Lyons and S. Lawrence (eds) *Social Work in Europe: Educating for Change*, Birmingham: Venture Press.

Lundy, C. and van Wormer, K. (2007) 'Social and economic justice, human rights and peace: The challenge for social work in Canada and USA', *International Social Work*, vol 50, no 6, pp 727–39.

Martinez, M.A. (2004) 'Spain', in A. Campanini and E. Frost (eds) *European Social Work: Commonalities and Differencies*, Rome: Carocci.

Mayntz, R. (2003) 'New challenges to governance theory', in H.P. Bang (ed) *Governance as Social and Political Communication*, Manchester: Manchester University Press.

Naldini, M. (2003) *The Family in the Mediterranean Welfare States*, London: Frank Cass.

NASW (National Association of Social Workers) (2008) *Code of Ethics of the National Association of Social Workers*, Washington, DC: NASW.

Paci, M., (2005) *New Works, New Welfare: Security and Freedom in the Active Society*, Bologna: Il Mulino (in Italian).

Pavolini, E., (2003) *The New Social Policies: The Welfare Systems between Institutions and Civil Society*, Bologna: Il Mulino (in Italian).

Payne, M. and Askeland, G.A. (2008) *Globalization and International Social Work*, Farnham: Ashgate.

Richan, W.C. (2006) *Lobbying for Social Change* (3rd edn), New York: Haworth.

Roth, W. and Briar-Lawson, K. (2011) (eds) *Globalisation, Social Justice, and the Helping Professions*, Albany, NY: State University of New York Press.

Saraceno, C. (ed) (2002) *Social Assistance Dynamics in Europe*, Bristol: The Policy Press.

Tonon Giraldo, S. (2005) 'Social work education', in M. Dal Pra Ponticelli (ed) *Social Work Dictionary*, Rome: Carocci (in Italian).

Toren, N. (1974) 'The structure of social casework and behavioural change', *Journal of Social Policy*, vol 3, pp 341–52.

Trivellato, P. and Lorenz, W. (2010) 'A profession on the move', in C. Facchini (ed) *Between Commitment and Profession: Social Workers as Welfare Subjects*, Bologna: Il Mulino (in Italian).

Turco L. (2000) 'A law of social dignity', *Social and Health's Prospects*, vol 20/22, p 1 (in Italian).

SIX

Social workers affecting social policy in Russia[1]

Elena Iarskaia-Smirnova and Pavel Romanov

At the Joint World Conference on Social Work and Social Development in Hong Kong in 2010 a set of values was formulated that defined the mission of social work and the development of social policy. It is assumed that these key values, and in particular the principles of social justice and empowerment, are shared by social work and social policy practitioners, educators and experts. In the history of the profession there are many examples in which social workers sought, and successfully achieved, politically significant changes in the social order. However, there were also periods of a decline in activism and a decrease in the role of structural or political social work.

This chapter presents the results of a study of the participation of Russian social workers in processes of structural changes. Interviews with social workers were conducted in several Russian regions. Case studies present mechanisms of changes evoked through counter-actions and compromises, individual activity or collective action, consolidation with social movements and other agents, through the implementation of new methods and forms of casework in the system of social services, or through the lobbying of legislative changes and the practice of institutionalised forms of conflict resolution in courts. Strategies for promoting social change, agents of change and institutional barriers are discussed in the theoretical context of professionalism as a value system and ideology.

Background

In the early 1990s Russian society changed drastically. It became more open and heterogeneous. This brought wealth to some and hardship to others. It was a time of major political changes and painful social transformations, which were accompanied by a dramatic growth in levels of of poverty and unemployment, homelessness and juvenile delinquency, drug and alcohol misuse, mental health issues, and HIV/AIDS (Green et al, 2000; Stephenson 2000, 2006; Pridemore, 2002;

Höjdestrand, 2003; Titterton, 2006; McAuley, 2010). Under conditions of a rapid decrease in the living standard during market reforms, the number of welfare client groups increased and it became evident that existing social institutions could not cope with these new social problems. Russia inherited from the Soviet period a complex system of social security based on public institutions, without professional social work and with very limited and often irregular cash benefits to different social groups (people with disabilities, single mothers, veterans, and so on – altogether making up more than 150 categories).

The 'professional project' (Larson, 1977) of social work has developed in Russia since 1991: new occupations, among them social worker, social pedagogue and specialist in social work, were officially introduced that year. At the same time, university training programmes were opened and several professional associations were established. By 2011 there were 175 university programmes in social work, covering the entire country. Currently the universities are involved in a process of transformation towards the Bologna system, which includes two levels of university education (a four-year bachelor programme and a two year master's programme), but many of them also continue to offer traditional five-year diploma programmes of 'specialists in social work'. The system has certain problems in the labour market for the graduates of such programmes. Due to the low salaries offered to qualified social workers, young university graduates are choosing other jobs.

During the 1990s a wide network of social services was established under the jurisdiction of the Ministry of Labour and Social Development (later renamed the Ministry of Healthcare and Social Development), and this social services network expanded rapidly from 2000. According to the 1995 Social Service Federal Law, 'the system of social service agencies includes organisations under the control of both federal and regional authorities, in addition to municipal organisations of social services. Social service can also be provided by organisations and citizens representing different sectors of the economy'. There are currently about 6,000 organisations with more than 500,000 employees providing services for older people, people with disabilities and families with children. Most of the services are public agencies designed in a similar way according to an exemplary standing order and regulated by common bureaucratic requirements.

The social welfare sector in Russia covers a variety of agencies that provide direct care and support to service users. The welfare sector of this system can broadly be split into adult services and family and child services. Adult services include residential nursing homes, day care, home help, work with people with disabilities, homeless people and job counselling for unemployed people. The main component of the family and child services is work with families, encompassing family care centres, rehabilitation facilities for children with disabilities and for children from families at risk, part-time day care facilities and nursing homes for children with learning difficulties. Outreach work with young offenders, drug addicts and homeless people is conducted mainly by non-governmental organisations (NGOs), which are active in the big cities.

Recent changes in the Russian social services include the rise of a third sector, a concern with social work professionalisation and the development of new managerialism (Romanov, 2008). The ongoing processes of social policy reforms in Russia are driven by a neo-liberal ideology and the government's efforts to make relations between the citizens and the state more efficient and effective. Due to the perceived ineffectiveness of a universalistic approach, the emphasis in solving welfare problem shifted to means testing. This has led to the cancellation of benefits in kind (for example, free access to public transportation, some medicines, vouchers to resorts for certain categories of clients) and to compensating them via monetary means.

These changes have reinforced bureaucratic forms of stabilisation. There is an ongoing debate about whether or not Russia is now a welfare state (a 'social state', as was stated in the post-Soviet basic law, the 1993 Constitution of the Russian Federation) or if it is typified primarily by laissez-faire arrangements. Marginalised individuals, families, groups or communities have not gained additional resources as a result of the new managerialism. Although means-tested assistance was supposed to increase the effectiveness of the social welfare system, it has had negative effects on the most vulnerable populations, especially single mothers who are the heads of low-income households. Having engaged in interactions with the social service system in the late 1990s and early 2000s, these single mothers were often frustrated by the inadequacy of assistance and the impossibility of improving their situations. Neither clients nor social workers were automatically empowered in a new way; heavy workloads which limited the initiative of social workers were not reduced.

According to Larson (1997, p 38), a successful professional project would have resulted in a 'monopoly of competence legitimised by officially sanctioned "expertise", and a monopoly of credibility with the public'. The processes of acquiring a monopoly for its service and status and upward mobility (collective as well as individual) in the social order (Evetts, 2003, pp 401–2) has been a difficult project for social work as an occupation in Russia. Since the beginning of the 1990s, its practice field developed separately from the field of professional training, while the situation in human resources of the social work services sector was characterised by low wages, labour shortage, a high turnover in personnel and insufficient opportunities for retraining. Flexible working hours provided much opportunity for women to undertake care work both in the family and in public services. Added to this, these positions were open while other job chances were scarce – "There are not very many options to find jobs, no choices" (interview with a social worker, 1996) – and were at constant risk of being closed down. This symbolic contract between women and the state was legitimised by the 'National plan of activities concerning the improvement of women's position in Russia and increasing their role in society up to 2000' which promoted a 'creation of additional working places for women by widening the network of social services' (National Plan, 1996). Our previous research (Iarskaia-Smirnova and Romanov, 2008) shows that, by adopting inadequate wage policies for social workers, the state has reinforced the societal assumption of cheap female labour as well as the lack of professionalisation of social work.

Since 2000 a reform has gradually taken place by which public social services are being converted into semi-autonomous organisations. The idea is to make social services capable of operating in a quasi-market, as they will be required to operate without guaranteed financing and to compete for budgeting with other providers. This reform was launched as an experiment in several regions in the early 2000s and the possibility of choosing the legal frame was opened up to all social service organisations by a federal law in 2010. It has made it possible for various types of organisations, including NGOs, to participate in social services market competition. It is assumed that management will become more flexible, possibilities for commercial activity will grow and the wages and motivation of workers will increase as well as offering opportunities for professional development.

Professional ideologies in social work

According to Julia Evetts (2003), professionalism can be seen as a value system or as an ideology. Social work ideology is an important concept in critical reflection of professionalisation (Souflee, 1993; Mullaly, 1997; Chiu and Wong, 1998; Evetts, 2003; Fook, 2003; Woodcock and Dixon, 2005). This includes the professional values and beliefs motivating people to act in order to realise these values, but it also goes beyond the framework of the profession, being incorporated into relations and discourses about social problems and ways to tackle them (Souflee,

1993). Professional ideologies in Russian social work are shaped and modified by various sources and reflect the post-Soviet legitimacy of care and control (Iarskaia-Smirnova, 2011).Throughout its short history in Russia, social work has undergone a constant process of change; the actual characteristics of social work education and training are (re)defined by the definition of professionalism, by highly ambivalent relations with contemporary Russian public policy, by the background of teachers and departments, by a philosophy and ideology of human rights and by international investments and exchange.

Placing social work ideology in a complex picture of theories, policies, philosophies and myths, it is possible to consider the various agents contributing to the constitution of shared knowledge and value base of the profession. In a changing societal context, this profession may lose its political basis and become less critical (see, for instance, Chiu and Wong, 1998). Ideology in socialist states combined elements of conservative and social democratic value systems, and while the early Soviet political rhetoric appealed to the values of self-government and equality, a shift was then made towards paternalism and totalitarianism. It was reflected in changes in the understanding of social problems, their causes and ways of tackling them, reforming social support and service provision. In today's Russia the principles of neo-managerialism in social work are infused by the ideologies of a neo-liberal welfare state. The intervention of market ideology (or 'businessology') in the 'caring' domain of social services (Harris, 2003) does not solve old difficulties, but rather adds new dilemmas, problems and contradictions. Dividing the poor into deserving and undeserving turned out to be a very useful means of rationalising the allocation of resources scientifically. By saving resources, ideologies of governmentality create a gap between clients and social workers.

What is the character of changes that might be induced by social workers and to which ideology do they correspond in today's Russia? These ideologies can operate on macro (society, state and market), meso (organisations and institutions) and micro (groups and actors) levels (Evetts, 2003, p 399). Correspondingly, the changes can be considered on macro (changes of policy and legislation, structure of service provision and nature of social work), meso (within an organisation – for example, new kinds of services, departments, directions of work in a concrete service – that is, some institutional transformations, concerning a rather broad circle of workers, administrators and clients) and micro (workplace, such as proposals to change the content or form of existing service provision) levels.

Practitioners themselves, on a micro level, contribute to the construction of the set of notions and values for an ideal client and the ideal technology for intervention, treatment and quality of work, as well as fulfilling the need for certain knowledge and skills. However, individual workers tend to share the way their institutions think.

On a meso level, an organisation is an environment for shaping social work legitimacy (Anleu, 1992). Social workers 'utilize the normative discourse in their relations with clients, their occupational identities and their work practices' (Evetts, 2003, p 399). Newcomers to an organisation are socialised and integrated. As Peter Blau (1960) showed in his research on welfare services in Chicago in the late 1950s, new caseworkers were typically full of sympathy for clients' problems but soon began to experience a 'reality shock' which made them change their orientation. They managed to cope with this disillusioning experience through consolidating with the collective, by telling jokes and stories about their clients. According to Mary Douglas (1986, p 92), 'Institutions systematically direct individual memory and channel our perceptions into forms compatible with the relations they authorize'. There are also examples where the individuals have the hope and eagerness for intellectual independence.

We can consider these discourses as everyday social work ideologies that exist in a form of 'tacit knowledge' (Zeira and Rosen, 2000). This knowledge is interconnected with dominant thinking on gender and social order. Thus the problems of a client might be, for example, an outcome of beliefs in traditional gender roles and traditional family definitions, which presuppose inequality and the subordination of women. This can be explained by the low level of abstraction in social work, which in Russia remains under-professionalised and focuses not on social structures but on cases and facts, with an emphasis on having knowledge of the legal rules and the qualities of a 'big motherly heart'. As such, the problems tend to be privatised, and structural inequalities are not taken into account. By contrast, some NGOs, such as crisis centres for women, which are run with the support of international donors, have developed a strong emancipatory view based on feminist ideology. Currently, a new understanding has formed that the various forms of violence against women are a problem worthy of state response (Johnson, 2009). Even so, an egalitarian and non-discriminatory ideology is lacking in public social services. Service users form their attitudes towards social work as they interact with social services and practitioners, while the general population builds an image of social work from the mass media. Some service users' associations, grassroots movements and NGOs use emancipatory ideology as a basis for their struggle to fulfil human rights and principles of independent living.

On a macro level, textbooks can legitimise certain value bases of a profession. Many Russian social work and social policy textbooks published since the early 1990s have been written from the ideological perspective of social pathology and represent a large incongruence between the dominant global social work discourse and the Russian understanding of social work theories and practice (see an analysis of 42 social work and social policy textbooks published between 1996 and 2006 in Iarskaia–Smirnova and Romanov, 2008). For example, mothers are generally presented from the point of view of a patriarchal state ideology while single mothers, in particular, are depicted as immoral, unfortunate and dangerous not only for their own children but also for society as a whole.

The first Russian Code of Ethics of social work was adopted in 1994 by the Association of the Social Services Employees. In 2003 it was revised ('Code of Ethics for the Social Worker and Social Pedagogue', 2003). The code is based on the *Code of the International Federation of Social Workers* (The Ethics of Social Work, Principles and Standards, International Federation of Social Workers, 1994) and defines social work as a 'complex of activities aimed at the satisfaction of social needs of a person'. It relates to policy involvement by emphasising social justice and humanism as professional values. It states that, 'according to their opportunities and the level of professional activity', social workers and social pedagogues influence the formation of the social policy that promotes the satisfaction of social needs of people and that they 'conduct active work improving the activity of social institutes, political structures, certain political leaders and local heads with the purpose of elimination of infringements of civil, political, economic, social and cultural human rights'.

Since the mid–1990s a growing number of social service organisations have elaborated and adopted different versions of Codes of Ethics. Some of these codes have been based on the translation of internationally accepted documents. The emphasis on human rights and social policy is not present in all versions of locally adopted codes. A thorough comparison of the different versions and the application of these regulations in practice has not yet been made, but there is some evidence to suggest that the Code of Ethics is used at least for the purposes of administration: "well, usually I refer to employees' instructions but sometimes I can also mention the ethical code if I'd like to appeal to morals" (interview with an administrator of a social service organisation, 2011).

University training programmes in social work do include courses on ethics as well as on social policy and research methods. While students are obtaining skills that facilitate critical reflection on policy issues and a consideration of the ethical dilemmas of the social work profession, because of the gap between university training and the professional field, ethical issues continue to be mostly theoretical and distinct from practice. However, some social service organisations have developed a reflexive holistic approach in working with clients and have become exemplary resource centres for others in terms of developed competences and a humanist philosophy of social work. They also conduct supervision and training courses for colleagues from other agencies.

On a macro level, the state contributed to the formation of the value base of the new profession by introducing special mechanisms to accumulate social prestige. In 1995 an award for the 'distinguished worker of social security of the population of the Russian Federation' was introduced by presidential decree, and in 2000 Social Worker's Day was established by the order of President Putin. The choice of this day, 8 June, can be traced back to reforms introduced by Peter the Great: on that day in 1701 the Russian emperor signed a decree assigning poor, sick and older people to poorhouses. Each summer since 2001, the regional departments of social security (or ministries of social development) have arranged concerts and costumed amateur performances at local theatres. This was an important building blocks in the process of making social work into a profession with its own proud history.

Case studies[2]

The ongoing research project began in 2010 after a call was sent to schools of social work for descriptions of cases showing the involvement of social workers in the formulation of new rules and principles of work – in an organisation, a local community, a region or on the national level – that positively affect the wellbeing of a population group. The goal of the study was to determine what structural changes in Russian social policy could be implemented from below, through the initiatives of social workers, and how these initiatives were structured by local conditions. Since then we have collected a dozen case studies primarily describing changes in the wellbeing of individuals and families as a result of individual efforts and their corresponding effects. Several cases reflect structural changes and a few others focus on formal institutional mechanisms designed to promote change. The data relate to change in eight regions of Russia: Kazan, Krasnodar, Moscow, Petrozavodsk, Saratov, St Petersburg, Tomsk and Volgograd. The collected cases depict more or less successful initiatives with diverse effects that were generated by the actions of the parents of children with disabilities with the support of social workers, and of public officials, of charities, of university teachers or researchers and other actors. In some cases the changes were peaceful while in other they were a consequence of conflicts that catalysed or hindered changes. The sustainability of changes induced has, at times, been problematic after the financing ended.

The main agents of change in the cases collected were social workers (formally termed 'specialists in social work') employed by public services and NGOs, public officials from departments of social security and education, researchers and university teachers, parents of children with disabilities and other citizens who can be the catalysts of change. The majority of cases relate to state employees. Some of the NGO employees identify themselves as social workers, while others distant themselves from this occupational group due to their regular institutional conflicts with social services: "Social workers only interfere when we try to promote changes" (interview with a specialist in a non-governmental service for children with complex disabilities).

The strategies adopted in the cases sought legal, institutional and societal changes, and can be grouped into four categories: the introduction of new technologies for casework, the consolidation of agents and alliance of resources, the mobilisation of collective action and institutionalised conflict:

- New technologies in social services constitute a new focus in social service policy. Examples of new technologies include methods that are often adopted through international cooperation: a network of social contacts; the mobilisation of resources of the social environment of a family; intensive family therapy at home; the active support of parents, and so on (in Volgograd, St Petersburg, Saratov). Usually, these changes are rooted in systemic models of social work, they often affect organisational modification in social services, and they are induced by changes in ideology.
- Consolidation of agents and alliance of resources are the most accessible forms of achieving changes. Sometimes social workers discover gaps in their own authority or in systemic arrangements which hinder their ability to help a client or to solve a problem. They appeal to an ombudsman or engage in advocacy, gain the attention of the mass media, public officials and members of local parliaments

and succeed in integrating several fragments of the social services system, for instance through making a special contract between the centre of social services and medical-social expertise in order to improve mechanisms of individual rehabilitation programmes. Sustainability is secured through updating work regulations and regular collaboration between different specialists and agencies. Interagency collaboration is a very important and an often successful part of social service policy in Russia. Sometimes such innovations lead to significant changes in the legal base and infrastructure of social services, as is the case in Perm, Tomsk and other regions. In some cases, an individual service user can be a catalyst of change. Thus, for example, a mother of a child with severe disability in Saratov motivated social workers at a rehabilitation centre to establish a club for children with special needs. The social workers have attracted charity and political resources and, as a result, several clubs for children and young people with disabilities were established in the city. Not all of these initiatives were successful. Many projects failed to materialise or ceased to exist due to a lack of resources or because of destructive conflicts.

- Mobilization of collective action is a strategy employed by civic groups, charities and NGOs. Parents of children with disabilities often become an engine of such change when they collaborate with active NGOs, social workers or teachers from public services and officials.
- Institutional forms of conflict are the strategy employed by NGOs when collecting information about the violation of legislation and human rights, making official claims and initiating negative sanctions against the violators. For instance, in Moscow in 2006 an NGO (the Centre for Curative Pedagogics) initiated court proceedings concerning the refusal of the social security department to enable parents of children with disabilities to identify and use proper services for children. Perspektiva, another NGO, succeeded in a court case in 2008 concerning the refusal of the airline Siberia to let a person in a wheelchair on board.

In this chapter we focus on two cases which, in our opinion, are characteristic of social work in today's Russia and illustrative of the strategies of change realised on different levels.

A new service for homeless people in Tomsk:[3] change at the institutional level

This project began in 1997 when a social work student, Gloria Vinogradova, became the leader of a small team advocating homeless people's rights. The members of the team had been selling donations of unsold cloth in second-hand shops, promoting these charity activities in the press, and writing appeals to various institutions to help homeless people get to a hospital or to a residential home. However, their major goal was to establish a shelter for homeless people in the city. This plan was difficult to realise as the municipal authorities refused to help, justifying this by referring to legislation which placed work with homeless people under the jurisdiction of the oblast (regional) authorities. These authorities said there were no homeless people in the region and thus there was no problem. Actually, in the oblast there are several residential homes for people who have no place to stay, but these are in remote regional towns while the majority of the homeless people are in the city.

This was a vicious circle that Gloria sought to break. As a member of the Evangelical Lutheran Church, she had met a missionary from the US who advised her to write a grant application to the Church, which she did successfully. After receiving initial funds to establish the refuge, she applied to the oblast and municipal departments of social security asking for premises for the new service. Even with grant money ready to be spent, it was still not an easy task. In her interview, the social worker describes her efforts to open the public centre as a fight with the system: "these are some games of the officials ... they kept silent for a long time ... maybe I was so persistent, I kept coming and asking them ... but [we] have annoyed them ... so that finally everything worked out" (interview with Gloria Vinogradova). The project could not be achieved without the support of the head of the city social security department, who helped to promote the initiative so that it could receive municipal support and funding to pay salaries for an administrator and an accountant, for utilities, and so on. Within two years, the premises were repaired, furnished and equipped, all necessary fiscal and legal negotiations had been achieved and finally, in 1999, the municipal institution, an overnight home called the 'Refuge of a Wanderer', was opened.

In addition to her work as a leader of a NGO, Gloria has become a middle-level manager of this municipal social service for homeless people. Here her efforts have focused on widening the functions of this agency, so that it would remain not only an overnight shelter but also become a service to help people with official documents, offer legal counselling and so on. In 2001 Gloria received another grant, this time from the European Initiative for Democracy and Human Rights (EIDHR), which made it possible to employ social workers and a legal consultant, to establish a database, to provide services (including a job search for clients) and undertake a sociological survey.

In a few years the refuge was successfully changed into a centre for social assistance for homeless people. The facility and the range of services were extended significantly and now include a department for acute social assistance (help with issuing passports and medical insurance), a temporary living ward for 100 people, an overnight ward and a ward for people after treatment for tuberculosis, as well as other services. The employees of the centre promote social inclusion: "homelessness is in fact a person's deprivation of society, it is marginality. And our task is ... to 'inscribe' a person into this society, to create social relations" (interview with Gloria Vinogradova). Gloria wanted to become the director of this service but her application was declined as she was seen by officials as 'too young'. As a result she worked first as a social worker and then as an administrator of one of the departments. Later, as an outreach worker, she also collaborated with other refuges and residential homes so that her clients could register for social security benefits, disability benefits, pensions and get a place in one of the residential facilities. As the new director was eager to develop the centre further, Gloria was satisfied: "The director has the wish and power to promote new functions, to find new perspectives, which pleases me. Thus, I think that my task is complete" (Gloria Vinogradova's own case description). However, the collaboration between the municipal organisation and the NGO was not successful: "the voluntary organisation, in fact, has quietly died, so to say, giving the place to the municipal service" (interview with Gloria Vinogradova). Later, Gloria left the centre to go to the US to study at an evangelic university. On graduation she returned to Novosibirsk, where she now works at a crisis centre for women.

As we can see, a social worker could not only establish a small NGO and raise international funds but also mobilise municipal structures of the public social security system and, as a result, create a new, large and successful social service organisation and ensure its sustainable development. This initiative was not easy to implement within the framework of the public social services where the institutions and positions are created from above and on the basis of strictly determined frames of activity. 'Bottom-up' initiatives are viewed with suspicion and thus require special qualities in agents of change. As Gloria puts it:

'Now, in general, at all levels of authority, one might say there is a similar situation. What would happen if an official doesn't budge? At the most [they] would wag a finger at [him], but would not even fire, because they all stick together. Well, he does not risk anything. And why stir if you don't need to?'

It was not only the individual energy of a social worker and that of additional participants in the process but also the existence of accessible resources (which can serve as an alternative to the statutory budget) that were important conditions for success. Crucially, these resources included the Church with its transnational networks, charities and foundations, networks with institutional partners and volunteer support, social work theoretical knowledge and the skills of independent thinking and fundraising acquired from university.

Inclusive education in Petrozavodsk: macro-level changes

In Russia today children with disabilities are entitled to receive education services in regular schools or in special institutions. Psychological-medical-pedagogical commissions have the authority to identify the type of educational setting deemed appropriate for a child with disabilities. The system of education in Russia has undergone deep changes and the schools have experienced transformations influenced by government reforms and the market economy. However various barriers still persist in efforts to introduce inclusive education (Iarskaia-Smirnova and Romanov, 2007).

Social workers in Russia are seldom involved in human rights movements or the promotion of new legislation. However, collaboration between the employees of social services and social movements and other public agencies can lead to structural changes that are aimed at improving the well-being of large groups of people. Such an exceptional example is that of Svetlana Driakhlitsyna from the city of Petrozavodsk, the capital of the Republic of Karelia, situated in the northwest of Russia near the Finnish border. Svetlana had been working as a social worker in a public agency and at the same time was a leader of the Karelia association of NGOs for people with disabilities. In 2004 she supported a court appeal by a group of parents who sought pre-school places for their children with disabilities. Prior to this appeal, the parents had made several unsuccessful attempts to find facilities for their children in kindergartens by approaching the city administration. The city court rejected the appeal and accepted the city department of education's explanation that it lacked the funds to provide accessible facilities.

After the Supreme Court of the Republic of Karelia failed to reverse the decision, the parents arranged for a press conference in a special library for visually impaired people. They came to the press conference together with their children, members of associations for people with disabilities and several active social workers, including Svetlana. The news about the violation of the children's rights was broadcast on all local television channels and published in local newspapers. Shortly after that, the case was again discussed by the Supreme Court and the original decision was reversed in 2006. Funding for the appeal was made available through the Tacis European project. However, by the time the appeal was accepted, the children were already seven years old and it was too late for them to go to a pre-school (although they were admitted to a special school for children with severe disabilities).

The court decision did not identify which authority – municipal or republic, education or social security – had responsibility for implementing the decision and funding this type of service for disabled children in the future. Thus, a similar case occurred in June 2006, when another two parents of children with disabilities attempted to enrol their children in pre-school services. The parents were better prepared this time and again NGOs and social workers from several agencies supported the petition in court. The subjects of the petitioned parties – the city administration, the ministry of finance, the Karelia Ministry of Education – all insisted they had a lack of jurisdiction. However, within a short time, in December 2006, the court decided to require the city administration to establish special facilities in regular pre-school settings in collaboration with the republic's government and Ministry of Education.

Further collaboration between the parents' movement, NGOs and social workers has led to additional structural changes. On 31 January 2008, new legislation was passed (Law of the Republic of Karelia, N 1168) regarding 'introducing changes in some legal acts of the Republic of Karelia concerning the provision of social support and social services for children with complex disabilities who cannot serve themselves' (Political Life of the Northwest, 2008). According to this law, children with disabilities who are enrolled in kindergartens or schools are entitled to have a salaried personal assistant and to receive 1,880 roubles (UK£37/US$59) as a monthly payment for transport. In addition, educational institutions that offer inclusive services are to be provided with an additional budget to develop an accessible environment. The implementation of this new law has given rise to several new issues, including the low salary of personal assistants and uncertainty regarding their tasks, the slow reconstruction of facilities, and so on. Nevertheless, it is clear that the alliance between social workers and the public can promote important changes at the political level.

Participation in this activity has led to a change in Svetlana's job situation. Having experienced pressure from the administration, she left public social service. She is still working as chair of the association of NGOs of people with disabilities in Karelia, and in 2011 she contributed to the promotion of new universal legislation, 'On providing access for people with disabilities and other citizens with low mobility to public buildings and transport', which is now under consideration in the government (Tsygankov, 2011).

Institutional conditions limit the initiative and field of possibilities for the employees of social services. According to Svetlana:

> 'Mostly, possibilities to achieve certain changes are possessed by the managers of social services or their deputies. The specialist in social work has no tools for her own action. From the very beginning, they had to perform functional duties, and ... their own initiative is not motivated, rather, it belongs to those who make the decisions.' (interview with Svetlana Driakhlitsyna)

In this case, there were several factors that contributed to the success of the social worker's endeavour. Being involved in international exchange programmes and further qualification programmes, Svetlana and some other social workers recognised and internalised the professional values of social work. As a social worker in a managerial position she increased her autonomy and ability to promote and maintain changes justified by the system. Svetlana was inclined to professional reflection and civic activism – she has long experience of combining work in a public service with civic activity. In 2009 she defended a thesis in the sociology of disability at St Petersburg State University. The geographical proximity of Karelia to Northern Europe also increases opportunities for international collaboration, for finding various resources and support.

Conclusion

The most characteristic feature of the Russian public sector in general, and of the social services sector in particular, is the persistence of the monopoly position of organisations providing public services and the limited possibilities for creating a competitive environment. During the last few years some experiments have taken place in this area, primarily in those fields supported by international foundations and expert groups. These innovations were directed towards increasing the effectiveness of social services as well as their management, with a great emphasis on measurable outcomes. Although the potential exists for all types of social services to participate in the process of budgeting in the framework of the so-called quasi-market processes, this process in Russia is limited by a lack of standardisation of services, a weak knowledge base concerning the methods of working with clients and standard regulation in this field, a shortage of skills in evaluating quality and effectiveness by many public organisations and NGOs, as well as a lack of knowledge of how to be competitive to promote good services, organisations and methods of work.

NGOs offering social services to the population have succeeded quite well in accumulating their human resources. Due to their flexible organisational structure, strong motivation and the high level of qualifications of their management and employees, many NGOs working with orphans, people with disabilities, survivors of domestic violence and other vulnerable groups of the population have developed professional skills, are involved in international cooperation and in many cases collaborate with local government, social services and universities. Having grown out of the service users' associations and grassroots movements, these NGOs employ an emancipatory and egalitarian ideology in their struggle to establish human rights and principles of independent living. NGOs located in large cities and funded by international and national foundations can provide an attractive labour market for qualified social work graduates as they offer better wages, encourage and support employees to improve professionally, and operate on the basis of project management (as opposed to the traditional bureaucracy that operates on the basis of centralised budget schemes), which is often associated with a flexible and lively organisational culture. However, the number of such organisations is rather limited and unstable due to the specific economic and political situation in Russia whereby large-scale involvement of foreign donors is not encouraged while national funds to support non-governmental activities are scarce. In addition, some major international donors and NGOs, which were previously very active in Russia, are decreasing their presence there.

Social workers are gradually acquiring new knowledge and skills to effect social change in a democratic egalitarian mode rather than following a paternalist scheme of thought and action. This is still the exception rather than usual practice. As we can see, capacity to promote social initiatives varies at different levels of the organisational hierarchy, while the professional autonomy of specialists is very limited. Several cases in our research exemplify such exceptions when the initiatives of social workers have led to structural changes.

The contemporary situation in Russian social work is featured by under-professionalisation and therefore a low degree of professional autonomy, as well as a lack of activism frameworks in the social services culture, an absence of critical reflection on social work practice, and the rigidity of governance. This is a background that tends to stifle initiatives to change the existing social order. However, recent evidence that local initiatives can bring about a transformation of the social work and social policy system has emerged. Social workers initiate positive changes through counter-actions and compromises, individual activity or collective action, consolidation with social movements and other agents, through implementing fundamentally new methods of casework into the system of social services or through the practice of institutionalised forms of conflict resolution.

It is important for government, foundations and the academic community in Russia to focus more on critical issues in social welfare and on the importance of developing conflict resolution skills, and to support the development of social services research. Democratic, egalitarian and non-discriminatory ideology is required in social services as well as in social work training. It is worth paying more attention to retraining programmes and to raising the level of skills of specialists who already work for social service agencies. University education in social work can have an impact on the enhancement of the professional identity of social work in the frames of critical social thinking with a focus on social justice and human rights. The impact of international cooperation on enhancing the professional identity of social work is a useful contribution to the development of structural social work.

Notes

[1] The study was conducted within the project 'A Comparative Analysis of Social Policy Processes in the Post-socialist Space' supported by the John D. and Katherine T. McArthur Foundation, and research findings from the 'Ideologies of Professionalism in a Welfare State' project carried out as part of the National Research University Higher School of Economics Academic Fund programme in 2012, grant no 12-05-0007.

[2] The authors thank Natalia Sorokina for help in coordinating this project.

[3] The authors thank Olga Melnikova from Tomsk University and Gloria Vinogradova from the Novosibirsk crisis centre for women for the materials and ideas.

References

Anleu, S.L.R. (1992) 'The professionalisation of social work? A case study of three organisational settings', *Sociology*, vol 26, no 1, pp 23–43.

Blau, P.M. (1960) 'Orientation towards clients in a public welfare agency', *Administrative Science Quarterly*, vol 5, pp 341–61.

Chiu, S.W.S. and Wong, V.C.W. (1998) 'From political to personal? Changing social work ideology and practice in Hong Kong', *International Social Work*, vol 41, no 3, pp 277–92.

'Code of Ethics for the Social Worker and Social Pedagogue' (2003) Moscow, http://socpedagogika.narod.ru/Kodeks.html (in Russian).

Douglas, M. (1986) *How Institutions Think*, New York: Syracuse University Press.

Evetts, J. (2003) 'The sociological analysis of professionalism: Occupational change in the modern world', *International Sociology*, vol 18, no 2, pp 395–415.

Fook, J. (2003) 'Critical social work: The current issues', editorial, *Qualitative Social Work: Research and Practice*, vol 2, no 2, pp 123–30.

Green, A.J., Holloway, D.G. and Fleming, P.M. (2000) 'Substance misuse in Russia: A partnership for policy change and service development', *International Journal of Drug Policy*, vol 11, no 6, pp 393–405.

Harris, J. (2003) '"Businessology" and social work', *Social Work and Society*, *www.socwork.net/sws/article/view/259/438*.

Höjdestrand, T. (2003) 'The Soviet-Russian production of homelessness: Propiska, housing, privatization', http://www.anthrobase.com/Txt/H/Hoejdestrand_T_01.htm

Iarskaia-Smirnova, E. (2011) 'Professional ideologies in Russian social work: Challenges from inside and outside', in S. Selwyn (ed) *Social Work Education in Countries of the East: Issues and Challenges*, Hauppauge, NY: Nova Science Publishers, Inc, pp 425–48.

Iarskaia-Smirnova, E. and Romanov, P. (2007) 'Perspectives of inclusive education in Russia', *European Journal of Social Work*, vol 10, no 1, pp 89–105.

Iarskaia-Smirnova. and Romanov, P. (2008) 'Gendering social work in Russia: Towards anti-discriminatory practices', *Equal Opportunities*, vol 7, no 1, pp 64–76.

Johnson, J.E. (2009) *Gender Violence in Russia: The Politics of Feminist Intervention*, Bloomington: Indiana University Press.

Larson, M.S. (1977) *The Rise of Professionalism: A Sociological Analysis*, Berkeley: University of California Press.

McAuley, M. (2010) *Children in Custody: Anglo-Russian Perspectives*, London: Bloomsbury Academic.

Mullaly, B. (1997) *Structural Social Work: Ideology, Theory, and Practice* (2nd edn), New York and Oxford: Oxford University Press.

National Plan (1996) 'National plan of activities concerning the improvement of women's position in Russia and increase of their role in the society up to 2000', no 1032, 29 August, www.owl.ru/win/docum/rf/plan.htm (in Russian).

Political Life of the Northwest (2008) 'The Law of the Republic of Karelia on social support of children with disabilities has been adopted', Political Life of the Northwest, 2 July, www.zaks.ru/new/archive/view/48379 (in Russian).

Pridemore, W.A. (2002) 'Social problems and patterns of juvenile delinquency in transitional Russia', *Journal of Research in Crime and Delinquency*, vol 39, no 2, pp 187–213.

Romanov, P. (2008) 'Quality evaluation in social services: Challenges for new public management in Russia', in G. Peters (ed) *Mixes, Matches, and Mistakes: New Public Management in Russia and the Former Soviet Republics*, Budapest: LGI, OSI, pp 9–53.

Souflee, F. Jr (1993) 'A metatheoretical framework for social work practice', *Social Work*, vol 38, no 3, pp 317–31.

Stephenson, S. (2000) 'The Russian homeless', in S. Hutton and G. Redmond (eds) *Poverty in Transition Economies*, London: Routledge, pp 14–34.

Stephenson, S. (2006) *Crossing the Line: Vagrancy, Homelessness and Social Displacement in Russia*, Aldershot: Ashgate

The Ethics of Social Work, Principles and Standards, International Federation of Social Workers, 1994 http://ethics.iit.edu/ecodes/node/3935

Titterton, M. (2006) 'Social policy in a cold climate: Health and social welfare in Russia', *Social Policy and Administration*, vol 40, no 1, pp 88–103.

Tsygankov, A. (2011) 'To dismount the barriers', Centre for political and social research of the Republic of Karelia, 18 May, http://politika-karelia.ru/?p=5845 (in Russian).

Woodcock, J. and Dixon, J. (2005) 'Professional ideologies and preferences in social work: A British study in global perspective', *British Journal of Social Work*, vol 35, no 6, pp 953–73.

Zeira, A. and Rosen, A. (2000) 'Unravelling "tacit knowledge": What social workers do and why they do it', *Social Service Review*, vol 74, no 1, pp 103–23.

SEVEN

Social workers affecting social policy in Spain

María-Asunción Martínez-Román

Social work in the welfare system in Spain

Ever since the current Constitution was passed by parliament in 1978, Spain has been organised territorially in municipalities, provinces and autonomous communities (regional level). All these bodies enjoy self-government in the management of their respective interests (Constitution, section 137). Within this decentralised structure, each level of the administration has its own responsibilities, but the central administration retains some basic control in order to guarantee equality within all territories. Each of the autonomous communities has its own government and adopts its own policies while following national policy guidelines. In addition, local authorities enjoy a degree of autonomy in their respective territories. In Spain there are different forms of social protection which are provided by the central government, the autonomous communities' governments and by local government.

Central government is responsible for the social security system, which is universal across territories. It comprises a contributory system based on social contributions made by workers and employers; a non-contributory pension system; social assistance benefits for the unemployed that are linked to annual income; and an economic benefit bonus, introduced in 2009 as a new temporary social security economic benefit in response to the economic crisis.

The central government promotes other basic policy guidelines at the national level, although the application of these guidelines is devolved to the local and autonomous administrations. There are general Acts concerning education, health, employment, children, equal opportunities, gender violence protection and dependence. In other areas, there is no national legislation but rather national plans agreed between the central and autonomous administrations, such as housing policy or programmes for the Roma population. Social assistance is also the responsibility of the autonomous communities and, since 1988, a programme funded jointly by all three levels of government (Plan Concertado de Prestaciones Básicas de Servicios Sociales en las Corporaciones Locales) has existed (Ministerio de Sanidad, Política Social e Igualdad, 2011).

The *autonomous communities* implement national policies and have the capacity to establish their own policies. Each of these regional governments can also introduce specific policies on the basis of their own social services Act. As a result there are 17 social services Acts, one for each of the regions. These Acts differ in terms of social rights, social services and social expenditure. All of them offer some common basic benefits and discretional minimum income services.

At *local government* level, municipalities with over 20,000 inhabitants have a legal obligation to deliver basic social services (Act 1985/7). Municipalities with fewer than 20,000 inhabitants provide social services supported by the provincial government (*diputación*).

The emergence of this decentralised administration model is causing major differences in social rights according to people's place of residence. While this has led to a demand for a general social services law, with a national scope that guarantees territorial equity (CERMI, 2011), some of the autonomous communities have rejected this option, noting that it contradicts the current Constitution. An example of the complexity of the design, implementation and evaluation of policies in this area is the slow development of the Promotion of Personal Autonomy and Care of Dependent Persons Act 2006/39. This national legislation represents a major step forward in the institutionalisation and universality of care – before its adoption this had remained the responsibility of families. The Act generated wide-ranging broad social debate and much support for the universality of social care. However, its implementation has taken diverse routes in the various regions and as a result has generated public debate and protests by individuals and families eligible for support. The main complaints have been the lack of territorial equity, delays in the assessment of eligibility for benefits, and delays in the provision of benefits or services when people do qualify for them. Other negative elements in the implementation of the law are the inadequacy of the financing model, a lack of information (lack of transparency and political use), scarce delivery of home-assistance services, day care centres, residences and alternative housing (58% of the total population served receive a low economic benefit for family care or non-professional care, which contradicts the Act, under which they should receive priority access to services such as home help, day or residential facilities). The development of these services would represent an important area for employment growth, and would support female members of families, who are usually the informal carers. Moreover, it would decrease the number of insecure jobs. Another unresolved issue is the coordination between health and social services in the care system for dependent persons (Casado and Fantova, 2007; Barriga et al, 2011; CERMI, 2011; CES, 2011). These dysfunctions in the implementation of the Act at the national level can contribute to a better picture of the complexity of citizens' access to recognised social protection rights, and the context in which professional social workers perform their professional duties.

An overview of contemporary social policy in Spain indicates that the country has made notable advances in social protection over the last decades. However, not all citizens enjoy adequate social protection, and Spanish social expenditure remains below the European Union average (Eurostat, 2011). Families (primarily women) continue to bear much of the responsibility for caring for their relatives, and difficulties in balancing work and family life are causing a breakdown of the traditional care model (Martínez-Román, 2005; Pérez-Díaz, 2010; Requena, 2010). The unemployment rate in 2010 was over 20% and the relative poverty rate increased in 2010 to 20% (INE, 2011). However, in response to the grave economic crisis in Spain in recent years public policies have resulted in cutbacks in social benefits and services. This has placed a major burden on families and voluntary organisations (Marbán and Rodríguez, 2008; Rodríguez-Cabrero, 2010).

The social work profession and its education structure

Contemporary university-based education for social workers (formerly termed *asistente social*/social assistant) has been recognised since 1981. The entry-level degree is *grado en trabajo social* (a social work undergraduate bachelor's degree). The second level of studies is *postgrado* (graduate studies, equivalent to a master's degree) and the third level is the *doctorado* (doctoral degree).

Parallel to the creation of a university degree, there has been a long process of professional development of social work in Spain. In order to understand this process, it is important to take into account the political, socioeconomic, and cultural context in Spain in the last decades, in particular the years of the Franco dictatorship (1939–75). This period was characterised by the international isolation of Spain and its underdevelopment. Franco established a Catholic state (National Catholicism), delegating the care assistance system to the religious organisations of the Catholic Church. These organisations delivered overtly ideological services that sought to provide healthcare to children, frail elderly people, disabled people and poorer people, especially those who lacked family support, as families had a legal obligation to care for family members.

In this context, women were assigned a dual social role as mothers and as caregivers so that they did not work outside the home. Women's opportunities for employment were usually limited to being nurses or teachers, and most educational institutions for women were affiliated with the Church. The social assistants' schools started in the 1930s in Spain and social work offered a new area of opportunity for women to be included in the labour market, but the Civil War (1936–39) disrupted its development. The major growth of these schools took place during the late 1950s, within the context of underdevelopment and serious social problems, and the government requested external financial assistance to promote economic policies. The social and political situation favoured the creation of new schools for the training of social assistants, mostly promoted by the Church, but also by other organisations. The development of Church-affiliated schools led to a period in education that was associated with a social commitment based on religious beliefs, and mainly targeted at women. However, there were other schools that had a more open educational point of view that should be acknowledged. These other schools were linked to a school of thought that was critical of the Church, advocating the recognition of social rights in response to the serious social problems and the inadequacy of public policies that were causing most of these social problems. This 'other Church' promoted important policies and activities that sought to improve unfair social structures, serving as an umbrella for activities considered politically incorrect and/or illegal by the authoritarian regime. It is important to consider that, at that time, there was no freedom of expression and therefore any questioning of policies was forbidden.

In 1957 there were only six schools of social work, and in 1958 another 11 were created. Ten of those new schools were linked to the Spanish Caritas, which was affiliated to the Catholic Church. Caritas had a primarily religious function but it also offered assistance in the case of serious individual and family situations. Furthermore Caritas promoted social development and implemented important moves towards community development such as the Plan Social Baza (Casado, 1969).

As was the case in other countries, the first stage of growth in the professionalisation and training in social work was a result of international influence (Hernández et al, 2004). From the end of the 1950s onwards, the Franco regime was the target of international pressure to adopt new social policies as a condition for obtaining financial aid for economic development. The international requirements included the need for incorporating qualified professionals in the social field, with social assistants among them, as documented in the First Economic and Social Development Plan (Act 1963/194). In one of the reports from the plan, the 'Health and social assistance final report' (Comisaría del Plan de Desarrollo Económico y Social, 1963), the urgent need to train 4,000 social assistants was underscored. At the same time, it was necessary to develop quality education in social work and for that the schools sought international assistance. The educational influence of social assistants' schools from Belgium and Switzerland should be emphasised, as well as the importance of training courses given by international experts from the United Nations and other specialised activities conducted by international specialists (Colomer, 2009; Gil-Parejo, 2010).

The 1964/1403 decree was the first legal regulation recognising educational training in social work. In 1964, 30 out of the 41 schools of social work were institutions linked to the Catholic Church. The Spanish Federation of Church Schools of Social Service (Federación Española de Escuelas de la Iglesia de Servicio Social, FEEISS) was established to represent the majority of educational institutions of social work. Colomer emphasises the difficulties that were present during the process of establishing the federation, given the sociopolitical context. We should consider that even merely the use of the word 'social' could have had negative political connotations under the Franco regime (Colomer, 2009). In 1967 the only educational institution independent of the Ministry of Education (Escuela Oficial de Asistentes Sociales) was created in Madrid. It had a role in controlling the other private schools. In 1968, the classification of occupations was regulated and recognised the Diploma of Social Assistant as coming under the category of Técnico de Grado Medio. The proposal for creating jobs for social workers under the development plans was never enforced. Public policies of the development plan were, in practice, driven by economic growth regardless of the social costs of growth, and public employment was not created for social workers, so the social work profession developed very slowly in a paternalistic context. The social policy regulations did not recognise social welfare as right, promoting individual charity and a very residual welfare policy based on the legal obligation of caring for families. However, there was also a part of society that was critical of the Franco regime and considered it necessary to introduce more structural change in the sociopolitical order in order to achieve more equitable economic and social development (Sarasa, 1993).

In 1967 the Federation of Social Workers' Professional Organisations (Federación de Asociaciones de Asistentes Sociales, FEDASS) was created to promote the profession, its objectives, methods and techniques. This federation contributed greatly to the professional development of social work. In the first national congress of social assistants (1968), the decision to change the professional title to 'social work' was adopted in order to distinguish the profession from the former charitable approaches (Llopis, 1984). At the same time, most of the schools of social work continued to belong to the Church but they became very heterogeneous, with some becoming more conservative or more critical and progressive than others. The II Economic and Social Development Plan highlighted the need for social development. The revision and updating of charity and social assistance legislation was determined to be one of the objectives of this Act (1969/1).

In the early 1970s, the III Economic and Social Development Plan (1972–75) emphasised, in its chapter on social assistance, that professional social action should be promoted and that new positions should be created to incorporate social assistants into the public administration. This meant the creation of new jobs in public administration, with better salaries and a higher social recognition, and in the opening session of the II National Congress of Social Assistants (1972), the minister of labour publicly recognised the professional work of social assistants (Hernández et al, 2004). However, employment options within public administration remained scarce. Some positions were created in companies, schools or social housing, but many social assistants (mainly women) were employed by non-profit organisations linked to the Catholic Church, such as Caritas, with very low salaries. Similarly, some jobs for social assistants were gradually created in non-profit organisations that offered social care services (Vázquez, 1971).

In the second half of the 1970s, after Franco's death in 1975, a process of democratic transition began. Another key factor in the development of the social work profession was the Act of 1977/3, which recognised social assistants as a profession in public administration (*cuerpo especial de asistentes sociales*).

Between the 1970s and 1980s, FEEISS, along with the rest of the schools and the professional body FEDAAS, made a significant contribution to achieving university-level recognition of social work. There was a remarkable milestone in 1981. Studies were integrated as an undergraduate programme under the title of Diplomado en Trabajo

Social (a three-year degree). The professional activity denomination was then changed to social work and the Ministry of Education established a national legal regulation for core academic content standards for all universities.

In addition to university recognition, the most important development of the profession took place when social workers became active participants in political parties and were able to access positions at the national level where decisions were taken about the design of social policies and concerning social work education (Domenech, 1991). During the first socialist government, a new model of social services was organised and public policy to support non-profit organisations as part of an effort to professionalise the social sector was adopted (Martínez-Román, 1997). Both of these developments led to the creation of new jobs for social workers.

An important turning point was the 1990 approval by the Ministry of Education, of social work and social services as a scientific area of knowledge within social and law sciences. This process had diverse consequences due to the fact that it reflected the recognition of the uniqueness of social work and distinguished it from other areas of knowledge such as political science, sociology and labour law. This recognition led to the creation of specific social work departments, and thus social work teaching staff no longer had to belong to other departments. The newly established departments could assign teaching duties in specific subjects related to social work and, in many universities, to social policy and social services. Social workers became members of committees responsible for the selection of faculty members and obtained consolidated positions through promotion. Since 1996 universities have established a network, the Conferencia de Directores de Escuelas Universitarias de Trabajo Social (Board of Directors of Schools of Social Work), as a way of promoting scientific improvements in this area of knowledge. Finally, the universities have stimulated research and publications intended to contribute to the enrichment of the academic, as well as the professional, fields of social work and social services (Alemán and Garcés, 1996, 1997; Prieto et al, 1996).

The integration of the former schools of social assistants into the universities was a long and difficult process. Indeed, the transition to universities was positive but not cost free. For example, in the former schools the degree required for teaching staff was the degree of social assistant. This meant that all teachers of social work methods and practice were social assistants, generally with professional experience. However, once the studies joined the university system, the rules for hiring teaching staff were changed. The situation was very heterogeneous within universities: some universities valued a specific degree and professional experience in social work to teach social work methods and practice, but others prioritised staff with five-year degrees in pedagogy, sociology or law. This was one of the causes of the mixed situation in the university curriculum, and also contributed to the distance between university educational training and professional practice. With the recognition of the social work and social services area of knowledge, professional experience was finally valued. Furthermore, access to a doctorate was promoted by social work teaching staff.

Another negative consequence of the transition to the university system was an increase in the number of students that was not proportionally matched by the increase in teaching staff, and which was exacerbated by a lack of recognition of the time teaching staff spent supervising students' fieldwork experiences.

Despite these achievements, in professional practice there was some dissatisfaction and a sense of being undervalued during the 1990s (Barbero, 2002). The three-year degree was an obstacle for professional promotion because other professions, which required a five-year degree (psychology, sociology and others), offered better opportunities. After a long advocacy process by both universities and social workers professionals, and as a result of the European convergence reforms, the Ministry of Education decided to remove all three-year degrees and to offer some general common guidelines for all studies. This autonomy led to very varied educational training profiles in social work. Another process aimed at guaranteeing basic standards for training in social work was promoted by the Board of Directors of Schools and Departments of Social Work, with the participation of all universities, and the General Council of Social Work[1] (Conferencia de Directores de Escuelas de Trabajo Social and Consejo General de Trabajo Social, 2005, 2007).

Since 2010, undergraduate programmes in social work have increased in length to four years (240 ECTS, equivalent to a bachelor's degree). Students who graduate from this programme are considered social work graduates. The educational training profile is still generalist and includes the writing of a mandatory final thesis. Those who complete an undergraduate degree are recognised as qualified professional social workers.

The reform of the Spanish university system came at the same time as a major economic, political and social crisis, that caused great differences and inequalities in the implementation of the curriculum in the different autonomous communities.

Social work and Spanish social policy

It is estimated that there are 49,000 social workers in Spain. The Consejo General de Colegios Oficiales de Diplomados en Trabajo Social (General Council of Social Work) is a national organisation representing all 37 associations of professional social workers; there is no specific professional union for social workers in Spain. The council is an active member of the International Federation of Social Workers (IFSW).

In 1999, the council approved its own national Code of Ethics (Consejo General de Colegios de Diplomados en Trabajo Social y Asistentes Sociales, 1999).[2] The general professional duties of social workers are described thus in the code:'the duties of a social worker are to plan, design, apply and establish changes in social policies and services for groups and communities. Social workers play roles of information, prevention, assistance, promotion, mediation, planning, management, evaluation, supervision and teaching' (Code, sec. 2).

The ethical commitment in the code incorporates the principles of social justice as well as the recognition of human rights (sec. 7, 10). It is also noteworthy that the code underlines social workers' duty to participate in the improvement of institutional policies by contributing with their knowledge of professional practice and experience. Social workers are also called on to promote the efficacy and efficiency of institutions for the benefit of service users and the community (sec. 25).

Regarding the social responsibility of social workers, a number of professional duties are outlined. They include contributing to the improvement of the quality of life of all persons through promoting policies that guarantee social justice. In addition, social workers are required to participate in social development, cooperating in the prevention of social difficulties and the improvement of quality of life (sec. 57), to promote and support the development of rules and policies (sec. 59), to condemn social situations that cause social inequality, alienation and social exclusion (sec. 60) and to help promote social consciousness in citizens and public authorities of the nature of individual, group and community problems as well as social needs (sec. 62).

The council has promoted activities defending professional activities. It has sought to strength the professional and educational profile of social work, has organised congresses and conferences, offered specialised training and supported studies and publications. In the 1980s the council was a pioneer in offering education and training on social services organisation and management topics. This new professional profile was demanded by the new employment opportunities in public administration and in the private sector.

The first social work congresses were held in 1968, 1972 and 1976. These were opportunities for showing the profession's identity and seeking social recognition. In the following years, several topics were debated: social services for all (1980); social welfare: a utopia? (1984); social work, current challenges (1988); professional intervention within the framework of Europe with no borders (1992); social work at the turn of the millennium (1996); social work's compromise and contribution to human development (2000); a world of a thousand cultures: globalising solidarity (2004); and social work: meaning and direction (2009). Social work teaching staff were active in the scientific committees of these congresses. In order to promote research in social work, the council offers an annual national award in social work research. In 2011 a new national award in social work was established, awarded to members of the parliament who are social workers and have made an outstanding contribution to promoting the law for personal autonomy and care of dependent persons. Other professional organisations, such as those in Catalonia and Málaga, also convene social work research awards.

There are a number of specialised publications in social work. The council has published *Servicios Sociales y Política Social* (Social Services and Social Policy) since 1984. Other professional social work organisations publish journals, the pioneer being the Catalan *Revista de Trabajo Social* (Social Work Journal), which was first published as a bulletin in 1960. Other journals are published in Madrid, Málaga, Galicia and Castilla-La Mancha. *Trabajo Social y Salud* (Journal of Social Work and Health) is edited by an organisation of the same name.

As a national professional body, the council presents reports and policy proposals to parliament, the ombudsman and at conferences. An example of involvement in the field of social policy is the council's creation of the Observatorio Nacional de Servicios Sociales (National Observatory of Social Services) in 2008. The origin for this was the lack of development of the mentioned 2006/39 Act, primarily because many regional governments blocked the development of the law for political reasons. The general council decided to promote discussion, analysis and social criticism of the violation of individual rights of people in situations of dependence, with the collaboration of universities and non-profit private entities. It has also supported social protest by organisations representing the rights of people in situations of dependence. The National Observatory of Social Services has continued to organise an annual conference on social policy and services and publishes a national annual report. At the same time, professional organisations at the provincial or regional level have also made significant contributions to policies at these levels and they are invited to present reports and policy proposals to the regional parliament, ombudsman, congresses and other fora. An example of this is the pioneering role played by the professional association of Barcelona and the Catalonia region. In 2009, the 'Social Work Manifesto in the Crisis' (Consejo General de Colegios de Diplomados en Trabajo Social y Asistentes Sociales, 2009) described the professional situation of social work in the context of the economic crisis faced by Spain. The document recommended that social workers participate in formulating municipal social service policies and, in particular, voice the needs, opportunities and aspirations of citizens. For example, the manifesto claims that social policies do not sufficiently promote social participation, even though this is formally recognised by regulations. It also underscores the need to explore the political and structural dimension of changes with the goal of furthering universal and structural social justice. Clearly, the crisis situation has had profound consequences on the profession. Social work feels obligated to condemn policies that consist of cutbacks to benefits and services, and it has formulated proposals and suggestions for social improvement and demanded political action.

Social work education in policy practice and professional involvement

Social policy, as a taught subject, has been part of the social work curriculum from 1983, since the integration of social work studies in universities. The national regulation for academic content included in the third year of study a compulsory subject entitled 'social policy and social wellbeing'.

In 1990, a new curriculum regulation for social work university studies (still a three-year degree) included social policy. The content guidelines for the course consisted of the structure, content and means of social action, and social and political analysis of current models. However, despite the common guidelines, each university has adopted a different profile in its social work programme (Rubiol, 1997; Mira-Perceval, 1999; Brezmes, 2008). In some cases, courses are adapted to the profile of social workers and take into account the need to train them to engage in policy practice, but in others this has not happened. Moreover, it is common among students to be sceptical about the possibilities of policy practice.

Meanwhile, the universities started to organise social work congresses in 1996 on social work, social services and social policy. Other topics have been: globalisation and social work (1998); social change, human relationships, new technologies: a future educational training approach (2000); violence challenges (2002); is another world possible? (2004); European social work in the 21st century (2006); a social and plural Europe (2008); and the right to the city (2010). These conferences have been a place for reflection and debate about social work and social policy. They have also included the presentation of studies conducted by social workers, many of whom combine their professional activity with part-time teaching in the university.

Universities publish scientific social work and social science journals that include articles based on professional practice experiences. These include the following journals (in chronological order): *Cuadernos de Trabajo Social, Acciones e Investigaciones Sociales, Alternativas, Cuadernos de Trabajo Social, Humanismo y Trabajo Social, Portularía, Revista de Trabajo Social, Atlántida. Revista de Ciencias Sociales, Pedagogía y Trabajo Social* and the newsletter *Boletín Informativo de Trabajo Social (BITS)*.

Since 2010, as already noted, there have been no common legal guidelines on social work training but some common guidelines between universities and the Social Work Council have been agreed on. Among the competences of the professional profile approved in 2003 by the council is one related to policy knowledge and practice. The guidelines include: (a) to identify contexts and procedures to cooperate in local and national policy; (b) to contribute to knowledge of best practices in his/her work team, organisation and other networks.

These guidelines are innovative in that they explicitly recognise the interplay between social policy, social work and policy practice. Considering the professional profile, it was felt that education in social work must be oriented to prepare social intervention professionals with a comprehensive understanding of social structures and processes, social change and human behaviour that will enable them to: (a) intervene in social and institutional contexts in which people live, and transform those contexts, including political and social ones; (b) participate in formulating and evaluating policies, social services and social initiatives; (c) contribute to active citizenship through the empowerment and the guarantee of human and social rights; and (d) work in preventing social problems (Conferencia de Directores y Consejo General de Trabajo Social, 2005, 2007).

According to the criteria, the social work curriculum should include five modules: (a) social work: concepts, theories, methods and practice; (b) the institutional context of social work; (c) processes and issues involved in social work; (d) legal and organisational tools for social work; and (e) practice in the field and a final thesis. The subject of social policy and social work is part of module b, the institutional context of social work (along with social services). Among the learning outcomes, the following can be highlighted: it is important that social workers be able to assess the consequences and implications of different orientations for social policy, but also to be able to know (and be competent in) social work's contributions to the design, development and evaluation of social policy.

A review of the social work curriculum in all 36 universities, undertaken by the author, and a comparison of the approaches adopted in the various schools and the common guidelines reveal that, in practice, each university has a large degree of freedom as to the setting of its curriculum. Indeed, differences emerge in the number of social policy courses in the content or in the approach to social work practice and in the number of ECTS credits;[3] 18 universities have at least 12 ECTS credits, but policy practice is not explicit in the course syllabus. However, policy practice is present in the syllabuses of some social work or social services courses. In short, the result is still great heterogeneity among universities. It is too soon to go into additional details because many universities are still at the beginning of the implementation of the new curricula. Clearly the goals of policy practice are best met by a multidisciplinary approach with contributions from all modules of the social work curriculum.

Professional involvement in policy practice: achievements and limitations

At the end of the 1960s and during the 1970s, examples of policy practice were most common in social work at the neighbourhood level, especially in new areas inhabited by Spanish migrant workers from rural areas. Social workers were committed to this population because of growing political, economic and social dissatisfaction in the context of underdevelopment (Colomer, 1993; Carrera, 2004). As political parties were banned, sociopolitical activity took place in neighbourhood associations.

After Franco's death, the transition to democracy was a time of raising consciousness and awareness, as well as of illegal political organisations, gathering people who wished to promote democracy and human rights. Social workers were involved among these professionally and, after the freedom of political parties was approved, they became activists with political responsibilities in the new social services.

In the 1980s, from a prominent political position in the socialist government and with the support of their professional organisations, social workers developed a new model of basic social services. This change in policies generated an important increase in public employment of social work, whereby social workers were considered a source of professional knowledge in primary social services (Domenech, 1991). There was also an increase in the number of social work students. Some sectors of the profession had reservations regarding this process or the way it developed in practice (Llovet and Ubieto, 1990; Alvarez-Uría, 1993; Brezmes, 2008; Barbero et al, 2009). While this period was very important for social work as a profession, it also created substantial costs as it tended to emphasise more individual work or work centred on the creation of new services or better jobs to the detriment of a sociopolitical commitment. The socialist government (1982–96) began to introduce neo-liberal policies which were enhanced under the conservative Partido Popular (1996–2004).

While social workers in government and in non-profit organisations have clearly played a major role in designing and implementing new policies (Domenech, 1991; De la Red-Vega, 1997; Corral, 2001; Gomá et al, 2009; Lima, 2009), there are few documented examples of policy practice in the professional literature. Social workers do not disseminate successful experiences, in many cases because their reports are integrated into those provided by the organisations they work for. Another reason is the lack of time for reflection about practice. There is also little evaluation of policy practice.

On the other hand, the journal of sessions of the Congress and Senate hearings offers evidence of policy practice by professional social workers at the invitation of the parliamentary committees. A large number of social workers have participated in the policy process leading to the adoption of legislation concerning social issues by providing professional practice expertise in the debating of provisional proposals and in their legal development afterwards. Social workers have contributed to the promotion of changes of public and organisational policies at different levels of the public administration – and still continue to do so. The non-profit organisations have also been professionalised and, in many cases, their managers or directors are social workers who have an important role in directing the policy of the organisation. Nevertheless, many front line professionals do not consider policy practice an integral part of their job, working at the individual level and siding with their organisations rather than with service users (Corral, 2001; Barbero et al, 2009).

The reasons for the reluctance of front line professionals to engage in policy practice can be linked to obstacles and constraints in their work. The first general obstacle is the lack of opportunities for effective social participation. However, in practice the situation is very heterogeneous and the most frequent scenario is that political action does not promote citizen participation (Pastor Seller, 2004). Information is often difficult to obtain as there is no culture of accountability. In fact, Spain is still a democracy in development (Navarro, 2002).

An obstacle related to the low level of democracy is that social policy can cause employment problems. On the one hand, when social workers are public sector employees they have legal obligations, so they are limited in what they can do. They can propose policy improvements internally, but may not make public their evaluations or proposals. On the other hand, social workers from non-profit organisations work in organisations that are largely dependent on public funding. As a result, many private non-profit entities have become recipients of public financial resources and are unwilling to risk their financial survival by raising issues of social justice.

Personal attitudes are also an obstacle. For instance, in a single organisation we can find social workers 'avoiding' barriers to advance the rights of service users while other professionals in the same organisation can act as gatekeepers who care more for their career than for the rights of service users (Martínez Román et al, 1996). Social workers should represent the interests of service users, but often they do not act with the goal of empowering to promote direct participation. Recent changes in social work education are a good chance to improve policy practice in this way (Martínez-Román, 2002, 2010). In other cases there are social workers who have low self-esteem about their work and do not believe that their professional practice can influence policy. There are also those who have abandoned policy practice because they suffer from burnout. Finally a near-passive attitude to politics undermines a readiness to engage in policy practice among many social workers. Inadequate training is another obstacle. Until now, policy practice per se has not been a subject of professional training or of continuing education.

Towards increased policy practice

The present crisis has produced new awareness of the increase of social problems and welfare cuts. Citizens are faced with difficulties in exercising their rights (Amnistia Internacional, 2011). To a large extent, it would appear that Spanish social policy has returned to an era in which the Catholic Church is again the last safety net. There is also a high rate of unemployment among social workers, with many working in temporary or precarious employment. Many professionals work in non-profit social agencies that are running out of funding, either public or private. However, the current socioeconomic and political situation has also led to a new social movement, driven by young people but involving people of all ages and called *indignados* (outraged). This has led to debate and reflection throughout Spain and it enjoys much social support.

Universities and professional social workers are participating in public policy design or, in other cases, are criticising the quality of such policies or even the lack of them. It is clear that the crisis situation has had profound consequences for the profession. Social workers feel compelled to condemn policies based on cutbacks in benefits and services, and they are formulating proposals and suggestions for improving quality of life, and demanding changes. The demise and destruction of public and private social services has been condemned. In order to further their goals, there is a search for alliances with other social groups for joint action. The most recent example of this has been the formation of the Alianza para la defensa del Sistema Público de Servicios Sociales (Alliance for the Defence of the Social Services Public System). This is a plural group of experts supported by the professional council with the participation of diverse professional groups, employers, unions and universities. The goal was to incorporate a consensual document in the political agenda of all political parties.

In relation to social work education, the sociopolitical situation is a good context in which to motivate and train students and professionals. It is an opportunity to promote a more systematic development of policy practice in education and training, with progression at different levels of complexity from the first to fourth year of undergraduate studies. The goals of policy practice are closely related to professional ethics so it is very important to ensure feedback between universities and professional practice. These are best met by a multidisciplinary approach with contributions from all modules in the curriculum. In the case of the master's programme, it is an excellent opportunity to integrate advanced study and professional experience. Also, it is an opportune time to increase publications describing good practice in policy practice.

Notes

[1] The Consejo General de Colegios Oficiales de Asistentes Sociales (General Council of Social Workers) as a representative of professional organisations replaced the Federación de Asociaciones de Asistentes Sociales (FEDASS).

[2] The council is currently reviewing this code in order to update it. Between 1976 to 1999, the FEDASS adopted the Ethics in Social Work Statement of Principles of the IFSW. However, the first Code of Ethics was adopted by the social workers of Catalonia in 1989.

[3] ECTS are the unit of academic credit under the new European system, the European Credit and Accumulation Transfer System. The new system allows the recognition of European mobility of students and offers joint degrees between European universities.

References

Alemán, C. and Garcés, J. (eds) (1996) *Administración Social y Servicios de Bienestar* (Social Administration and Wellbeing Services), Madrid: Alianza.

Alemán, C. and Garcés, J. (eds) (1997) *Política Social* (Social Policy), Madrid: McGraw-Hill.

Alvarez-Uría, F. (1993) 'La crisis del trabajo social' (The social work crisis), *Claves*, no 34, pp 49–53.

Amnistía Internacional (2011) *Derechos a la Intemperie: Obstáculos para Hacer Valer los Derechos Económicos, Sociales y Culturales* (Obstacles to Access Economic, Social and Cultural Rights), Madrid: Sección Española de Amnistía Internacional.

Barbero, J.M. (2002) *Trabajo Social en España* (Social Work in Spain), Zaragoza: Mira Editores.

Barbero, J. M., Feu, M. and Vilbrod, A. (2009) 'Representaciones de la profesionalidad y debilidad de la formación' (Professional social image and weakness of training), *Servicios Sociales y Política Social*, no 88, pp 31–53.

Barriga, L., Brezmes, M.J., García, G. and Ramírez, J.M. (2011) *VI Informe de Evolución de la Ley de Promoción de la Autonomía Personal y Atención a las Personas en Situación de Dependencia, Cuatro Años Después* (VI Report of the Implementation Process of the Promotion of Personal Autonomy and Care for People in Situations of Dependency Act), Coruña: Colexio Oficial de Traballo Social de Galicia.

Brezmes, M. (2008) *El Trabajo Social en España: Una Profesión para la Democracia* (Social Work in Spain: A Profession for Democracy), Murcia: Editum–Universidad de Murcia.

Carrera, N. (2004) 'El reencuentro del método del trabajo social comunitario' (Back to the community social work method), *Servicios Sociales y Política Social*, no 66, pp 133–7.

Casado, D. (1969) *Plan Social Baza* (Baza Social Plan), Madrid: Cáritas Española.

Casado, D. and Fantova, F. (eds) (2007) *Perfeccionamiento de los Servicios Sociales en España* (Improvement of Spanish Social Services), Madrid: SIPOSO-FOESSA.

CES (2011) *Memoria Sobre la Situación Xocioeconómica y Laboral, España 2010* (2010 Spanish Social, Economic and Labour Situation Report), Madrid: Consejo Económico y Social de España.

CERMI (2011) *Derechos y Servicios Sociales: Por un Sistema de Servicios Sociales Universal, Garantista y de Calidad: Un Derecho Básico para la Igualdad y el Desarrollo Humano* (Social Services and Rights: Promotion of a Quality and Universal Social Services System: The Basic Right to Equality and Human Development), Madrid: Cinca.

Colomer, M. (1993) 'El trabajo social como respuesta a las necesidades sociales' (Social work to meet social needs), *Servicios Sociales y Política Social*, no 31/32, pp 75–8.

Colomer, M. (2009) *El Trabajo Social que yo he Vivido* (My Living Experience with Social Work), Barcelona: Impulso a la Acción Social-Consejo General de Colegios Oficiales de Trabajo Social.

Comisaria del Plan de Desarrollo Económico y Social (1963) *I Plan de Desarrollo Económico y Social para el periodo 1964-1967* (First Economic and Social Development Plan), Madrid: Presidencia del Gobierno

Conferencia de Directores de Escuelas de Trabajo Social y Consejo General de Trabajo Social (2005) 'Libro blanco de grado en trabajo social' (Social work degree white book), Madrid: Agencia Nacional de Evaluación de la Calidad y Acreditación, www.aneca.es/var/media/150376/libroblanco_trbjsocial_def.pdf.

Conferencia de Directores de Escuelas de Trabajo Social y Consejo General de Trabajo Social (2007) 'Criterios para el diseño de planes de estudio de títulos de grado en trabajo social' (Guidelines for the design of the social work degree curriculum), www.cgtrabajosocial.es/madrid/documentos/planes_estudio_titulo_grado_bcn07.pdf?phpMyAdmin=56fb57517a30c73c99b2110d086f072c.

Consejo General de Colegios de Diplomados en Trabajo Social y Asistentes Sociales (1999) 'Código deontológico de la profesión de diplomado en trabajo social/asistente social' (Social work national code of ethics), www.ifsw.org/p38000297.html.

Consejo General de Colegios de Diplomados en Trabajo Social y Asistentes Sociales (2009) 'Manifiesto trabajo social ante la crisis' (Social work manifesto in the crisis), www.cgtrabajosocial.es/manifiesto/index.htm.

Corral, L. (2001) 'El preocupante deterioro de las políticas sociales en España' (The alarming decline of social policy in Spain), *Servicios Sociales y Política Social*, no 54, pp 101–8.

De la Red-Vega, N. (1997) 'Política social y trabajo social' (Social policy and social work), in C. Alemán and J. Garcés (eds) *Política Social* (Social Policy), Madrid: McGraw-Hill, pp 531–52.

Domenech, R. (1991). 'La evolución del trabajo social en España en la década de los años 80' (The evolution of social work in Spain during the 1980s), *Servicios Sociales y Política Social*, no 20, pp 14–18.

Eurostat (2011) 'Population and social conditions', *Statistics in Focus* 17, Luxembourg: Publications Office of the European Union.

Gil-Parejo, M. (2010) 'La institucionalización del trabajo social en España 1958–2000 (The institutionalisation of social work in Spain 1958–2000), PhD thesis, Madrid: Universidad Autónoma de Madrid.

Gomá, R., Arenas, J. and Figueras, C. (2009) 'Una mirada al trabajo social desde diversas formaciones políticas' (An inside look at social work from different political groups), *Servicios Sociales y Política Social*, no 86, pp 91–102.

Hernández, S., Martínez-Román, M.A. and Redero, H. (2004) 'Memoria y género: Historia del trabajo social en Alicante 1960–1980' (Memory and gender: The history of social work in Alicante 1960–80), in AEIHM, *VIII Taller: Las Mujeres Como Agentes de Asistencia Social II*, Universidad de Alicante, Asociación Española de Investigación de Historia de las Mujeres-AEIHM (Spanish Association of Research on the History of Women) VIII Workshop.

INE (Instituto Nacional de Estadística (National Institute of Statistics) (2011) www.ine.es/en/inebmenu/mnu_analisoc_en.htm.

Lima, A. (2009) 'La profesión del trabajo social' (The social work profession), *Servicios Sociales y Política Social*, no 86, pp 9–41.

Llopis, B. (1984) 'Qué ha sido y qué ha representado la FEDASS en la vida de la profesión de trabajadores/asistentes sociales' (The influence of the Spanish Federation of Professional Social Workers), *Servicios Sociales y Política Social*, no 3, pp 29–30.

Llovet, J. and Ubieto, R. (1990) *Los Trabajadores Sociales: De la Crisis de Identidad a la Profesionalización* (*Social Workers: From Identity Crisis to Professionalization*), Madrid: Popular.

Marbán, V. and Rodríguez, G. (2008) 'Panoramic view of the social third sector in Spain: Environment, development, social research and challenges', *Revista Española del Tercer Sector*, no 9, pp 13–39.

Martínez- Román, M.A. (1997) 'Política social, pobreza y exclusión social' (Social policy, poverty and social exclusion), in C. Alemán and J. Garcés (eds) *Política Social* (*Social Policy*), Madrid: McGraw-Hill, pp 479–504.

Martínez- Román, M.A. (2002) 'Pistas para el diseño de políticas sociales: Escuchando a las mujeres'(Clues for the design of social policy: Listening to women), in J.M. Tortosa (ed) *Mujeres Pobres: Indicadores de Empobrecimiento en la España de hoy* (*Women in Poverty: Impoverishment Indicators in Spain*), Madrid: FOESSA, pp 127–51.

Martínez- Román, MA (2005) 'Reflexiones sobre las Políticas públicas: Promoviendo la aplicación de la igualdad de oportunidades a las familias con personas en situación de dependencia' (To reflect on public policy: Promoting equal opportunities for families with dependent people), in E. Guillén (ed) *Sobre problemas y respuestas sociales*, Barcelona: Hacer, pp 195–214.

Martínez-Román, M.A. (2010) 'La incorporación de los usuarios en la educación teórica y práctica de los trabajadores sociales: ¿Convergencia con Europa?' (Incorporating users in social work education and training: European convergence?), *Miscelánea Comillas. Revista de Ciencias Humanas y Sociales*, vol 68, no 132, pp 223–39.

Martínez-Román, M.A., Mira-Perceval, M.T. and Redero, H. (1996) 'Sistema público de servicios sociales en España' (The public system of social services in Spain), in C. Alemán and J. Garcés (eds) *Administración Social y Servicios de Bienestar* (*Social Administration and Wellbeing Services*), Madrid: Alianza, pp 203–46.

Ministerio de Sanidad, Política Social e Igualdad (2011) www.msps. es/politicaSocial/portada/home.htm.

Mira-Perceval, M.T. (1999) 'La formación para el trabajo social en España: Planes de estudio: Niveles y exigencias'(Social work education in Spain: Curriculum, degrees and standards), *Revista de Servicios Sociales y Política Social*, no 39, pp 91–6.

Navarro, V. (2002) *Bienestar Insuficiente, Democracia Incompleta: Sobre lo que no se Habla en Nuestro País* (*Insufficient Wellbeing, Incomplete Democracy: Unspoken Matters in our Country*), Barcelona: Anagrama.

Pastor Seller, E. (2004) 'La participación ciudadana en el ámbito local, eje transversal del trabajo social comunitario' (Citizen participation at the local level, a key for community social work), *Alternativas. Cuadernos de Trabajo Social*, no 12, pp 103–37.

Pérez-Díaz. J. (2010) 'Perspectivas demográficas en España: Efectos a largo plazo de la crisis' (Demographic perspectives in Spain: Effects of a long-term crisis), *Revista del Ministerio de Trabajo e Inmigración*, special issue 2, pp 23–45.

Requena, M. (2010) 'Los cambios familiares en España y sus implicaciones' (Family changes in Spain and their implications), *Revista del Ministerio de Trabajo e Inmigración*, special issue 2, pp 47–67.

Rodríguez-Cabrero, G. (2010). 'El gasto público social' (Social public expenditure), *Revista Economistas*, no 123, special issue, pp 193–201.

Rubiol, G. (1997) 'La formación de los trabajadores sociales: Análisis comparativo de Europa, América Latina, Estados Unidos y España' (Social work education: A comparative analysis of Europe, Latin America, United States and Spain), *Revista de Servicios Sociales y Política Social*, no 39, p. 39–51.

Sarasa, S. (1993) *El servicio de lo social* (About Social Celivery), Madrid: INSERSO.

Vázquez, J. (1971): *Situación del Servicio Social en España* (Social Work Situation in Spain), Madrid: Instituto de Sociología Aplicada.

EIGHT

Social workers affecting social policy in Sweden

Katarina H. Thorén and Tapio Salonen

Introduction

The Swedish welfare system is known as a comprehensive and redistributive welfare state, with diverse institutions providing public support and social services. Despite the existence of a broad welfare state system, less is known of the extent to which professional social workers are active in reforming, changing, or otherwise affecting social policies in Sweden. In other words, in what way are they engaged in policy practice activities as part of their practical work? In this chapter we will present and describe the role of Swedish social workers in policy practice activities, with a specific focus on the shape and boundaries of such practices in the Swedish welfare state context. More specifically, we will discuss social work in relation to Swedish social policy, social work education and its teaching of policy practice skills, and social workers' engagement in policy practice.

This contribution highlights the Swedish case, which is often unreflectively perceived of as an example of an interventionist and universal welfare state. In Sweden, professional social workers[1] play a significant role in the implementation of social policy and a majority of Swedish social workers are employed within the large public welfare sector. Although public welfare institutions, such as municipal social services, are important vehicles for social policy implementation, professional social workers can also be found in other settings such as schools, mental health services, voluntary and non-profit organisations, the healthcare system, residential care units, substance abuse treatment, care of older people and people with disabilities, correctional services, employment services and immigration services. Social work is a rather large profession in Sweden; it enjoys a relatively high professional status, and social work education has a long tradition in the country (Meeuwisse and Swärd, 2007). Most social workers have a university degree, and an education in social work consists of a three and a half year programme with both theoretical and practical components.

Thus, social work is a strong and stable profession, training combines clinical skills with social policy knowledge, and the research environment is active and growing. Nevertheless it is less clear in what way social workers engage in policy practice activities in their professional and practical work. In fact, it has been argued that social workers are relatively unengaged in policy practice activities attempting to influence social policy (Dellgran, 2008; Rolfer, 2009). Similarly, it has been claimed that social workers do not play an effective role in current policy debates, which limits their engagement in policy practice. Such professional passivity is remarkable, since social workers in Sweden have traditionally been active in transforming and shaping social policy (Qvarsell, 2003).

The role of professional social workers is in a transitional stage in the Swedish welfare state context, and the boundaries for policy practice activities are also changing. The question is how they are changing and what implications this has for social policy and social work. In this chapter we will discuss social workers' current engagement in policy practice in Sweden and the institutional context for such engagement. The aim is to examine the knowledge and tools that social workers have to participate in policy practice engagement. In particular, the following questions will be explored: what are the institutional boundaries for social workers' policy practice engagement? What is the importance of policy practice in the social work discourse in Sweden? Does social work education in Sweden prepare social workers to engage in policy practice, and, if so, in what way? To what degree do social workers engage in policy practice in order to influence social policy? What are the factors that influence social workers' involvement in policy practice and what are the implications of this?

The Swedish welfare state and the social work context

Clearly, the welfare system creates the broad boundaries for both the social policy context and social workers' opportunities to engage in policy practice. Sweden is known for its generous universal and redistributive welfare state that includes several social protection schemes and social services (Esping-Andersen, 1996; Salonen, 2001; Kangas and Palme, 2005; Bergh, 2009). The Swedish system has its roots in the early 1900s, when visions of national welfare policies, financial security and the right to social services on equal terms began to develop.

In the formative years of the Swedish welfare state, social workers were important actors and they were active in the social political debate and in reforming social policies (Qvarsell, 2003; Meewisse and Swärd, 2000). One example is the formation of the Central Association of Social Work (Centralförbundet för Social Arbete – CSA) in 1903. The CSA was a cooperative body comprising a number of related associations with socially progressive ideas. During the beginning of the 20th century the CSA was especially engaged in the issues of poverty, child protection, and housing but the CSA was also an important actor in the formation of new and additional organisations which focused on various social policy issues (Larsson, 2000). The members of CSA and the related associations were engaged in vast array of social concerns, which they frequently addressed in public debate (Pettersson, 2011). During this period the CSA also initiated several investigations of contemporary social problems and supported social policy reforms proposed to deal with these problems. These reforms included increased state responsibility for handling poverty and other social ills. Many well-known social workers, such as Gerda Mayerson and Agda Montelius, were affiliated with the CSA and were very active in the social and political processes that led to social policy transformation and the development of the social work field in Sweden. Over the years the CSA has served as a think tank and a leading organisation for social policy and social work issues, though this was particularly the case during the first decades of the 20th century. While the organisation is still active and a central organisation within the social work field, it is less involved directly in social policy reforms today (Pettersson, 2001). The CSA's current activities focus mainly on conference arrangements, the provision of small research grants in the area of social policy research and supporting publications within the social policy area.

Another organisation that has been important for the social work profession is the Swedish Association for Social Workers (SSR), which was founded in 1958. The SSR is the trade union with which many university-educated social workers are affiliated, and its mission is to promote and develop the professional role of social workers and to improve their working conditions. One of the SSR's major tasks is to offer counselling to individual members regarding working conditions and to represent them in negotiations with employers. Other important tasks are lobbying, advocacy and additional activities that attempt to influence the government and employers. It also seeks to influence public opinion on matters relating to social work practice and general social policy issues (Wingfors, 2004). Finally, the SSR attempts to affect the quality and conditions of social work education and that of other similar disciplines. The SSR's current activities in relation to policy practice will be discussed later in the chapter. In addition to the SSR, some social workers, primarily those lacking a professional university degree, are also affiliated with the Vision trade union (previously called SKTF). Vision comprises primarily publicly employed workers in municipal- and county-level services.

Between the 1930s and 1970s the Swedish welfare state modernised and adopted a wide-ranging welfare system, introducing public benefit systems and social services that supported large groups in Swedish society. There was a strong consensus in Sweden for welfare state development and this consensus encompassed diverse actors, including political parties, the labour movement and other civil society organisations. Due to this strong welfare state consensus there was less need and motivation for social work professionals to engage in social and political issues. Holgersson (2001) argues that social workers' new role as public officials within public welfare organisations created little space for individual actions on the part of social workers.

The 'Swedish model' took shape after the Second World War and since then has often been depicted as an example of an ideal type welfare state model. Social work has been an integral part of the Swedish welfare system, with several formal regulations for social work practice and public social service organisations in which social workers have an important role. Despite this strong welfare state and access to services for large groups, the welfare system has also been a target for political debate and institutional changes. Since the end of the 1970s the Swedish model has been questioned on both political and ideological terms and many traditional welfare characteristics have changed over the last decades. In the 1990s Sweden experienced a severe economic recession that amplified criticism of the welfare system. As a result of both this criticism and economic difficulties, the welfare system underwent significant cutbacks and institutional changes (SOU, 2000:3; Hvinden and Johansson, 2007). A number of social services moved away from institutional regulation and towards increased flexibility, local adaptation and individualization (Sunesson et al, 1998). The institutional changes affected many of the groups with whom social workers work, as well as the working conditions of the social workers themselves.

The institutional changes initiated in the 1990s have sought to renew the public welfare sector in terms of efficiency, freedom of choice and privatisation, with the goal of creating competition (Sunesson et al, 1998). New forms of management such as performance measurement and New Public Management strategies are now integral parts of many public social service organisations (Wolmesjö, 2005; Berg et al, 2008). Social service organisations are facing shrinking resources, and selected services are increasingly being contracted out to private providers, especially those engaged in the care of older people, drug abuse treatment and institutional care for children and young people. The social work field extends increasingly to both non-profit and for-profit organisations (Bergmark and Lundström, 2008) even though both the voluntary, non-profit and the for-profit sectors are still relatively small in the Swedish welfare system (Lundström and Svedberg, 1998; Chartrand, 2004; Svedberg and Olsson, 2010). Interestingly, while these welfare state changes have affected the role of social work and social workers, they have taken place without many objections from the social work profession.

Organisational context and areas of practice

Despite the institutional changes in the Swedish welfare state, the typical organisation of social work practice remains intact. Municipal social services are still the prime place of work for social workers and they are the largest organisational arena in which social work is conducted in Sweden (Lundström and Sunesson, 2000; Bergmark and Lundström, 2008). The municipal social services include a larger service called 'individual and family services' (*individ-och familjeomsorgen* – IFO), which provides financial support for people with economic needs, child protection and family support service, and various services for adults, primarily those with substance abuse or mental health problems (Bergmark and Lundström, 2008). The social services also engage in the care of older people and people with disabilities. The municipal social services are an important part of the welfare state structure in Sweden and these make up 45% of municipal spending.

The municipal social services, and in particular the individual and family services are generally staffed with trained social workers. Social work within the social services is regulated primarily by the Social Service Act (Socialtjänstlagen – SoL), which is national legislation concerning individuals' right to support and services from the municipality. The Act also stipulates the municipalities' responsibilities for child protection and investigation processes. In its initial paragraph, the Act also spells out that clients' self-determination and individual preferences should be respected and taken into account within the social services. Furthermore, the professional aim of the social services is to liberate and develop individuals' own resources and integrity. A fundamental starting point is the focus on the needs of the individual and the understanding that the social services must take a broad view of the individual's situation, problems and resources. These professional principles are stated in both the legislation and in the SSR Code of Ethics (2011). On the other hand, within the administrative boundaries of the Social Service Act, social workers in the municipal social services have a dual role as they are both providing help and support while, at the same time, acting as public officials responsible for controlling clients' behaviour (Salonen, 1998; Svensson, 2001; Järvinen, 2002; Thorén 2008). The duality in many social workers' professional positions might create a situation which limits the social workers' potential to engage in policy activities that raise questions concerning their clients.

Each local social service organisation is headed by a 'social service board', which is a political body constituted by local politicians. The social service board takes larger budget decisions and oversees the general financial trends of the local social services. The daily activities and the formal decision-making of social workers are delegated in a hierarchical order from the politicians, through the managerial level to the professional social workers. Work within the social services is influenced by both political decisions and institutional changes at the macro level, which consequently affect the structure and orientation of social work practices (Bergmark and Lundström, 2008). In effect, this means that many Swedish social workers are employed in organisations that are heavily influenced by political decisions and in which politicians are ultimately responsible for their practices. Bergmark and Lundström (2008) also claim that the core structure of social work in Sweden is shaped within the social services and requires social service employees to have an ability to understand the politically driven work that they perform. The question is whether they have this understanding of their work.

Another aspect of the organisation of social work relates to current professional trends. This is particularly true of the growth of specialisation in Swedish social work by which many broad social work areas are becoming more and more organised into smaller and specialised segments and areas. Liljegren (2008) discusses this specialisation process and how it creates tensions between new forms of professional segments. For example, substance abuse treatment is becoming increasingly specialised in terms of who is working with this kind of problem. A parallel process is the medicalisation of substance abuse treatment, which makes it a healthcare concern rather than a social work concern. This creates a situation in which social workers, with a more holistic perspective on these issues, are becoming more and more removed from this kind of social problem and further removed from a situation in which they can raise social and political questions related to the field. Another example is the social work with poverty and unemployment, which is gradually becoming more and more individualised and bureaucratic, and decoupled from its structural causes. This development is also removing social workers from seeing the greater picture of many current social problems, and, hence, limits their possibilities of reacting on a sociopolitical level. The specialisation of social work is affected by, and affects, social policies that are related to each specialised field. Many social policies increasingly relate to social problems as individual failings rather than as structural limitations, and this leads to more individually focused social work rather than macro-level social work. There is also a risk that the specialisation of the profession will lead to a greater gap between policy and practice for social workers.

The trend towards evidence-based practices within social work may also contribute to distancing social workers from social policy matters since their focus becomes whether interventions are scientifically proven to be effective rather than problematising social injustices in society (Bergmark and Lundström, 2006; Jergeby, 2008).

The social work profession and its education structure

While it is difficult to offer a firm definition of who is considered to be a professional social worker in the Swedish context, the term is used here to describe professionals with a bachelor's degree in social work (*socionomexamen*) or similar degrees from other disciplines. Most social workers both within the social services and other social work organisations do, in fact, have a social work degree and for some specialised positions a social work degree is a prerequisite. There are currently approximately 40,000 practising social workers in Sweden. There are 16 social work programmes that lead to a social work degree. The programmes consist of three and a half years (seven semesters) of university studies and include both theoretical courses and field training. Social work studies take the form of a generalist education with the aim of providing a broad knowledge of social work and other related disciplines. Social work is a recognised academic field within the university system and social work research is also well established and growing in Sweden, with several active researchers and PhD students. The research is wide ranging and interdisciplinary and examines a large variety of social work questions. Research on policy practice issues is less developed, although a number of social work scholars are interested in social policy research and issues relating to inequality, poverty and social politics (Johansson, 2002; Thorén, 2008; Ulmestig, 2007; Angelin, 2009; Salonen, 2011).

How are social policy and policy practice skills taught to future social workers? Social policy courses are offered in virtually all social work programmes in Sweden and the assumption is that social workers require this knowledge base in their education. As such, social policy courses are taught both on the undergraduate and graduate levels, although the direction and content of specific social policy courses vary to some extent between universities in Sweden. Unlike some countries, there is no division in Swedish social work education between clinical social work and social policy, as the social work programme is a broad social science education entailing both clinical social work and structural and policy-oriented social work knowledge.

An examination of the various syllabuses and course descriptions of social policy courses reveals that social work students gain social policy knowledge about rather broad and theoretical knowledge such as welfare state theories, the historical development of Swedish social policy and the welfare state, how social policy affects various populations, and comparative social policy. There is virtually no specific Swedish social work literature relating to the subject of policy practice and students get little practical training in how to work professionally at the policy level.

Social work and social policy in Sweden

There are no clear descriptions, definitions or explicit targets in terms of how social policy issues should be performed in social work in Sweden. Professional Codes of Ethics can shed light on this. In the Swedish case, it would appear that social workers have a responsibility to promote social justice, in relation to both society in general and in relation to the people with whom they work (SSR, 2011). The Code of Ethics notes that social workers should represent democratic civic ideals including human rights, humanity and solidarity. Their work should also contribute to a good and worthy life for citizens and develop the welfare structure of the society. For example, the Swedish Code of Ethics states: 'The social worker has a specific responsibility toward individuals and groups in vulnerable situations' (SSR, 2011, p 14). Social workers are expected to challenge unjust policies and practices and have a professional duty to bring to the attention of their employers, policymakers, politicians and the general public situations in which resources are inadequate or where the distribution of resources, policies and practices are oppressive, unfair or harmful. Thus social workers are obliged to contest social conditions that contribute to social exclusion and stigmatisation and to work towards social inclusion. These statements are clear and straightforward with regard to the expectation that social workers engage in work tasks that include policy practice and policy reforms. While these descriptions and definitions of social work do not explicitly say that social work in itself is active in political engagement, they do underscore that a sociopolitical perspective on social work and social problems is part of the professional social work field.

Policy practice in reality

There is currently no systematic knowledge about social workers' engagement in policy practice as part of their profession in Sweden. But the common view is that social workers are silent and rather passive in sociopolitical debates and processes and that they have, in general, abandoned issues such as poverty, inequality and marginalisation (Dellgran, 2008). Early social work in Sweden had a clear-cut commitment to social policy issues and social reforms which sought to reduce inequality, poverty and other injustices in society (Pettersson, 2001; Aronsson, 2008; Holgersson, 2008). These issues appear to be generally overlooked in practical social work.

Although it would appear that today social workers are relatively unengaged in the sociopolitical debate and in policy practice, there are some individual attempts to question various social issues at the local level. There are examples in which individual members have criticised their own municipalities. These issues have often been related to the working situation of the social workers or the local organisation of social work, but they also include situations that have implications for clients or social policy in the long term. In such cases social workers have acted as whistle-blowers and reported problematic situations to their trade unions (SSR and Vision), and thereafter been supported by their union in further legal processes. For example, the SSR has been involved in protests when some local municipalities have tried to lower the qualifications for certain social work positions in the municipalities. Another way in which social workers or social work organisations can be involved in the policy process in Sweden is the formal legislation process. When the parliament proposes a new policy or legislation in Sweden, various interest groups or experts are asked to comment formally on the proposal. For example, when a new piece of legislation was proposed for the school system, the association for school social workers replied to the legal proposal. Another example is how the association for healthcare social workers commented on a proposal about a social work licence for social workers within the health care sector. Furthermore, the SSR is often involved in this kind of policy-making process but it is still a rather limited function for social workers in general. Since July 2011, there is a new legal requirement (Lex Sarah) for staff within the municipal social services that requires them to report any kind of abuse within the social services to the service provider, and the service provider must investigate and remedy the situation or remove the reported abuse. The National Board of Health and Welfare should also be notified if it is found that the abuse is serious. This form of legal formality does not generate an obvious policy practice engagement, but it can highlight situations that might illuminate the need for policy practice actions.

Another response to social workers' sociopolitical silence is a project called 'Project Mission Welfare' (Projekt Uppdrag Välfärd), which has attempted to raise interest in the sociopolitical debate among politicians and social workers. This project was founded by the SSR and highlights the need for greater political awareness among social workers themselves. Part of this project was a survey and interviews about the social workers' own working conditions. The survey asked 400 social workers within the municipal social services how they perceived their work situation. The result was very discouraging in regards to their workload and potential to follow the intentions of the Social Service Act. In brief, many social workers felt that they could not provide adequate support, resources or services according to clients' legal rights (Akademikerförbundet SSR and Novus, 2010). The project has also published a book entitled *A Quest for Social Policy: A Debate that Disappeared* (*Spaning efter socialpolitiken. Om en debatt som försvann*) (Rolfer, 2009), in which various stakeholders such as social workers, social work professors, politicians and union representatives expressed their views on the lack of sociopolitical engagement among social workers and society in general. Another example is a demonstration in December 2009 in Stockholm, which was conducted by a large number of social workers from the various social service departments in the city administration. The reason for the demonstration was major cuts in the city's social services and the consequences these cuts would have for both service users and social workers.

Alongside more traditional forms of policy practice, we can also see new forms of sociopolitical movements in the social media. One example in Sweden is a number of appeals and 'groups' on Facebook. For example, the Facebook page 'Lets break the silence' (*Nu bryter vi tystnaden*) is an initiative by social workers and the trade union Vision. The aim of it is to highlight the fact that poverty and injustice are growing in Sweden and that social workers' working situations, especially in the municipal social services, are terrible. These new forms of manifestations, appeals and groups in social media might create new avenues for social workers to engage in sociopolitical activities.

What are the reasons for the apparently low level of social work engagement in policy practice in Sweden? One possible explanation is that most social work in Sweden takes place within organisations that are heavily influenced by a sociopolitical context. This is due to the fact that the boundaries and opportunities to affect social policy are constrained and complex. Contradictions between social policy goals and professional values place social workers in a difficult situation when they actually deliver social policy to clients. First, social workers must follow policy directives, and second, they want to provide clients with support and help from a social work perspective. In the Swedish context, the role of social workers is increasingly twofold. On the one hand, they are often employed as public officials in a political organisation; on the other hand they are required to be the watchdog over their clients and to implement policies that do not support clients or that create difficult working conditions for the social workers themselves. As argued earlier, social workers in the Swedish social work context often have double roles as helpers and controllers because of the public organisation of social work in Sweden. This means that they use both carrots and sticks when working with clients, according to the Swedish social work organisation and legislation (Salonen, 1998; Järvinen, 2002; Thorén, 2008).

In this kind of professional and organisational situation social workers can choose between various strategies for their responses and resistance to social policies and social structures that they might find difficult and problematic in relation to their clients' situations. Thus, social workers' responses can take the form of 'exit', 'voice', or 'loyalty' (Hirschman, 1971). The 'voice' strategy means some type of policy practice action or protest on behalf of the social workers. The 'exit' strategy implies that they leave the organisation and their position in order to object to the situation or the policy. The 'loyalty' strategy means that the social worker is loyal to the organisation and/or the policies that they are required to implement. With a welfare system with large public social service organisations, and very few non-profit, private, or volunteer social service organisations, social workers will probably find it difficult to question the organisations, policies or other kinds of political decisions. In a new study of Nordic social workers' attitudes towards their work, many social workers said that they liked their work but claimed that they had little opportunity to influence more general organisational changes (Meeuwisse et al, 2011). This means that the 'loyalty' strategy is most likely, while the possibility that Swedish social workers will opt for 'voice' is narrow. The risk for limited space for responses and resistance can also be amplified with New Public Management strategies and the increased use of performance measures as a way to steer and control social work practices (Berg, 2008). The 'exit' strategy seems to be used more often within social work, especially in the municipal social services in Sweden. Many social workers leave or want to leave their work when they find it difficult, either for themselves due to high demands and little resources or when it becomes hard to support their clients in reasonable ways (Akademikerförbundet SSR and Novus 2010; Meeuwisse et al, 2011). Dissatisfaction and staff turnover rates are especially high within the area of financial support in the municipal social services. What is also pertinent is that social workers in financial support are more inclined to explain clients' economic hardships and poverty with individual explanations rather than structural causes. Such standpoints will probably affect their willingness and ability to conduct policy practice activities concerning poverty and marginalisation as part of their professional work.

Another reason for diminishing social policy interest on the part of Swedish social workers may be that this type of activity is being abandoned in favour of social work that focuses more on therapeutic and treatment-oriented activities at the individual level (see also Specht and Courtney, 1994 for a comparison with the US; Dellgran, 2008). This can be seen as a remarkable development because policy activism has traditionally been in social work areas, both in Sweden and internationally. The lack of policy practice involvement can probably be linked to social work education and how it prepares social work students to be engaged in social policy and policy practice as part of the work. As mentioned earlier, social policy courses appear in most social work programmes in Sweden but they tend to focus on knowledge and literature on welfare state theory and social policy development ·rather than on policy practice skills. It is possible that Swedish social work students may benefit from more precise skills on how to engage in policy practice (Mendes, 2003, Weiss et al, 2006).

Conclusions

In this chapter we have examined and described the current situation of social workers' policy practice involvement within the Swedish welfare state. We can see that it is a major challenge for professional social workers to focus on structural social policy issues, since an individualised approach to social work and social problems is currently dominant in social work practice in Sweden. This individual-oriented social work creates a discrepancy between practical work at the individual client level and more socially oriented policy work. We also argue that the structure of the Swedish welfare state with a large public sector and politically controlled social services creates barriers for social workers to engage in policy practice activities since that would basically mean that they are questioning their own employers. In such a context it becomes difficult to give voice to sociopolitical concerns. Instead, it is easier and less risky to become loyal and 'follow the rules'. Other factors that we also believe limit policy practice engagement are the development of performance measure and New Public Management strategies, which put the focus on outcome measures rather than the root causes of inequalities and injustices that many client groups experience in their lives. The individualisation and performance measures seem to constrain social workers' opportunities to engage in policy practice actions. Specialisation and medicalisation are developments that also appear to limit policy practice activities as the social workers become experts on small segments of their field and thereby have difficulties in comprehending how various social problems are linked to wider sociopolitical factors. This makes it more difficult for social workers to influence and make a difference in relation to larger social policy issues.

But policy practice does not necessarily need to be all about grand social policy reforms; it can also be about minor and local issues and concerns as well as intra-professional issues. It appears that social workers have greater motivation and engagement in issues about their own working situation than about their client populations. Social workers are also better supported by their trade unions on such issues, and these activities can also influence and shape a debate that is greater than the initial issue. Nevertheless, we argue that social workers in Sweden are rather passive and silent.

Social work education in Sweden offers a solid university degree but clearly the social work profession would benefit from increased policy practice skills and learning how to do this kind of work effectively as part of their profession. Social work students receive a good understanding of social policy from their education, but in practice they tend to think structurally but act individually. This tension between structural and individual perspectives is in fact embedded in the core of professional social work and shapes both limits and possibilities for the professional role in a changing society. Without an awareness of social policy framework and structural factors constituting social risks and problems social workers will get lost in practice.

Note

[1] Individuals with a social work degree equivalent to a Bachelor of Social Work, which in the Swedish context is referred to as *socionom*.

References

Akademikerförbunder SSR and Novus (2010) *Social workers in the municipal social services about their working conditions*, unpublished presentation of survey, Stockholm: Akademikerförbunder SSR and Novus.

Angelin, A. (2009) 'The double logic of powerlessness: A study of long-term unemployment and income support taking among young adults', Diss . Lund: Lund University (in Swedish).

Aronsson, P. (2008) 'From poor relief women to modern social workers', in H. Swärd and M-A. Egerö (eds) *The Politics of Conditions: Poverty Premises and Community Action: Now and Then*, Malmö: Egalité (in Swedish).

Berg, E., Barry, J. and Chandler, J. (2008) 'New public management and social work in Sweden and England', *International Journal of Sociology and Social Policy*, vol 28, no 3–4, pp 85–90.

Bergh, A. (2009) *The Capitalistic Welfare State*, Stockholm: Norstedts akademiska förlag (in Swedish).

Bergmark, A. and Lundström, T. (2006) 'Towards an evidence-based practice: The directions for social work', *Socialvetenskaplig Tidskrift*, vol 13, no 2, pp 99–112 (in Swedish).

Bergmark, Å. and Lundström, T. (2008) 'Individual and family services in the municipal social services: The conditions for social work', in Å. Bergmark, T. Lundström, R. Minas and S. Wiklund (eds) *The Social Services in the Spotlight: Organization, Resources and Activities – Examples from Work with Children and Youth, Income Support and Substance Abuse*, Stockholm: Natur och Kultur (in Swedish).

Chartrand S. (2004) 'Work in voluntary welfare organizations: A sociological study of voluntary welfare organisations in Sweden', Diss. Stockholm: Stockholm University.

Dellgran, P. (2008) 'The professionalization of poverty and the escape from the exercise of authority', in H. Swärd and M-A. Egerö (eds) *The Politics of Conditions: Poverty Premises and Community Action – Now and Then*, Malmö: Egalité (in Swedish).

Esping-Andersen, G. (ed) (1996) *Welfare States in Transition: National Adaptations in Global Economies*, Oxford: Oxford University Press.

Holgersson, L. (2008) *Social Policy and Social Work: History and Ideas*, Stockholm: Norstedts juridik (in Swedish).

Hirschman, A. (1971) *Exit, Voice, and Loyalty: Responses to Decline in Firms, Organizations, and States*, Cambridge, MA: Harvard University Press.

Hvinden, B. and Johansson, H. (2007) *Citizenship in Nordic Welfare States: Dynamics of Choice, Duties and Participation in a Changing Europe*, London: Routledge.

Jergeby, U. (2008) *Evidence-based Practice in Social Work*, Stockholm: Gothia (in Swedish).

Johansson, H. (2001) 'In the shadow of social citizenship: The right to social assistance during the 1980s and 1990s', Diss. Lund: Lund University (in Swedish).

Järvinen, M. (2002) 'The helping universe: A power perspective on the meeting between client and system', in A. Meeuwisse and H. Swärd (eds) *Perspectives on Social Problems*, Stockholm: Natur och kultur (in Swedish).

Kangas, O. and Palme J. (eds) (2005) *Social Policy and Economic Development in the Nordic Countries*, Basingstoke: Palgrave.

Larsson, S. (2000) 'Voluntary organization in social work', in A. Meeuwisse, S. Sunesson and H. Swärd (eds) *Social Work: A Textbook*, Stockholm: Natur och Kultur (in Swedish).

Liljegren, A. (2008) Professional boundary work: Social workers in Sweden. Diss. Göteborg: Göteborgs universitet, 2008. Göteborg.

Lundström, T. and Sunesson, S. (2000) 'Social work is taking place in organisations', in A. Meeuwisse, S. Sunesson and H. Swärd (eds) *Social Work: A Textbook*, Stockholm: Natur och kultur (in Swedish).

Lundström, T. and Svedberg, L. (1998) 'Swedish voluntarism in an international perspective. An introduction', *Socialvetenskaplif tidskrift*, vol 5, no 2-3, pp 106-127.

Mendes, P. (2003) 'Teaching social policy to social work students', *Australian Social Work*, vol 56, no 3, pp 220–33.

Meeuwisse, A., Scaramuzzino, R. and Swärd, H. (2011) 'Everyday realities and visionary ideals among social workers in the Nordic countries: A matter of specialization and work tasks?', *Nordic Social Work Research*, vol 1, no 1, pp 5–23.

Meeuwisse, A. and Swärd, H. (2007) 'Cross-national comparisons of social work: A question of initial assumptions and levels of analysis', *European Journal of Social Work*, vol 10, no 4, pp.481–96.

Pettersson, U. (2001) *Social Work, Politics, and Professionalization: The Historical Development in the US and Sweden*, Stockholm: Natur och Kultur (in Swedish).

Pettersson, U. (2011) *From Poor Relief to Social Services: Social Work and Extra-parliamentary Work*, Lund: Studentlitteratur (in Swedish).

Qvarsell, R. (2003) 'CSA and social policy around the early 1990s', *Socialvetenskaplig Tidskrift*, vol 10, pp 2–3 (in Swedish).

Rolfer, B. (2009) *A Quest for Social Policy: A Debate that Disappeared*, Stockholm: Premiss and Akademikerförbundet SSR.

Salonen ,T. (1998) 'Client', in V. Denvall and T. Jacobson (eds) *Everyday Concepts in Social Work. Ideology, Practice, and Theory*, Stockholm: Publica (in Swedish).

Salonen, T. (2001) 'Sweden: Between Model and Reality', in P. Alcock and G. Craig (eds) *International Social Policy*, Basingstoke: Palgrave.

Salonen, T. (2011) *Welfare Not for Everybody* , Stockholm: Save the Children (in Swedish).

SOU 2000:3 (2000). *Welfare at the crossroads: The development during the 1990s*, Ministry of Health and Social Affairs, Kommittén Välfärdsbokslut, Stockholm: Fritzes (in Swedish).

Specht, H. and Courtney, M.E. (1994) *Unfaithful Angels: How Social Work has Abandoned its Mission*, New York: Free Press.

SSR (2011) *Social Workers' Code of Ethics, the Swedish Association for Social Workers*, Akademikerförbundet SSR: Stockholm (in Swedish).

Sunesson, S., Staffan Blomberg, S., Edebalk, P-G., Harrysson, L., Magnusson, J., Meeuwisse, A., Petersson, J. and Salonen, T. (1998) 'The flight from universalism', *European Journal of Social Work*, vol. 1, no. 1, pp 19-29.

Svedberg, L. and Olsson, L-E. (2010) 'Voluntary organisations and welfare provision in Sweden', in A. Ewers and A. Zimmer (eds) *Third Society Organizations Facing Turbulent Environments*, Baden-Baden: Nomos Verlag.

Svensson, K. (2001) 'Instead of jail? A study of caring power, punishment, and social work within the probation services' Diss. Lund: Lund University (in Swedish).

Thorén, K.H. (2008) 'Activation policy in action: A street-level study of social assistance in the Swedish welfare state', unpublished doctoral dissertation, University of Chicago.

Ulmestig, R. (2007) 'On the borders of poor relief? A study of labour market policies and social assistance', Lund University (in Swedish).

Weiss, I., Gal, J. and Katan, J. (2006) 'Social policy for social work: A teaching agenda', *British Journal of Social Work*, vol 36, pp 789–806.

Wingfors, S. (2004) 'The professionalization of the social work profession', Gothenburg University (in Swedish).

Wolmesjö, M. (2005) 'Management functions in transitions: Changes in the professional roles of first-line managers in municipal elder and disability care', unpublished doctoral dissertation, Lund University (in Swedish).

NINE

Social workers affecting social policy in the US

Richard Hoefer

Social work in the context of the US welfare system

The US has long been considered the only major industrialised country in the world with a residual social welfare system. The US welfare system relies on means testing for many of its major income maintenance and food aid programmes, so individual Americans must usually be poor to receive government assistance. Levels of social expenditure are low relative to national GDP and are volatile, with conservative politicians taking away what liberal elected officials are able to bestow when power shifts to Republicans from Democrats. The 2011 debate at local, state and national levels regarding cutting spending rather than raising taxes from historic low levels is one indication of the power of conservatives in American politics, as exemplified by Republicans winning control of the House of Representatives in the elections in 2010.

Jansson (2005) describes some of the contextual factors that explain the US 'reluctance' to embrace a welfare state. He emphasises the US belief that providing charity encourages idleness and dependency, that social problems will yield to simple programmatic solutions, that everyone has equal chances to succeed, that free markets are the best way to solve many problems of inequality and poverty and, indeed, that a certain amount of inequality is a positive thing. In addition, he argues that the division of programmatic financial responsibility into state-run and national government-run programmes, with both relying on private, non-profit organisations for implementation, has created a confusing lack of responsibility for aiding people in need. Jansson further notes the presence of racism and prejudice, which affect responses to solving social problems, many of which are seen as connected to failures on the part of people of colour and minority status.

Within this context of contest and debate, Blau and Abramovitz (2004) argue that the social work profession is also an arena of struggle, with clashes between those who work to change individuals (containment orientation) and those who work to change society (change orientation). The social work profession has strains of both traditions still living within its current structures and culture. Two primary historical patterns exist, the more individually oriented and conservative Charity Organization Society (COS) movement and the more reform-oriented liberal-leaning Settlement House Movement.

The Charity Organization Society approach to alleviating need is based on a scientific investigation of the causes of poverty and assessments of individual situations to determine how best to assist the individual. The COS movement first began in England and had found its way to the US by 1877. Blau and Abramowitz (2004, p 241) indicate that COS leaders claimed to have a new approach to ending poverty but in fact retained 'the old social welfare ideology of individual responsibility, elimination of outdoor relief, and the repression of pauperism'. Jansson (2005, p 156) describes the work of the volunteer 'friendly visitors', who were almost always white, well-to-do, English-speaking and female, as doing 'detailed research on the motivations, history and living arrangements of families as they decided whether and how to help destitute people'. Eventually, this approach to helping became known as casework (Jansson, 2005), a methodology refined over the years and practised by social workers even today.

The Settlement House Movement had a different approach. Jansson states that workers in settlement houses were 'somewhat more reform oriented, more inclined to decrease the personal distance between paid staff and neighborhood residents, and less convinced that helping could be reduced to a science' (2005, pp 157–8). While Jansson believes that the differences between the Charity Organization Societies and the Settlement House Movement were substantial and led to 'frequent conflict between the two groups' (p 158), Blau and Abramovitz (2004, p 242) warn that 'one should not exaggerate the differences' because 'both drew volunteers from the privileged classes who sought to reduce the gap between the rich and the poor'.

The social work profession in the US developed from these two elements, often veering back and forth from the relatively strong progressivism and liberalism of reformers such as Jane Addams to the more conservative views of Mary Richmond and others interested in changing individuals. Without strong trade union support, as existed in most European countries, social work in the US developed in the late 1800s and early 1900s only as a result of finding wealthy supporters who would bankroll aid to the poor, immigrants and other unfortunates who were harmed by the emergent industrialist system (Jansson, 2005). Even today, tensions in emphasis of practice viewpoints (individually focused micro practice versus organisational and reform-focused macro practice) exist. These differences are evident in organisational politics within the National Association of Social Workers (NASW, the largest organisation for social workers in the US) and the Council for Social Work Education (CSWE), the nationally recognised accrediting body for social work education.

Overview of the social work profession and its education structure

In the early part of the 20th century, friendly visitors and settlement house workers attended meetings of the National Conference of Charities and Corrections, where they tended to vie for ascendency in the emerging profession of social work (Jansson, 2005). Popple and Leighninger (2008, pp 10–13) discuss the debate regarding the status of social work at length. One of the key aspects of this debate is the definition of a 'profession' as opposed to any other occupation. In 1915, at the annual meeting of the National Conference of Charities and Corrections, Abraham Flexner declared that the field of social work, while it had some attributes of a profession, lacked others, and could thus not be declared to be a profession. Flexner argued that social work lacked 'an educationally communicable technique' (Popple and Leighninger, 2008, p 11) because the field was so broad – too many things were being called 'social work' and thus little could be said to be outside of the field. A lack of specificity made it impossible to teach students how to perform social work tasks. Another problem with calling social work a profession lay in the idea that social workers did not take individual responsibility for achieving success in solving problems, but rather they referred their cases to specialists in other fields or in other organisations. Social workers, according to Flexner, mediated between clients with problems and the true sources of aid which lay beyond the social worker's abilities (Popple and Leighninger, 2008). Ever since 1915, social work has been trying to live up to Flexner's definition of profession. This has resulted, by and large, in social work being promoted as casework, rather than as social action and with private practice-oriented with individual social workers being able to diagnose and treat clients as they see fit, similar to medicine (Flexner's ideal of a profession) (Popple and Leighninger, 2008).

This interpretation has been contested since social work began, and various victories have been won by advocates for a more socially conscious and reform-oriented approach to social work. Popple and Leighninger (2008) argue that social work is really a 'policy-based profession' not a 'market-based profession' as they call Flexner's model (which they argue is outmoded, if it ever was correct). Currently, all schools of social work in the US are accredited by the CSWE, 'a nonprofit national association representing more than 3,000 individual members, as well as graduate and undergraduate programs of professional social work education' (CSWE, 2011a). According to its mission statement,

> CSWE aims to promote and strengthen the quality of social work education through preparation of competent social work professionals by providing national leadership and a forum for collective action. CSWE pursues this mission through setting and maintaining policy and program standards, accrediting bachelor's and master's degree programs in social work, promoting research and faculty development, and advocating for social work education. (CSWE, 2011b)

The CSWE has jurisdiction over all accredited professional social work educational programmes (and those programmes seeking accreditation) at the bachelors and masters levels, but not at the PhD level of education. As of February 2011, the CSWE had accredited 471 Bachelor of Social Work (BSW) programmes and 208 Master of Social Work (MSW) programmes. In addition, 24 BSW and 18 MSW programmes were 'in candidacy', (CSWE, 2011c), meaning that they were in their first years of existence and were showing how they met the requirements to be accredited. The process of accreditation is developed and overseen by the CSWE's Commission on Accreditation (COA). The set of accreditation standards currently in use was developed in 2007 for implementation in 2008 and were revised in 2010. These are called the Educational Policy and Accreditation Standards (EPAS) (CSWE, 2010a). As of October 2010, all programmes seeking accreditation or reaffirmation of their previous accreditation must follow these standards. Compared to earlier educational and accreditation standards, the 2008 EPAS were intended to be competency-based, to be more flexible and allow for more innovation, to permit social work educational programmes to be more responsive to their particular organisational and social context and to focus on the outcomes of education, rather than the inputs (CSWE, 2010b, slide 7).

The CSWE requires that graduates have attained competency in 10 core areas of social work practice. Without going into detail, these core competencies are listed in Table 9.1 (more detail is available from the source document, CSWE, 2010b). It is interesting to note the mix of competencies that were accepted by the stakeholders in social work education to be required of all graduates. Most of the competencies do not fit easily into either 'micro' or 'macro' niches in their entirety. A few, such as Competency 5, 'Advance human rights and social and economic justice' and Competency 8, 'Engage in policy practice to advance social and economic wellbeing and to deliver effective social work services', are decidedly macro in focus. And yet, Competency 10, 'Engage, assess, intervene and evaluate with individuals, families, groups, organizations, and communities' would be easily recognised by Mary Richmond as her classic casework approach to social work (Richmond, 1922). Thus, while accommodations have been made on both sides of the Charity Organization Society versus Settlement House debate, the two positions remain enmeshed in an active struggle for primacy in social work education and practice in the US.

Table 9.1: Council on Social Work Education's 10 core competencies

Competency 1: Identify as a professional social worker and conduct oneself accordingly
Competency 2: Apply social work ethical principles to guide professional practice
Competency 3: Apply critical thinking to inform and communicate professional judgments
Competency 4: Engage diversity and difference in practice
Competency 5: Advance human rights and social and economic justice
Competency 6: Engage in research-informed practice and practice-informed research
Competency 7: Apply knowledge of human behavior and the social environment
Competency 8: Engage in policy practice to advance social and economic well-being and to deliver effective social work services
Competency 9: Respond to contexts that shape practice
Competency 10: Engage, assess, intervene, and evaluate with individuals, families, groups, organizations, and communities

Source: CSWE, 2010b

Social work competencies are achieved through classroom instruction but are also learned through social work's signature pedagogy, field education (CSWE, 2010b, p 8). A signature pedagogy 'represents the central form of instruction and learning in which a profession socializes its students to perform the role of practitioner' and field education is what is used in social work field education. The CSWE further comments:

> The intent of field education is to connect the theoretical and conceptual contribution of the classroom with the practical world of the practice setting. It is a basic precept of social work education that the two interrelated components of curriculum – classroom and field – are of equal importance within the curriculum, and each contributes to the development of the requisite competencies of professional practice. (CSWE, 2010b, p 8)

It is not clear in the CSWE material how classroom and field are of equal importance, yet field is the 'central form of instruction'.

Involvement of social workers in social policy: guiding educational and professional statements

The principle that social workers should be involved in social policy is well established in both educational policy statements by the CSWE and guidelines set forth in the NASW Code of Ethics (2008). After discussing these two areas of guiding educational and professional statements, we will turn to the empirical record of actual involvement.

The full text of the CSWE Educational Policy Accreditation Standard relating to policy practice (Educational Policy 2.1.8) reads:

> *Engage in policy practice to advance social and economic well-being and to deliver effective social work services.*
>
> Social work practitioners understand that policy affects service delivery, and they actively engage in policy practice. Social workers know the history and current structures of social policies and services; the role of policy in service delivery; and the role of practice in policy development. Social workers
> - analyze, formulate, and advocate for policies that advance social well-being; and
> - collaborate with colleagues and clients for effective policy action. (CSWE, 2010b)

One could reasonably argue that the purpose and aim of social workers' policy practice is laid out in the earlier EPAS, 2.1.5 which states the following competency:

Advance human rights and social and economic justice.

Each person, regardless of position in society, has basic human rights, such as freedom, safety, privacy, an adequate standard of living, health care, and education. Social workers recognize the global interconnections of oppression and are knowledgeable about theories of justice and strategies to promote human and civil rights. Social work incorporates social justice practices in organizations, institutions, and society to ensure that these basic human rights are distributed equitably and without prejudice. Social workers

- understand the forms and mechanisms of oppression and discrimination;
- advocate for human rights and social and economic justice; and
- engage in practices that advance social and economic justice. (CSWE, 2010b)

These two standards, taken together, provide a very strong statement regarding the need and purposes of policy practice as primary components of social work practice in the US.

This impression is reinforced by sections within the NASW Code of Ethics. According to Hoefer (2012, p 22), 'There are several parts of the *Code of Ethics* (last revised in 2008) which indicate that being involved in advocacy is one part of a professional social worker's job description.' He cites sections 6.01, 6.02 and 6.04 of the code, stating that the ethical imperative for advocacy is clearest in section 6.01. Section 3.07 addresses the ethical demands on administrators for advocacy for adequate resources for clients (subsection a) and the need for fair and open benefit allocation principles (Subsection b) (see Table 9.2 for the exact text of these sections).

If we can say that policy practice and advocacy are close enough in meaning to be interchangeable, then it is clear that major social work organisations in the US strongly support social workers being active in politics and advocacy. Haynes and Mickelson (2009) indicate that both the CSWE and the NASW have increased their support for the importance of advocacy and political action in recent years.

As noted earlier, the field of social work in the US has had a significant stream of reform-minded, if not radical, adherents since its early days. While the proponents of a more individualistically oriented profession won many of the ideological battles of the early years of the 20th century, the debate continued. Walz and Groze (1991) describe the 1960s as a period of social work activism, with social work devoting

**Table 9.2: Sections of the National Association of Social Workers'
Code of Ethics relating to advocacy**

Section	
6.01 Social Welfare	Social workers should promote the general welfare of society, from local to global levels, and the development of people, their communities, and their environments. Social workers should advocate for living conditions conducive to the fulfillment of basic human needs and should promote social, economic, political, and cultural values and institutions that are compatible with the realization of social justice.
6.02 Public Participation	Social workers should facilitate informed participation by the public in shaping social policies and institutions.
6.04 Social and Political Action	(a) Social workers should engage in social and political action that seeks to ensure that all people have equal access to the resources, employment, services, and opportunities they require to meet their basic human needs and to develop fully. Social workers should be aware of the impact of the political arena on practice and should advocate for changes in policy and legislation to improve social conditions in order to meet basic human needs and promote social justice. (b) Social workers should act to expand choice and opportunity for all people, with special regard for vulnerable, disadvantaged, oppressed, and exploited people and groups. (c) Social workers should promote conditions that encourage respect for cultural and social diversity within the United States and globally. Social workers should promote policies and practices that demonstrate respect for difference, support the expansion of cultural knowledge and resources, advocate for programs and institutions that demonstrate cultural competence, and promote policies that safeguard the rights of and confirm equity and social justice for all people. (d) Social workers should act to prevent and eliminate domination of, exploitation of, and discrimination against any person, group, or class on the basis of race, ethnicity, national origin, color, sex, sexual orientation, gender identity or expression, age, marital status, political belief, religion, immigration status, or mental or physical disability.
3.07 Administration	(a) Social work administrators should advocate within and outside their agencies for adequate resources to meet clients' needs. (b) Social workers should advocate for resource allocation procedures that are open and fair. When not all clients' needs can be met, an allocation procedure should be developed that is nondiscriminatory and based on appropriate and consistently applied principles.

Source: NASW, 2008

more efforts at advocacy, a greater emphasis on solving the needs of the
poor and becoming a more multicultural profession. These shifts were
more or less halted in the 1970s as social work became 'industrialised'
and social work students became less interested in working with poor
people, and more interested in creating a private practice. In 1975, about
one out of every six (17%) first-year graduate students indicated that
they were interested in working in direct services or clinical practice;

a decade later this had increased threefold to more than one of every two students (52%) (Walz and Groze, 1991). This change away from working with poor people to working with higher-income and better-educated clients continued into the 1980s, as employee assistance programmes proliferated in employment settings and insurance plans began to cover some mental health concerns. Walz and Groze indicate that the social work students of the 1970s and 1980s were different from earlier students. They state: 'Findings point to a group that reflects the conservative trend in society, seems less committed to the concerns of poor people, and appears to be less oriented towards social action and advocacy as a part of practice' (Walz and Groze, 1991, p 502).

A few years later, Harry Specht and Mark Courtney (1994) authored an influential book along these same lines, called *Unfaithful Angels: How Social Work Has Abandoned its Mission*. In it the writers detailed how the profession had turned its back on poor people in order to use the methods of psychotherapy and to chase higher status as a profession. They also castigated social work organisations such as the NASW for using whatever limited political capital they possessed to work for licensure laws and reimbursement payments to licensed social workers rather than emphasising the expansion of welfare programmes to assist the poor. As they had intended, Specht and Courtney (1994) created considerable controversy. Haynes and Mickelson (2009) take issue with this attack on the social work profession's culpability for 'abandoning' its mission. The gist of their argument is that social work has *two* missions: one is social change, while the other is assisting individuals deal with their pain. To choose one over the other is incorrect – both are needed and valuable.

Clearly, the profession of social work in the US has not been able to settle this '100 Years War' regarding the chief mission of social work. Thus, it is little wonder that social work and the social work educational establishment have not been able to, either. The next section examines US social work education and training for policy practice and other macro areas.

Education and training in policy practice

The CSWE has enunciated the need for graduates of social work programmes at the bachelor and master levels to be able to demonstrate core competency in policy practice (CSWE, 2010b). Less information is available on the actual achievement of this competency. This section brings together the limited research on coursework in policy practice and other macro topics.

When McNutt (1995) charted the extent and types of macro concentrations in social work graduate programmes in the mid-1990s, he categorised 'macro' education as planning, community organisations and administration. Separate concentrations in policy practice were rare. The University of Houston began a concentration in political social work (Fisher, 1995) but, as of the fall 2010 semester, had revised its curriculum to change this 'concentration' to a less ambitious 'specialisation' (University of Houston, 2011). The University of Texas at Arlington combined an internship in a state legislator's office with a course on advocacy and social policy to form an initiative to increase political content in its macro curriculum area (Hoefer, 1999a). Not much else is known about policy practice programmes at that time.

While firm figures are not available, it appears that social work education has not moved towards increasing the number of courses on policy practice or macro practice in general in the last decade. Policy-related field opportunities are available at only one-third of BSW programmes, for example (Dickinson, 2007). Instead, due to falling student demand for macro practice, instructors are attempting to influence student interest in policy courses by employing innovative classroom techniques.

Over a decade ago, Hamilton and Fauri (2001) suggested that instructors seek to increase students' feelings of efficacy in political social work, believing that this would later pay off in increased political participation by these alumni. Tower and Hartnett discuss an internet-based assignment that impresses students with the ease of becoming involved in political processes using this medium. Their major conclusion after using this assignment is, 'Involving students in policy practice during their social work education may instill the importance of policy practice, give them the confidence to participate in policy practice, and experience the ease with which one can participate' (Tower and Hartnett, 2011, p 65).

Other authors provide additional thoughts on teaching macro practice, including policy practice. Carey (2007) and Manalo (2004) advise instructors to use experiential learning projects; DiRigne (2011) shows how to use current legislation and media resources to interest students in social policy work. Ersing and Loeffler (2008) believe that adding information on social capital to the curriculum is vital for students to become better policy practitioners. Hardina and Obel-Jorgensen (2009) and Reisch and Staller (2011) describe the importance of increasing students' abilities to handle confrontation and conflict in their field setting and in the classroom. Sather et al (2007) incorporate a service learning component in policy courses to interest students more in policy and research. Wolfer and Gray (2007) argue that the decision case method should be used to teach legislative policy advocacy.

All of these ideas have logic and at least some level of research support for their effectiveness in overcoming student reticence to study policy practice and incorporate it into their lives as social workers. Still, because there is only a limited amount of time devoted to policy practice in the curriculum, it would not be a great surprise if social workers advocate only infrequently once they graduate. The next section examines the research that has been conducted to understand how much social workers employ policy practice in the US.

Involvement of social workers in social policy: actual engagement in policy practice

As discussed earlier, both the CSWE and the NASW support the idea of social workers engaging in policy practice. There is still a question, however, of the extent to which actual social workers comply with these precepts.

Hoefer (2012) argues that the literature regarding advocacy in social work can be divided into two types: 'How to do' advocacy, sometimes based on research relating to effectiveness of particular efforts and sometimes not, on the one hand (Patti and Dear, 1981; Mahaffey and Hanks, 1982; Albert, 1983; Salcido, 1984; Richan, 1996; Haynes and Mickelson, 2009), and 'Is advocacy happening?' research, on the other hand. This second type can be further divided into exhortations to do more advocacy (Cohen, 1966; Amidei, 1987) and empirical research to determine how much advocacy is being done by social workers (Wolk, 1981; Pawlak and Flynn, 1990; Ezell, 1991, 1993; Mary et al 1993; NASW, 1995; Hartnett et al, 2005). A considerable amount of this literature is now more than a decade old. Conclusions, such as that social workers are more liberal (NASW, 1995), more activist than the general population (Ezell, 1993; Hamilton and Fauri, 2001) and active to about the same degree as other professions and business executives (Wolk, 1981), are probably still true but a good deal of this particular literature is now rather dated. Little research on individual social workers emerged during the first decade of the 21st century to validate these older conclusions.

Fortunately, research on advocacy never died, but it shifted away from focusing on individual advocacy efforts to looking more closely at the organisational basis of policy practice. In recent years, the pace of publication on this topic has increased, spurred to some extent by the creation of the *Journal of Policy Practice* (formerly the *Social Policy*

Journal). This newly focused research examines organisations more than individual behaviour and brings in the new technologies of the internet age. Kimberlin (2010) provides an excellent overview of advocacy and non-profit (not necessarily human services or social work) organisations. Her primary conclusions are that advocacy by non-profit organisations is difficult to define and measure but also that, citing Bass et al (2007), 'most organizations had participated in some type of advocacy, and that nonprofit executive directors felt strongly that advocacy was a critical component of achieving mission-based goals. Nonetheless, a substantial minority of organizations had not participated significantly in advocacy activities' (Kimberlin, 2010, p 170).

Hoefer (1999b, 2000a, 2000b, 2001, 2002, 2005) and Hoefer and Ferguson (2007) exclusively studied human services interest groups active in both legislative and regulatory issues, at the national level and at the state level in four states. Among other findings, this series of research articles emphasised the ability of researchers to understand which tactics of legislative and regulatory lobbying were empirically more effective than others. Importantly, Hoefer cautions that what is effective in one state may not be effective in another, so that advocates must be well-versed in local political culture and approaches (Hoefer, 2000b). This approach, imported from political science, was a sharp break from the primarily individually based social work literature on advocacy that came before.

Additional recent research has looked at the organisational context of social work policy practice, particularly as undertaken by NASW state chapters. The NASW was selected as the starting point for research for three reasons: its Code of Ethics calls strongly for advocacy on the part of social workers the state NASW chapter is usually the strongest focal point for social work political action in any state and it is relatively easy to contact member of this professional group. Hamilton and Fauri (2001), Hartnett et al (2005) and Scanlon et al (2006) provide results examining the role of NASW state chapters in advocacy. Hamilton and Fauri (2001) documented that social workers who were members of the NASW were more likely to be active in policy influence attempts than non-members. Hartnett et al, in surveying NASW chapter directors, note that NASW-belonging social workers are encouraged by 100% of NASW chapters to engage in political action, and that, in 91% of chapters, members are active (Hartnett et al, 2005, p 77). Still, these authors indicate that they did not survey the NASW membership regarding their participation levels and that 'Anecdotally, it appears that relatively few members in each chapter are actively involved in assisting in electoral and legislative goals' (p 77).

Scanlon et al (2006) describe what the NASW chapters do in terms of advocacy (as opposed to what the members do). Almost all engage in coalitions (95%), lobby (90%) and encourage members to run for office (90%). High percentages have a political action committee to help elect sympathetic candidates to office (86%), track legislation status (86%), endorse candidates (82%), conduct 'get out the vote' (GOTV) campaigns among members (82%), attempt to influence government administrative policy (81%) and support candidates financially (81%). Other activities receive less frequent mention (Scanlon et al, 2006, p 48). When executive directors of NASW chapters were asked how effective their organisation's efforts were, their average response was 'slightly less than effective' (Scanlon et al, 2006, p 48).

The arena of cyberactivism is an important emerging arena for social workers. McNutt (2006) argues that because of its newness, special efforts should be made to evaluate its effectiveness, and which specific techniques are most beneficial. Edwards and Hoefer examined the use of the internet and particularly of interactive Web 2.0 advocacy techniques for advocacy by social work organisations. Their findings show that 'Social work organizations make good use of their web sites for some advocacy activities and grossly underutilize the Web forum for others. Furthermore, social work organizations do not use Web 2.0 often for advocacy' (Edwards and Hoefer, 2010a, p 220). The strongest elements of social work organisations' websites were 'providing information to raise awareness' (90%); followed by 'have online advocacy documents' (67%); 'have statement of organization's point of view' (65%); 'facilitating identification of decision-makers' (59%); 'asking people to contact decision-makers' (59%); 'providing contact information to decision-makers' (59%); and 'providing guidance on how to contact decision-makers' (59%) (p 231). (It should be noted that NASW state chapters account for the vast majority of these last four web-based techniques). No other element was found by Edwards and Hoefer (2010a) to be used by more than 36% of the organisations. In a follow-up study comparing NASW state chapters with American Nursing Association state-level organisations, Edwards and Hoefer (2010b) indicate that, while neither set of organisations uses its websites well for advocacy, social work organisations are consistently better when there is a significant level of difference in use of particular web-based advocacy components.

A final area of policy practice and advocacy relates to the NASW Code of Ethics' call to 'facilitate informed participation by the public' (NASW, 2008) (including clients) to be active in shaping policy. Rome et al (2010) provide results showing how frequently this occurs in the context of direct service workers and their clients. Unfortunately, they find, 'it is far from common practice for social workers to encourage their clients to engage in political action' (Rome et al, 2010, p 206). The three most common political activities that clients were encouraged to do were to register to vote (33.6% of surveyed social workers did this 'often' or 'always'), to vote in general elections (33.7%), and to follow the news (31.7%).

One of the issues in trying to assess how much policy practice occurs by social workers and human services organisations is the lack of a clear definition of the term. Even the analogous term of advocacy has dozens of reported definitions (Schneider and Lester, 2000). Another issue relates to measurement. While there are accepted ways of measuring individual-level political participation, until recently no validated and reliable instrument was available to measure organisational-level advocacy efforts. Fortunately, this gap has been filled. Donaldson and Shields (2009) developed the 24-item Policy Advocacy Behavior Scale and pilot tested it on agencies in different fields of practice. This scale gathers information relating to agency behaviours, not individual social workers' actions. While scores were not particularly high, the pilot testing did show that many agencies have staff who attend hearings to provide testimony, participate in policy working groups with government officials, distribute information to clients about legislation that would affect them, write letters to the editor and opinion pieces for the media, and many other policy-related activities. The amount of policy activity being undertaken at the local level is currently simply not known, but with Donaldson and Shields' instrument now available, it is hoped that more research will emerge to fill the gaps in our knowledge on this topic.

Summarising this section, we see that the level of actual policy practice among social workers is lower than would be expected, given the stances of the CSWE and the NASW. Before discussing what encourages and what discourages policy practice and political participation by social workers in the US, we will turn to some examples of policy practice in action.

Specific examples of policy practice

The NASW is the largest social work organisation in the US and it seems to be the nucleus around which much political advocacy occurs. While it should not be considered the only social work organisation with ties to advocacy, much of the research cited in this chapter uses NASW members and state organisations as the study population. The examples provided in this section will likewise refer to the NASW for the most part, even though this may overstate the importance of this one association.

The NASW national organisation and most NASW state chapters have a political action committee (some are more active than others, with a few having trouble finding board members to serve), almost all have their own websites to provide information to members, and all work to inform NASW members in their state of opportunities for political participation. These activities would all fit into the meaning of policy practice. The NASW was very involved in supporting healthcare reform in the US when the legislation passed on 30 March 2010, and is working to maintain it as law against attacks. Another legislative priority for 2010 was to promote more educational loan forgiveness programmes for social work graduates.

The NASW website at the national level has considerable information for viewers relating to legislative, executive and judicial branch policy practice opportunities and techniques. Among other information, NASW has information on how to contribute financially to office holders and candidates, why one should get involved (including running for office), resources for social work candidates, and information on which candidates have been endorsed by social work political action committees. The state-level NASW websites contain information that is similar but directed specifically to the needs and priorities determined by the state chapter's volunteers and staff. Some consist primarily of outdated material, while others have up-to-date information and use interactive social media techniques to keep social workers interested and engaged in current policy efforts (Edwards and Hoefer, 2010a).

What explains why some social workers are engaged in policy practice?

The gap between NASW's and CSWE's written support for policy practice and the level of advocacy actually undertaken by social workers is puzzling. One of the more interesting questions relating to policy practice is: why are some social workers engaged and others are not? Another is: what are the factors that impede or encourage involvement? The theory of civic voluntarism (Verba et al, 1995) is very useful for explaining the level of social worker engagement in policy practice and a number of authors use its basic ideas (Ritter, 2008; Lane and Humphreys, 2011; Hoefer, 2012).

Verba et al (1995) describe nine variables (grouped into three categories) that explain participation in politics (see Table 9.3). Without going into detail here about how these variables were measured, Verba et al (1995, p 285) summarise their work thus: 'To give a reductionist version of our findings, political interest is especially important for turnout; civic skills, for acts requiring an investment of time; and money, for acts involving an investment of money.'

Table 9.3: Variables associated with political participation (Verba et al, 1995) and advocacy (Hoefer, 2012)

Verba et al 1995 (tested with social workers by Ritter, 2008)	Hoefer 2012
Dependent variable: Political participation	**Dependent variable**: Advocacy
Independent variables	**Independent variables**
Resources: • time • money • civic skills	External characteristics: • participation in other organisations • time • skills
Psychological engagement: • political interest • political efficacy • political information • partisanship • family influences	Internal characteristics: • education level • interest • values • sense of professional responsibility
Recruitment networks	

Sources: Verba et al, 1995; Ritter, 2008; Hoefer, 2012

Hoefer (2012) builds on Verba et al, presenting a model adjusted to fit social workers. He includes seven independent variables affecting the dependent variable of level of advocacy (see Table 9.3). Many of the variables are the same or overlap, such as interest, time, skills and participation in other organisations, but Hoefer adds professional education, values, and sense of professional responsibility to the mix.

Ritter (2008) tested the specifics of the Civic Volunteerism Model (along with a number of demographic variables) by surveying a national sample of social workers. Her results show that much of the model applies to the general body of social workers. Two demographic variables were important: being a member of the NASW and living in an urban area increased the likelihood of being politically active. Political skill levels were found to be low and did not affect the level of political participation, nor did level of family income or amount of free time. Ritter did find that the levels of psychological engagement for four of the five tested variables (political interest – local politics, not national – political efficacy, information and family influences) had significant impacts on participation levels. Level of partisanship did not affect social worker participation. Finally, social workers who were part of recruitment networks were more active politically, as the model suggests. Ritter's work thus largely validates the tenets of the Civic Volunteerism Model for social workers, providing a clear understanding of the factors that lead to political participation and, most likely, policy practice. This conclusion is strengthened by Lane and Humphreys (2011), who used the model to organise a survey of nearly 500 social workers who ran for elected office. The components of the model seem to hold true for this population as well.

Barriers to policy practice have been identified by a number of authors (Berry, 2003; Karger and Hernandez, 2004; Hartnett et al, 2005; Rocha et al, 2010). Important negative factors at the individual level include deficiencies in self-efficacy, time and other resources, as discussed in the Civic Voluntarism model. Organisational factors are a lack of support for social workers by their employers and limitations set by the Internal Revenue Service on lobbying by non-profit organisations (Rocha et al, 2010).

Assessing expected developments in the engagement of social workers in policy practice

Two paths lay before the social work profession in the US. Both begin with the realisation that potent political forces at local, state and national levels and a debilitating recession have decimated government budgets, made poor people scapegoats and led to unrelenting pressure to eliminate significant swaths of the social safety net. It is expected that social workers will choose between two paths forward in the face of these facts.

The first path is to give up, at least for the time being, and allow the river of public opinion and political opportunism to run its course. At some point, the facts will be too clear and the damage so great that something will need to be done to reverse the current and to improve the situation. The point of this path will be to survive in the short run, even while preparing for creating change in the long term.

The second path is to engage in more active policy practice now, focusing on maintaining as much as can be kept in terms of tax equity, social services and solidarity. This requires expanded efforts by social workers to understand the political system and the techniques by which change can occur. Some advocates may choose to walk the halls of power while others occupy parks to demand a more just system. The point of this path will be to expand the base of people working for the values of the social work profession and to improve their ability to make a difference.

The future of social work's engagement in policy practice in the US is likely to be one of these two paths. If the past is prologue, then we will find US social workers dividing their efforts, with some taking the first path, and others taking the second. The relative proportion on one road compared to the other is unknown. Still, just as in the 1930s and 1960s, when vast change was overtaking society, larger numbers of social workers embraced the importance of policy practice and became strong, skilled advocates for social justice. It is vital that we use the principles that stress the importance of advocacy and incorporate them into our everyday practice reality if we are to remain true to the best of social work history and ideals.

References

Albert, R. (1983) 'Social work advocacy in the regulatory process', *Social Casework*, vol 64, no 8, pp 473–81.

Amidei, N. (1987) 'The new activism picks up steam', *Public Welfare*, vol 45, no 3, pp 21–6.

Bass, G., Arons, D., Guinane, K. and Carter, M. (2007) *Seen but Not Heard: Strengthening Nonprofit Advocacy*, Washington, DC: Aspen Institute.

Berry, J.M. (2003) 'The lobbying law is more charitable than they think', *Washington Post*, 30 November, p B01.

Blau, J. and Abramovitz, M. (2004) *The Dynamics of Social Welfare Policy*, New York: Oxford University Press.

Carey, L. (2007) 'Teaching macro practice', *Journal of Teaching in Social Work,* vol 27, no 1, pp 61–71.

Cohen, W. (1966) 'What every social worker should know about political action', *Social Work*, vol 11, no 4, pp 7–11.

CSWE (Council on Social Work Education) (2010a) 'Educational Policy and Accreditation Standards', March, www.cswe.org/File.aspx?id=43974.

CSWE (Council on Social Work Education (2010b) 'Implementation of the 2008 EPAS: Quality assurance report and discussion', paper prepared for the 2010 Annual Program Meeting, Portland, OR, 14–17 October, www.cswe.org/File.aspx?id=43974.

CSWE (Council on Social Work Education) (2011a) 'About CSWE', www.cswe.org/About.aspx.

CSWE (Council on Social Work Education) (2011b) 'Mission statement', www.cswe.org/About.aspx.

CSWE (Council on Social Work Education) (2011c) 'Current number of social work programs', www.cswe.org/Accreditation.aspx.

CSWE (Council on Social Work Education) (2011d) 'About the CSWE accreditation', www.cswe.org/Accreditation.aspx.

Dickinson, J. (2007) 'A survey of policy practice placements in BSW education', *Journal of Policy Practice*, vol 6, no 1, pp 47–63.

DiRigne, L. (2011) 'Teaching social policy: Integration of current legislation and media resources', *Journal of Teaching in Social Work*, vol 31, no 2, pp 224–31.

Donaldson, L. and Shields, J. (2009) 'Development of the policy advocacy behavior scale: Initial reliability and validity', *Research on Social Work Practice*, vol 19, no 1, pp 83–92.

Edwards, H. and Hoefer, R. (2010a) 'Are social work advocacy groups using Web 2.0 effectively?', *Journal of Policy Practice*, vol 9, no 3, pp 220–39.

Edwards, H. and Hoefer, R. (2010b) 'A tale of two professions: A comparative analysis of Web 2.0 advocacy on social work and nursing websites', paper presented at the Annual Meeting of the Association for Research on Nonprofit Organizations and Voluntary Action (ARNOVA), Alexandria, Virginia, November.

Ersing, R. and Loeffler, D. (2008) 'Teaching students to become effective in policy practice: Integrating social capital into social work education and practice', *Journal of Policy Practice*, vol 7, no 2, pp 226–38.

Ezell, M. (1991) 'Administrators as advocates', *Administration in Social Work*, vol 15, no 4, pp 1–18.

Ezell, M. (1993) 'The political advocacy of social workers: A post-Reagan update', *Journal of Sociology and Social Welfare*, vol 20, no 4, pp 81–97.

Fisher, R. (1995) 'Political social work', *Journal of Social Work Education*, vol 31, no 2, pp 194–203.

Hamilton, D. and Fauri, D. (2001) ' Social workers' political participation: Strengthening the political confidence of social work students', *Journal of Social Work Education*, vol 37, no 2, pp 321–32.

Hardina, D. and Obel-Jorgensen, R. (2009) 'Increasing social action competency: A framework for supervision', *Journal of Policy Practice*, vol 8, no 2, pp 89–109.

Hartnett, H., Harding, S. and Scanlon, E. (2005) 'NASW chapters: Executive directors' perceptions of factors which impede and encourage active member participation', *Journal of Community Practice*, vol 13, no 4, pp 69–83.

Haynes, K. and Mickelson, J. (2009) *Affecting Change: Social Workers in the Political Arena* (7th edn), Boston, MA: Prentice Hall.

Hoefer, R. (1999a) 'The social work and politics initiative: A model for increasing political content in social work education', *Journal of Community Practice*, vol 6, no 3, pp 71–87.

Hoefer, R. (1999b) 'Protection, prizes or patrons? Explaining the origins and maintenance of human services interest groups', *Journal of Sociology and Social Welfare*, vol 26, no 4, pp 115–36.

Hoefer, R. (2000a) 'Making a difference: Human service interest group influence on social welfare program regulations', *Journal of Sociology and Social Welfare*, vol 27, no 3, pp 21–38.

Hoefer, R. (2000b) 'Human services interest groups in four states: Lessons for effective advocacy', *Journal of Community Practice*, vol 7, no 4, pp 77–94.

Hoefer, R. (2001) 'Highly effective human services interest groups: Seven key practices', *Journal of Community Practice*, vol 9, no 3, pp 1–13.

Hoefer, R. (2002) 'Political advocacy in the 1980s: Comparing human services and defense interest groups', *Social Policy Journal*, vol 1, no 1, pp 99–112.

Hoefer, R. (2005) 'Altering state policy: Interest group effectiveness among state-level advocacy groups', *Social Work*, vol 50, no 3, pp 219–27.

Hoefer, R. and Ferguson, K. (2007) 'Moving the levers of power: How advocacy organizations affect the regulation-writing process', *Journal of Sociology and Social Welfare*, vol 34, no 1, pp 83–108.

Hoefer, R. (2012) *Advocacy Practice for Social Justice* (2nd edn), Chicago: Lyceum.

Jansson, B. (2005) *The Reluctant Welfare State. American Social Welfare Policies: Past, Present and Future*, Belmont, CA: Brooks Cole.

Karger, H. and Hernandez, M. (2004) 'The decline of the public intellectual in social work', *Journal of Sociology and Social Welfare*, vol 31, no 3, pp 51–68.

Kimberlin, S. (2010) 'Advocacy by nonprofits: Roles and practices of core advocacy organizations and direct service agencies', *Journal of Policy Practice*, vol 9, no 3/4, pp 164–82.

Lane, S. and Humphreys, N. (2011) 'Social workers in politics: A national survey of social work candidates and elected officials', *Journal of Policy Practice*, vol 10, no 3, pp 225–44.

McNutt, J. (1995) 'The macro practice curriculum in graduate social work education: Results of a national study', *Administration in Social Work*, vol 9, no 3, pp 59–74.

McNutt, J. (2006) 'Building evidence-based advocacy in cyberspace', *Journal of Evidence-Based Social Work*, vol 3, no 3, pp 91–102.

Mahaffey, M. and Hanks, J.W. (1982) *Practical Politics: Social Work and Political Responsibility*, Silver Spring, MD: NASW Press.

Manalo, V. (2004) 'Teaching policy advocacy through state legislative and local ballot-based advocacy assignments', *Social Policy Journal*, vol 3, no 4, pp 53–67.

Mary, N., Ellano, C. and Newell, J. (1993) 'Political activism in social work: A study of social work educators', in T. Mizrahi and J. Morrison (eds) *Community Organization and Social Administration*, New York: Haworth. pp 203–23.

NASW (National Association of Social Workers) (1995) 'Political involvement high', *NASW News*, vol 40, no 9, p 1.

NASW (National Association of Social Workers) (2008) 'Code of Ethics', www.socialworkers.org/pubs/code/code.asp.

Patti, R.J. and Dear, R.B. (1975) 'Legislative advocacy: One path to social change', *Social Work*, vol 20, pp 108–14.

Pawlak, E. and Flynn, J. (1990) 'Executive directors' political activities', *Social Work*, vol 35, no 4, pp 307–12.

Popple, P. and Leighninger, L. (2008) *The Policy-based Profession: An Introduction to Social Welfare Policy Analysis for Social Workers*, Boston, MA: Pearson.

Reisch, M. and Staller, K. (2011) 'Teaching social welfare history and social welfare policy from a conflict perspective', *Journal of Teaching in Social Work*, vol 32, no 2, pp 131–44.

Richan, W.C. (1996) *Lobbying for Social Change* (2nd edn), New York: The Haworth Press.

Richmond, M. (1922) *What is Social Case Work? An Introductory Description*, New York: Russell Sage Foundation.

Ritter, J. (2008) 'A national study predicting licensed social workers' levels of political participation: The role of resources, psychological engagement, and recruitment networks', *Social Work*, vol 53, no 4, pp 347–57.

Rocha, C., Poe, B. and Thomas, V. (2010) 'Political activities of social workers: Addressing perceived barriers to political participation', *Social Work,* vol 55, no 4, pp 317–25.

Rome, S., Hoechstetter, S. and Wolf-Branigin, M. (2010) 'Pushing the envelope: Empowering clients for political action', *Journal of Policy Practice,* vol 9, no 3, pp 201–10.

Salcido, R.M. (1984) 'Social work practice in political campaigns', *Social Work*, vol 29, pp 189–91.

Sather, P., Weitz, B. and Carlson, P. (2007) 'Engaging students in macro issues through community-based learning', *Journal of Teaching in Social Work*, vol 27, no 3, pp 61–79.

Scanlon, E., Hartnett, H. and Harding, S. (2006) 'An analysis of the political activities of NASW chapters', *Journal of Policy Practice*, vol 5, no 4, pp 41–54.

Schneider, R. and Lester, L. (2000) *Social Work Advocacy: A New Framework for Action*, Belmont, CA: Brooks Cole.

Specht, H. and Courtney, M. (1994) *Unfaithful Angels: How Social Work Has Abandoned its Mission*, New York: Basic Books.

Tower, L. and Hartnett, H. (2011) 'An internet-based assignment to teach students to engage in policy-practice: A three-cohort study', *Journal of Policy Practice*, vol 10, no 1, pp 65–77.

University of Houston (2011) 'MSW specialization', www.sw.uh.edu/academics/gcswcurriculum.php.

Verba, S., Schlozman, K. and Brady, H. (1995) *Voice and Equality: Citizen Voluntarism in American Politics*, Cambridge, MA: Harvard University Press.

Walz, T. and Groze, V. (1991) 'The mission of social work revisited: An agenda for the 1990s', *Social Work*, vol 36, no 6, pp 500–4.

Wolfer, T. and Gray, K. (2007) 'Using the decision case method to teach legislative policy advocacy', *Journal of Teaching in Social Work*, vol 27, no 1, pp 37–59.

Wolk, J. (1981) 'Are social workers politically active?', *Social Work,* vol 26, no 4, pp 283–8.

TEN

An international perspective on policy practice

Idit Weiss-Gal and John Gal

The point of departure for this volume is that social work is a profession that embodies the values of social justice and human rights, and embraces social change as a means to achieve these values (Hare, 2004). As such, changing social welfare policies is an important, indeed crucial, aim of social work interventions because those policies can facilitate the furthering of these values by changing the environment in which service users live (Cummins at al, 2011). Policy practice is the form of social work practice that focuses on affecting social welfare policies (Jansson, 2008).

Our explicit goal in this book has been to explore the nature of policy practice in social work in eight countries with diverse social work legacies and patterns and different welfare regimes. In order to do this, four principal questions have dominated the country chapters that constitute the bulk of this study. The first relates to the importance of policy practice in the social work discourse. In other words, the volume has sought to explore the place of policy practice in Codes of Ethics, formal documents of social work organisations and the professional literature in the countries examined. The second question endeavours to examine social work education, the degree to which it prepares social work graduates to engage in policy practice and the manner in which it does so. The third question seeks to understand better the actual engagement of social workers in policy practice, in terms of the extent of this engagement and the forms that this takes in different countries. A fourth and final question focuses on the factors that contribute to involvement by social work professionals in policy practice in the various national settings. This concluding chapter attempts to bring together the responses offered to these questions by the country experts that authored each of the chapters of the book. By doing so, we seek to offer some more general responses to these issues on the basis of an examination of the similarities and the differences that emerge in the different country cases.

Thinking about how policy practice is defined

'Policy practice' is the term employed here to describe the policy-related activities of social workers. While a more formal definition of this term was offered in Chapter One, it is perhaps worthwhile reiterating that the underlying assumption in this volume has been that policy practice can be distinguished from other interactions between social workers and the policy arena. In particular, policy practice is distinct from civic voluntary political participation, which comprises a wide range of political activities that social workers do or can do as members of the societies in which they live, such as voting in local, state or national elections, actively work for a political party or candidate, or persuading others how to vote.

By contrast, the term 'policy practice' refers specifically to professional activities that seek to change or promote social policies which are directly related to the specific problems of the service users and social groups with whom the social workers work. As such, these interventions are undertaken as part and parcel of the social workers' daily practice in order to meet their service users' needs or address their problems in a better way. These activities are political in the Lasswellian sense that they relate to the process by which it is decided who gets what, when and how (Lasswell, 1936). Or, as Bruce Jansson (2003, p 289) noted, they refer to efforts by individuals 'in governmental and nongovernmental settings to secure their policy wishes by developing and using power resources'. However, unlike civic voluntary political participation, policy practice refers to the inherently political activities that social workers do as part of their professional responsibility in order to affect policies that have an impact on services users, and it does not refer to social workers' voluntary political activities as active citizens of the society of which they are part.

The examples of social worker engagement in policy-related activities in the various chapters of this volume reveal that the distinction between civic political participation and policy practice is not always clear-cut and may be better perceived as two poles of the continuum depicted in Figure 10.1.

Figure 10.1: The civic political participation–policy practice continuum

Civic political participation		Policy practice

There can be little doubt that a social worker participating in a campaign for public office on behalf of a specific candidate (civic political participation) or efforts by a social worker to change policies determining access to social care services in the locality in which she is employed (policy practice) represent clear-cut examples of the two poles. Other types of intervention in the policy sphere are not so clear cut. Thus, for example, social worker involvement in social action such as a sit-in or letter-writing campaign which is focused on social problems or policies that diversely affect disadvantaged groups may be construed as either policy practice or civic political participation. This will depend on the specific nature of the social action but also on the organisational context in which it occurs. If this type of activity is not organised by the social worker's place of employment but by external organisations and takes place after working hours, it will be closer to the civic political participation pole. However, if there is a direct link between the policy-related activities and the specific problems of the social worker's service users or if the activity is initiated by a professional recruitment network then it will be nearer to the policy practice pole.

Policy practice in the social work discourse

An obvious initial arena for examining the impact of policy practice in social work is the profession's discourse. The social work discourse is made up of the body of written and oral knowledge and thought created by social work professionals, educators and scholars in a given society. It includes professional Codes of Ethics, formal documents and declarations of social work organisations as well as diverse forms of professional literature and professional debate.

An examination of the place of policy practice in the Codes of Ethics – perhaps the key document in any profession (Banks, 2006) – reveals that, although the explicit term 'policy practice' did not appear in any of these texts in the eight countries studied here, most Codes of Ethics do require social workers to engage in activities aimed at influencing policy in order to further social justice. Indeed it would appear that a cross-national exchange of ideas, often through the good offices of the International Federation of Social Workers (IFSW), has contributed much to this trend. More specifically social workers are required to contribute to the development of social policy (UK), to advocate for change in policy (US), to promote socially just policies (Australia), to influence the formation of social policy (Russia), to plan, design, apply and establish changes in social policies (Spain), to play an active role in the promotion, development and advancement of integrated social policies (Italy) or to support policies that further social justice (Israel).

Besides these explicit demands, all of the Codes of Ethics also contain implicit sections which require social workers to engage in activities that can be linked to policy practice. For example, while there is not an explicit call for engagement in policy formulation in the Swedish code, the document does note that social workers are expected to play an important role in community planning and the development of social support programmes.

However, differences also emerge, particularly with regard to the extent to which issues of policy-related activities are referred to in the codes in different countries. In the Codes of Ethics in the UK, the US and Australia, there is extensive reference to social workers' requirement to engage in activities that seek to influence policy. Moreover these activities are regarded as an integral and crucial part of professional social work practice. Throughout the British Code of Ethics (BASW, 2012), one can find strong legitimacy for social workers to 'bring to the attention of their employers, policy makers, politicians and the general public situations where resources are inadequate or where distribution of resources, policies and practice are oppressive, unfair, harmful or illegal' (BASW, 2012, p 9) or 'be prepared to challenge discriminatory, ineffective and unjust policies, procedures and practice' (BASW, 2012, p 14). In the US the Code of Ethics contains several references to participation in activities aimed at influencing policy. For example, 'social workers ... should advocate for changes in policy and legislation to improve social conditions in order to meet basic human needs and promote social justice' (NASW, 2008, section 6.04). Similarly, the 2010 Australian Association of Social Workers Code of Ethics refers to social policy involvement in different places in the code and expects social workers to achieve social justice by 'promoting policies and practices that achieve a fair allocation of social resources' (AASW, 2010a, p 8).

In Italy, Russia, Spain and Israel the Codes of Ethics contain statements that support and promote participation in policy practice activities, but these references tend to be more limited in their extent and in their detail. For example, there is a general statement in the Italian Code of Ethics on the need for social workers to play an active role in the promotion, development and advancement of social policies aimed at fostering social and civic advancement emancipation and responsibilities and to alert the authorities and the general public to social problems such as poverty, oppression or inequality. In the Russian Code of Ethics ('Code of Ethics for the Social Worker and Social Pedagogue, 2003, section 3.2) social workers are requested to 'influence the formation of the social policy promoting fair satisfaction of social needs'. In the same vein, the Spanish Code of Ethics states that: 'The duties of social workers are to plan, design, apply and establish changes in social policies and services for groups and communities' (Consejo General de Colegios, 1999, section 2).

Israel is a good example of a country in which the place of policy practice was expanded in the latest Code of Ethics (Israel Association of Social Workers, 1995), although it stills remains relatively marginalised. While in an early version of the code there was no clear reference to engagement in efforts to influence social policy, in the 1995 publication it is stated that social workers should 'support policies and legislation aimed at enhancing social conditions and furthering social justice' (Israel Association of Social Workers, 1995, section 2.6).

The importance attributed to policy practice in the US and Australian Codes of Ethics is also reflected in prominent documents of the social work profession in these countries. In the US policy practice is regarded as a core competency of social work by the Council of Social Work Education (CSWE), and both the CSWE and the National Association of Social Workers (NASW) have increased their support for the importance of engagement in policy practice in recent years. In Australia, official statements by the AASW endorse the involvement of social workers in policy-related activity and perceive policy advocacy as a core professional requirement. The AASW Practice Standards defines social policy as one of the six core areas of social work practice. In addition, the AASW National Social Policy Committee (NSPC), formed in 2006, has been active in promoting an activist social policy agenda within the social work profession.

In other countries reference to the policy involvement by social workers in formal social work documents is much more limited. In the English case, although the Code of Ethics underscores that social workers are required extensively and clearly to engage in policy change, the current National Occupation Standards for Social Work relates only vaguely to engagement in policy. In Italy and Russia the place of activities within the realm of policy practice in the discourse of social work organisations (such as the Professional Register in Italy) is virtually non-existent.

Between these two poles are the Swedish, Spanish and Israeli cases. In the past the discourse of Swedish social work organisations, in particular the Central Association of Social Work and the Swedish Association for Social Workers (SSR), reflected a commitment to engage in policy practice and, more recently, there have been attempts by social work representative organisations to increase policy awareness and involvement on the part of social workers. In Spain there has been limited reference to policy-related activities in formal social work documents, though professional conferences organised by either the General Council of Social Work or university-based schools of social work have tended to serve as forums in which calls for social work involvement in social policy have been made. These calls have intensified in recent years. In particular, the severe economic crisis at the end of the first decade of the 21st century led to a demand issued at the 2009 Spanish Social Work Congress for social workers to participate in formulating municipal social policies and give voice to the needs of citizens. In Israel, calls for social work intervention in social policy debates dominated social work conferences in the 1970s and 1980s. Uniquely, specific references to the term 'policy practice' have also emerged in official state publications. In a recently published report of the State Commission on Reform of Local Social Care Services (State of Israel, the Ministry of Welfare and Social Services, 2010), policy practice was described as one of the social workers' intervention methods. The report also notes that social workers 'should engage in the formulation of social policy of other social services, local authorities, and the state' (State of Israel, the Ministry of Welfare and Social Services, 2010, p 36).

Between-country differences emerged with regard to the place of policy practice in unofficial, generally academic, social work literature. Explicit discussion of policy practice is most extensive in the US. Here there has been growing discussion of, and increased reference to, policy practice over the last three decades. This literature, be it in the form of journal articles or of books, deals with a wide range of questions ranging from the conceptualisation of policy practice and the normative justification for it, through examination of the actual engagement of social workers in policy practice, to a discussion of the factors that contribute or shape this level of engagement (see, most recently, Colby, 2008; Jansson, 2008; Ritter, 2008; Chandler, 2009; Haynes and Mickelson, 2009; Rocha et al, 2010; Hoefer, 2012). Indeed a journal devoted to policy practice, the *Journal of Policy Practice*, has been published regularly since the early 2000s. In Israel too there has been growing discussion of, and publication on, policy practice in the last decade. These have included a special issue on policy practice in a leading social work professional journal (Weiss-Gal and Ben-Arieh, 2009), the 2012 issue of the social work association bulletin and a book devoted entirely to policy practice (Weiss-Gal and Gal, 2011).

By contrast, the place of policy practice or the engagement of social workers in policy-related activities in the professional literature in other countries is more circumspect. In Australia, while policy-related issues have emerged in the literature – primarily in academic journals (for example, Mendes, 2003a; Pawar 2004; Zubrzycki and McArthur, 2004) – most of the leading Australian social work texts contain very limited discussion of the actual policy involvement of social workers. In England 'policy practice' as a concept is barely discussed, though policy issues have been examined in some journal articles, and the link between social work and social policy has been the topic of a small number of books (Denny, 1998; Adams, 2002; Dickens, 2010; Hothersall and Bolger, 2010; Simpson and Connor, 2011). Generally the emphasis in these has been on the impact of social policies on service users and on social workers, rather than on actual social work engagement in policy change, although the Simpson and Connor volume is a fairly explicit attempt to argue for engagement. In Spain reference to the policy involvement of social workers in the social work academic literature has been very limited despite the relatively large number of professional publications that exist in this country. Similarly, in Sweden the issue of social policy involvement has generated relatively little interest in professional publications, although a handful of authors have expressed concern over the limited degree of social work engagement in social policy formulation. This criticism has found expression recently in a publication that explores attitudes towards social workers' involvement in sociopolitical debate and in a social media initiative on the part of social workers and a trade union.

In the Russian case there is no evidence of a discussion of involvement in policy practice in the social work literature. Likewise, in the professional discourse in Italy there are no publications or published studies specifically devoted to social workers' involvement in policy practice.

Table 10.1 presents a schematic overview of the place of policy practice in the eight nations discussed in the country chapters. The three columns on the left relate to the place of policy practice in the social work discourse. Broadly speaking, the findings in the table reflect three groupings of countries. The first of these is the US, which is the only country in the study in which policy practice is prominent in all three facets of the social work discourse. A second grouping comprises two countries where there is a similarly high degree of congruence with regard to the lack of discussion of policy-related social work activity in the discourse. While there is explicit (albeit limited) reference to policy-related activities in the Codes of Ethics in Italy and in Russia, policy practice is absent in other facets of the social work discourse in these countries. Finally, the place of policy practice in the social work discourse in a third grouping of countries included in this study (Australia, England, Israel, Spain and Sweden) is uneven. In these countries, there are discrepancies in the degree to which policy practice is prominent in the various facets of the discourse. Although policy-related activities are relatively prominent in the Codes of Ethics in these nations, policy practice tends to be discussed to a much lesser degree in either professional documents or in the literature.

Table 10.1: Policy practice in social work discourse and education

Country	Discourse: Codes of Ethics[a]	Discourse: other professional documents[b]	Discourse: professional literature[c]	Education[d]
Australia	explicit; extensive	extensive	limited	existent
England	explicit; extensive	non-existent	limited	weak
Israel	explicit; limited	limited	extensive	existent
Italy	explicit; limited	non-existent	non-existent	non-existent
Russia	explicit; limited	non-existent	non-existent	weak
Spain	explicit; limited	limited	limited	existent
Sweden	implicit; limited	limited	limited	weak
US	explicit; extensive	extensive	extensive	existent

Notes:

[a] Refers to the degree to which social workers are required to engage in policy-related activities.

[b] Refers to the importance attributed to engagement in policy practice or policy-related activities.

[c] Refers to research on, and the conceptualisation or discussion of, policy practice or policy-related activities in social work journals or other publications.

[d] Refers to the degree to which applied policy practice is taught in schools of social work.

Education for policy practice

Substantial between-countries differences emerged with regard to the place that social worker engagement in policy formulation is related to in social work education (see the fourth column in Table 10.1). In four of the countries studied, specifically the US, Spain, Israel and Australia, alongside the study of diverse aspects of social policy there are also some applied policy practice courses in the curricula. However their extent is still limited and they are not necessarily offered in all schools of social work. In the other countries, while courses on social policy are generally common, policy practice, with its emphasis on providing tools for intervention in policy arenas, hardly exists as a distinctive component for study.

In the US the CSWE has clearly enunciated the need for graduates of social work programmes at the bachelor and master levels to be able to demonstrate core competency in policy practice. As such, there is a requirement for all schools to include courses on policy practice in their curricula. Less data exists on the actual achievement of this competency. While firm figures are not available, it appears that in general social work education has not moved towards increasing the number of courses on policy practice over the last decade. Complementing this requirement, there is an ongoing professional debate in the literature and in diverse professional forums on how to teach policy practice or how to increase interest and involvement in this area. Due to falling student demand for macro practice, instructors are attempting to gain student interest in policy courses by employing innovative classroom techniques (Carey, 2007; Sather et al, 2007; Wolfer and Gray, 2007; Ersing and Loeffler, 2008; Hardina and Obel-Jorgensen, 2009; DiRigne, 2011; Reisch and Staller, 2011; Tower and Hartnett, 2011).

Social policy, as a specific subject of teaching, has been part of the social work curriculum in Spanish schools of social work from 1983, ever since the integration of social work studies into universities. The then national legal regulation for academic programmes included in the third year of studies a compulsory subject entitled 'Social Policy and Social Wellbeing'. In 1990, a new curriculum regulation for social work university studies included 'Social Policy'. The content guideline of the course consisted of the structure, content and means of social action, and social and political analyses of current models. Since 2010 there have been no common legal guidelines on social work training but some standards have been agreed on between universities and the Social Work Council. Among the competencies of the professional profile approved in 2003 by the Council Consejo de Colegios General is one related to policy knowledge and intervention. The guidelines include: (a) to identify contexts and procedures to cooperate in local and national policy; and (b) to contribute to knowledge of best practices within his/her work team, organisation and other networks. These criteria explicitly recognise the interplay between social policy, social work and policy practice. A review of the social work curriculum in all 36 university-based schools of social work, undertaken by María Asunción Martínez-Román, and a comparison of the approaches adopted in the various schools and the common criteria reveal that, in practice, each university has a great degree of freedom in the setting of its curriculum. Indeed differences emerge in the number of social policy courses, in the content or in the approach to social work practice and in the number of credits offered for this subject. Eighteen universities have at least 12 credits, but policy practice is not explicit in the course syllabus. However, policy practice is present in, at least, some specific syllabuses of social work or social services courses.

Prior to the early 2000s, training in policy practice in Israel, as distinct from the more theoretical study of social policy, was absent in social work education. However, over the last decade policy practice has begun to be better integrated into social work education. Following calls in the literature in Israel (Weiss et al, 2006) and in the wider social work world (Pierce, 2000) to adapt social work training so that it conveys the understanding, knowledge and skills that will encourage students to engage in policy practice, there has been impressive movement towards the introduction of more applied policy practice courses in most social work schools in Israel on both the undergraduate (Kaufman, 2005) and graduate levels (Weiss-Gal and Savaya, 2012). Of all schools of social work in Israel, 80% currently offer either compulsory or elective courses on policy practice to Bachelor of Social Work (BSW) students. Although advanced social policy courses are included in the curricula in all seven schools which offer Master of Social Work (MSW) degrees, these courses tend to be descriptive or analytical. Nevertheless, in five of the schools policy practice is integrated in the teaching programme. Finally, policy practice is now incorporated, to a certain degree, in in-service training for social workers (Eytan et al, 2009).

In Australia the AASW Education and Accreditation Standards (2010b) identify social policy analysis and development as a core component of social work practice. As a result, all 28 schools of social work are obliged to include social policy as a mandatory subject. However, the form and extent of this component in social policy education appears to vary considerably between the schools, and the impact of these courses still appears to be limited. This can be linked to the fact that most social policy subjects are taught separately from social work theory and practice subjects, leaving social work students with the impression that social policy is simply about theoretical knowledge, without any need for practical application. Few students, for example, complete their fieldwork practicums in social policy agencies and the AASW does not require social policy to be taught by qualified social workers, or even by lecturers with some direct practice experience in social policy activities. Consequently, this leaves open the possibility of social policy subjects being taught in a highly theoretical manner with little practice-based application (Ife, 1997; Mendes, 2003b).

In England, although social policy has long been a component in social work education (Burgess and Taylor, 2005) and social work education still emphasises the role of sociology, ethics and human rights, the policy involvement of social workers is not yet an integral part of studies. Changes now being discussed in these studies may offer potential for the integration of policy-oriented practice in the curriculum. A key area which has entered the capability framework for the new degree is that of 'Rights, Justice and Economic Well-Being: Advance human rights, and promote social justice and economic well-being'. This may serve as an avenue for introducing policy practice into the social work curriculum.

In Sweden social policy courses are offered in virtually all social work programmes and the assumption is that social workers require this knowledge base in their education. As such social policy courses are taught both on the undergraduate and graduate levels, though the direction and content of specific social policy courses vary to some extent between universities in the country. There is no division in Swedish social work education between clinical social work and social policy, as the social work programme is a broad social science education entailing both clinical social work and structural and policy-oriented social work knowledge. However, an examination of the various syllabuses and course descriptions of social policy courses reveals that social work students gain social policy knowledge about broad and theoretical areas but there is virtually no specific Swedish social work literature relating to the subject of policy practice, and students get little practical training in how to work professionally at the policy level.

University-level training programmes in social work in Russia include courses on ethics as well as on social policy and research methods. However, the emphasis in studies in this country is primarily theoretical and the courses include very limited policy practice component. In Italy policy practice is absent from the programme of studies. While there are general courses on the principles and history of social work and on methods, social policies and the organisation of social services, none deals with specific methods or clients' problems or modules specifically on human rights, social justice, advocacy or policy practice.

Actual involvement in policy practice

There is a dearth of empirical data on the policy involvement of social workers and in most of the countries included here (and elsewhere, for that matter) no systematic studies on the actual involvement of social workers in policy practice exist. In a small number of countries (primarily the US and Israel) studies do exist but these provide only partial answers to the question of what is the current level of social worker involvement in policy practice. With regard to the US, Hoefer (Chapter Nine) notes that the empirical research on the amount of advocacy undertaken is more than a decade old and not all of it is focused on policy practice, as defined in this volume. However, he estimates that 'the level of actual policy practice among social workers is lower than would be expected, given the stances of the CSWE and the NASW' (p 174).

Weiss-Gal (Chapter Four) posits that an examination of Israeli social workers' involvement in policy practice over the last six decades reveals both an increase in involvement and greater diversity with regard to both the characteristics of the social workers engaged in policy practice and the strategies they have adopted. The increase of engagement in, and diversification of, policy practice among Israeli social workers is reflected in a recent study of the involvement of social workers in the deliberations of parliamentary committees in the Knesset, Israel's parliament (Gal and Weiss-Gal, 2011). The findings indicated that, during the period studied (1999–2006), social workers participated in 14% of relevant parliamentary committee meetings. It is notable that social workers were party to between a third and a half of the meetings of six different parliamentary committees. At the same time, Weiss-Gal (Chapter Four) concludes that 'although policy practice is an emergent form of social work practice in Israel, to a large extent it remains relatively marginalised in the field'.

While no systematic data on the involvement of social workers in policy practice in the other six nations exists, all the national experts estimate that this involvement tends to be marginal and that there is a wide discrepancy between discourse (at least as it reflected in the national Codes of Ethics) and practice, and all concur that practice does not match the rhetoric. When describing the Swedish case, Thorén and Salonen contend that social workers do not generally participate in sociopolitical debates and that they have abandoned issues such as poverty, inequality and marginalisation. Mendes (Chapter Two) claims that, despite the AASW commitment to promoting more equitable social policy outcomes, in Australia 'many (perhaps most) social workers do not participate in policy activities' (p 32). In the same vein, Graeme Simpson concludes that for most English social workers policy practice is 'hardly likely to become a mainstream activity' (p 47). Nevertheless he notes that social workers are engaged in helping shape policy at a local level through various working groups and committees with varying degree of success. In the Italian case, Campanini and Facchini emphasise that Italian social workers are much more focused on the 'dimension of individual relationships in their professional work with clients' (p

93) than on aspects of policy, and in Russia Iarskaia-Smirnova and Romanov claim that, while 'social workers are gradually acquiring new knowledge and skills to effect social change in a democratic egalitarian mode rather than following a paternalist scheme of thought and action ... this is still an exception rather than usual practice' (p 116).

Though there is very little empirical data on policy practice in the Spanish case, it appears that social workers clearly do engage in policy practice in this country although it is still limited in comparison to other types of practice. Indeed, this engagement is apparently much more extensive than that in most of the other countries included in the study and similar to that in the US and Israel. Martínez-Román notes that there is documentation of the major role that social workers in government and in non-profit organisations have played in designing and implementing new policies (Domenech, 1991; De la Red-Vega, 1997; Corral, 2001; Gomá et al, 2009; Lima, 2009). In addition, the journal of sessions of the Congress and Senate hearings offers evidence of policy practice by professional social workers at the invitation of parliamentary committees. Many social workers have participated in the policy process leading to the adoption of legislation concerning social issues by providing professional practice expertise in the debate process of provisional proposals and the later legal development of them.

Although the finding that policy practice is not a predominant social work intervention is not surprising, the actual diversity of forms that social worker policy practice engagement takes across the nations studied in this volume is. Five routes by which social workers engage in the policy process emerge in this study.

Policy practice by proxy

A common route through which social workers seek to affect social policies is by way of autonomous or semi-autonomous social work organisations. While these organisations represent social workers, when the intervention into the policy process takes the form of leadership- or organisation- level statements, lobbying efforts or participation in the policy discourse, it relieves rank-and-file members of the need to be involved directly in policy involvement. Professional organisations operating outside the state realm, such as the NASW in the US and the Swedish trade unions, or within the boundaries of the state, as in the case of the Professional Register in Italy, are examples of this type of organisation. Hoefer, for example, cites research that describes the involvement of NASW chapters in advocacy, coalition building, lobbying and efforts to track legislation status and attempt to influence government administrative policy. As an organisation, the NASW was very much involved in supporting healthcare reform in the US when the legislation passed in March, 2010, and continued working to maintain the law against attacks intended to retrench it.

The Australian AASW NSPC is another example of this type of involvement. The NSPC is involved in making submissions to government inquiries, issuing media releases, developing position statements in areas such as child protection, housing, mental health and Indigenous affairs, establishing partnerships with other stakeholders such as welfare advocacy groups and schools of social work, and motivating social workers and the AASW to provide an informed and effective voice on social policy (Cheron-Sauer, 2008).

In Spain, the General Council of Social Work is regularly invited to present reports and policy proposals to various bodies involved in the policy formulation process. A specific example of its involvement in social policy formulation is the creation in 2008 of the Observatorio Nacional de Servicios Sociales (National Observatory of Social Services). In response to the lack of development of the 2006 social services legislation due to the opposition of some regional governments, the General Council decided to promote discussion, analysis and social criticism in response to the violation of individual rights of people in a situation of dependency, with the collaboration of universities and non-profit organisations.

Policy practice through recruitment networks

In contrast to the policy practice involvement by proxy described above, in this type of engagement social workers seek to influence policy by participating directly in activities initiated and organised by social work organisations. Here the organisations serve as recruitment networks for social workers and involvement is by the grassroots in the framework of the organisations. Thus, for example, in England the Social Work Action Network (SWAN) is a loose coalition of members who share the aim of practice, which seeks to recapture the essence of a campaigning social work, committed to social justice. The West Midlands network has been at the forefront of campaigns against current policies, notably the attempts by Birmingham City Council to save in excess of £30m by increasing the thresholds for a service, a move which would remove support and services from many disabled people. In Sweden, trade unions representing social workers have been engaged in a number of projects that seek to encourage the involvement of social workers in the social policy process. These have taken the form of a publication in which various stakeholders such as social workers, social work professors, politicians and union representatives expressed their views on the lack of sociopolitical engagement among social workers, and a Facebook page 'Lets break the silence' (*Nu bryter vi tystnaden*), initiated by social workers and the trade union SKTF that seeks to highlight how poverty and injustice are growing in Sweden and the deterioration in social workers' working conditions. Another example is a campaign by the Australian Council of Heads of Schools of Social Work (ACHSSW) that involved rank-and-file social work practitioners and students contesting Australian government policies concerning the rights of refugees seeking asylum. The ACHSSW initiated a citizen-driven People's Inquiry into Detention in order to expose the abuses of long-term detention and to place the stories of those in detention on the public record. Social workers assisted the inquiry by testifying and submitting written submissions, and the first report of the inquiry, *We've Boundless Plains to Share*, was released in November 2006 at a national social work conference in Perth.

Finally, the significance of professional recruitment networks in providing an avenue for policy practice among social workers is reflected in studies on social work in the US cited by Hoefer. Thus Hamilton and Fauri (2001) found that social workers who were members of the NASW were more likely to be active in attempts to influence policy than non-members. Hartnett et al (2005) note that social workers belonging to the NASW are encouraged by 100% of NASW chapters to engage in political action, and that, in 91% of chapters, members are active.

Academic policy practice

Due to the greater autonomy that characterises it and the existence of both relevant data and critical approaches within it, social work academia is an additional route through which social workers engage in policy practice (Sherraden et al, 2002). Social work academics can utilise their professional status and access to policy makers and the media in order to influence policy. They also contribute to the policy process through research and the publication of findings that have implication for policy. The country experts in this volume cite diverse cases in which social work academics have played a role in policy-related activities, often in conjunction with social workers in the field. One example of this is the struggle against food insecurity in Israel during the early years of the 2000s. In this case, academics and students from the school of social work at Ben Gurion University formed a coalition of social workers and activists in a struggle to reintroduce school lunches as a response to the findings of a study that they undertook which revealed a high level of food insecurity among poor people in Israel. The public struggle resulted in the passage of legislation in the Israeli parliament that led to the establishment of a school lunch programme in elementary schools throughout the country in 2004 (Chapter Four).

The civil society route

Not only social work organisations but also diverse advocacy organisations, social movements and indeed social welfare provider organisations serve as the framework for the policy practice activities of social workers. These organisations play a major role in the policy formulation process in different countries, and the issues that they engage in often relate to service users and to social welfare policy and services (Schmid et al, 2008; Kimberlin, 2010). Social worker involvement in policy practice as members or employees of these organisations, or in conjunction with them, appears to be a more viable option in different countries than direct engagement on the part of social workers who are civil servants. This is clearly the case in Russia, where norms and formal regulations severely restrict the involvement of social workers employed by the state in policy-related activities. A good example of this type of policy practice is that of social work student Gloria Vinogradova, who became a leader of a small team advocating homeless people's rights in the city of Tomsk. The team sought to establish a shelter for the homeless in the city by overcoming claims by the municipal and regional authorities that there were no homeless people in the region. The efforts eventually culminated in the establishment of a municipal overnight home called the 'Refuge of a Wanderer' in 1999 from funding raised by the Evangelic-Lutheran Church in the US. Similarly, social workers in Australia have participated in welfare lobby groups such as the Australian Council of Social Service and the associated State and Territory Councils of Social Service and are involved in broader social change activities including local and national electoral politics and global campaigns for human rights.

The 'insider' route

Policy practice undertaken by social workers who are civil servants and engage in this practice directly within the context of their workplace is one of the major forms that this type of intervention takes in some of the countries studied in this volume. Social workers engaging in direct policy practice employ a wide range of policy practice strategies. These include legislative/legal advocacy (submissions to government inquiries, letters to cabinet ministers, participation in a government committee), social action with external (public and media advocacy, networking and partnerships with other welfare bodies) and internal foci (community development) and research and policy analysis (development of position papers, initiated inquiries to expose problems and suffering and place the stories of suffering on the public record).

It appears that much of the involvement of rank-and-file social workers in policy practice takes place within local agencies, neighbourhoods and communities. This is the case in Australia, England, Israel, Spain, and the US. The case of Svetlana Driakhlitsyna, a social worker in the city of Petrozavodsk in the northwest of Russia is an example of this form of policy practice. In 2004 she supported a court appeal by a group of parents who sought pre-school places for their children with disabilities despite the refusal of the municipal authorities to offer such places. While the original appeal to the Supreme Court of Karelia was dismissed, an intensive media campaign by the parents and social workers led to the original decision being reversed in 2006.

In a number of country cases described in this volume, social workers' policy practice engagement takes the form of testifying in the deliberations of parliamentary committees at the regional or national levels. Thus in Spain a large number of social workers have played an active role in the legislative process at the invitation of parliamentary committees. Similarly in Israel the author reports on the findings of a study that revealed that many social workers, a third of whom were employed at the time by municipal social welfare agencies, participated in the deliberations of these committees in the Israeli parliament.

Factors that influence policy practice involvement

Clearly, the factors that influence the policy practice involvement of social worker are numerous and inevitably differ from country to country to a certain degree. Nevertheless, all the volume's contributors employ similar frames of reference or sets of factors or explanations in order to explain the levels and forms of social workers' engagement in policy practice. Figure 10.2 presents these frames.

As can be seen in Figure 10.2, it is suggested that there are four broad interrelated sets of factors that explain the level and form of involvement of social workers in policy practice in the eight countries studied in this volume. These include the sociopolitical context within

Figure 10.2: Explanatory factors for policy practice

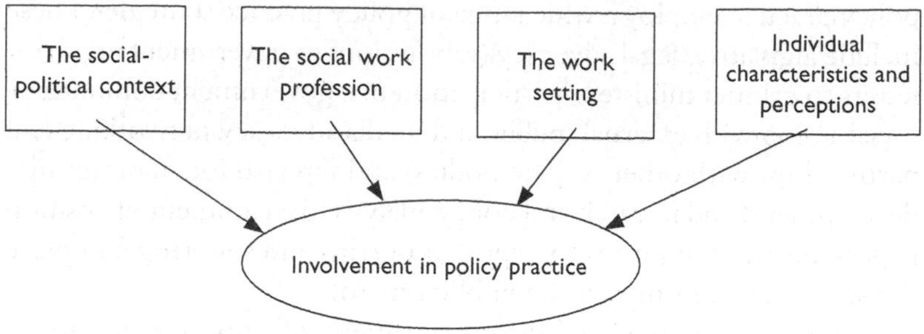

which the profession operates in the different national settings; the specific characteristics of the social work profession; the nature of the work settings in which social workers are employed; and finally a set of individual characteristics and perceptions.

All of the authors regard the sociopolitical environment in which social work has operated over time as crucial in understanding the involvement of social workers in the policy process. This set of factors can relate to the political or welfare regime in a specific nation, to the dominant ideologies that hold sway in a particular society and to its manifestations in social and economic policies in a set time period, as well as to more structural factors, such as the severity of social problems or the levels of inequality that exist in a nation. Obviously, as path dependency theory shows (Pierson, 2000), there is a temporal dimension that is crucial when discussing such factors, whereby developments or critical events at a specific point of time can lead to trajectories that have a significant impact over long periods of time.

The impact of political regime on social worker involvement is perhaps most striking in the Spanish case. The transformation in the mid-1970s from the Franco dictatorship to democracy had major implications for the social work profession in general, and for policy practice in particular. At the end of the 1960s and during the 1970s, policy practice on the part of social workers took place only at the neighbourhood level, especially in new areas inhabited by Spanish migrant workers from rural areas. After Franco's death, the democratic transition led the way to the growing involvement of social workers in the formulation of new social services and social policies. This trend was particularly strong during the 1980s with the establishment of the socialist government because of the major role that social workers played in this administration.

The dominance of specific ideologies in public discourse is clearly an additional facet of the sociopolitical environment that has affected social work engagement in policy practice. In different countries, the rise of critical perspectives in the late 1960s led to social work embracing structural approaches and a tendency by many within the profession to perceive social change as a central component in their professional project. This was certainly the case in English, American and Italian social work. Similarly, as Simpson underscores in his discussion of the English case, the rise of neo-liberalism in recent decades and its undeniable influence on social and economic thinking and policies in liberal democracies are regarded by many of the contributors as a crucial factors in the reluctance by social workers to engage in policy practice.

The social work profession itself is, of course, another major factor in the attempt to understand better the policy practice involvement of social workers. Professional trends within social work, the characteristics of the social work professional association or trade union and their perceived role in policy practice, and the scope and content of social work education are all components in this cluster.

More specifically, some of the national experts (in countries such as Australia, Israel, Italy and Sweden) explicitly link trends towards individualisation or clinicalisation the profession to the limited involvement of social workers in policy practice. For example, Mendes claims that narrow definitions of professionalism in Australia which emphasise the development of clinical therapeutic interventions with individuals at the expense of broader systemic approaches inhibit involvement in policy practice. Weiss-Gal asserts that the marginality of policy practice in social work in Israel can be traced to the fact that social work in Israel is dominated by an individualistic ideology that understands distress, be it that of individuals, families or, communities, primarily through intra-psychic psychological processes. This reflects both the ongoing impact of the therapeutic model dominant in US social work and alongside it the intensive professionalisation process that has sought to link Israeli social work to more prestigious clinical professions such as psychology and psychiatry.

The characteristics of social work professional associations and trade unions are also factors that influence social workers involvement in policy practice. These include the level of commitment to policy practice by the specific organisation and its structure and leadership. The strength of the association can also be another crucial factor. In the Australian case, the low levels of membership in the AASW and the fragmentation of social work organisations are seen by Mendes to be a major factor in the limited engagement of social workers in policy practice in that country. More specifically, the formation in 1975 of the Australian Social Welfare Union as a trade union for all social welfare workers, rather than just social workers, split the AASW and precipitated a gradual decline in activism. From 1985 onwards there was – with minor exceptions – little organised branch commitment to social action or reform. The fact that the AASW has often selected leaders at a state and national level that were employed by public sector agencies is regarded as a factor that impedes them from expressing critical views in the public sphere.

Finally, social work education is a central component in the manner in which the profession has an impact on engagement in policy practice. All the national contributors attribute policy practice's marginality in social work practice to the limited attention it enjoys in the professional socialisation process. While it is not clear whether education leads to practice or vice versa, it would appear that socialisation towards engagement in this type of practice and the provision of tools with which to undertake policy practice will be likely to increase the readiness of practitioners to incorporate policy practice in their interventions. The chapters in this volume indicate that incorporation of policy practice in social work education goes hand in hand with higher levels of engagement in policy practice on the part of social workers in the field. This is apparent in the US, Israel and Spain. By contrast, in national settings in which the level of engagement in policy practice in national settings is particularly low (Russia, Sweden, Italy and England), there is little or no socialisation to this type of practice in the social work education system. It is not surprising, then, that most national experts suggest changes in social work education in order to increase policy practice engagement.

The work settings of social workers are an additional factor that affects the form that policy practice takes, the routes chosen by social workers seeking to influence policy and the degree to which professionals are able to engage in this type of practice. The types of work settings in which social workers are employed – in particular whether these are within the realm of the state or beyond it – the organisational norms that frame the types of activities undertaken by social workers and that define the relationship between the workplace and the formal policy arena and the specific micro-level interactions between management and staff within the contours of the workplace will play a major role in if, and how, social workers engage in policy practice.

The adoption of managerialism as a consequence of the adherence to the principles of New Public Management in the social services in countries such as England and Italy has deprived social workers of opportunities to engage in policy-related activities within the framework of their workplace. Mendes claims that many Australian social workers are employed by government departments or government-funded agencies, which may restrict them from speaking out against government policies. This will lead to social workers choosing alternative routes to influence the policy process. Similarly, in Sweden and in Russia, the dominant norms within the state sector in these countries dictate a strict hierarchical structure that leaves policy involvement in the hands of the political echelons and limits the possibilities for rank and file social worker involvement in this process.

On a more specific level the Australian and US chapters in this book concur that the provision of support from the employing agency can increase social workers' involvement in policy practice. Hoefer (Chapter Nine) notes that 'Organisational factors are a lack of support by employers of social workers and limitations set by the Internal Revenue Service on lobbying by non-profit organisations.' In the same vein, Mendes explains the low levels of social workers involvement in policy practice by the possibility that they hold a professional identity linked more closely to their agency (Centrelink or state and territory government child protection services) rather than to social work per se. Weiss-Gal claims that the marginality of policy practice in Israel is influenced by the nature of the workplace environment of many social workers. Local social care services are underfunded and understaffed and, as a result, social workers are overwhelmed by large case loads. Moreover, due to the adoption of protective legislation, they are often occupied by statutory activities that leave little time to move beyond casework. As policy practice has not been identified as an integral part of the tasks of most social workers employed in social care, nor been encouraged by management, motivation to engage in this type of practice has been limited.

A final set of factors that affects policy practice by social workers relates to the individual social worker. Some of the chapter contributors relate to individual characteristics that may impede or encourage involvement in policy practice. These can be grouped into four main categories: sociodemographic characteristics; personal values; political self-efficacy; and professional ideology, primarily perceptions on social problem, social work and its main goals and tasks. Also important are the employment status of the social worker and the impact of professional recruitment networks.

For example, Martínez-Román claims that the personal attitudes of Spanish social workers are one obstacle to policy practice. These attitudes include a lack of belief that professional social work can influence policy and a lack of interest in politics. With regard to Sweden, Thorén and Salonen link the low level of willingness to engage in policy practice among social workers in the area of financial support within the municipal social services to their individual (rather than structural) explanations of their clients' economic hardship and poverty.

In the same vein, Mendes associates the low level of engagement of Australian social workers in policy practice with the social workers' perception that policy activism is incompatible with professional practice. Relying on a small-scale purposive study of 10 activist social workers, he found that personal background, experiences and beliefs play a key role in promoting the involvement of these social workers in social justice activism. For most of his interviewees, social work education primarily reinforced their existing beliefs and values. Equally, social work values, skills and identity tended to complement rather than shape their activist commitment. Other key factors that enhanced their social activism appeared to include working in senior or management positions that permit considerable practice autonomy, a belief that social action is a core requirement of social work practice, a commitment to a broad social justice agenda that transcends social work practice per se and a greater engagement with broader social and political movements than with specific professional social work structures and networks.

Responding to what he describes as one of the more interesting questions relating to policy practice – why are some social workers engaged and others are not? – Hoefer presents an explanatory model based on the theory of civic voluntarism (Verba et al, 1995). More specifically, he has identified two groups of variables that affect readiness to engage in policy practice: external characteristics, including participation in other organisations, time and skills; and internal characteristics that include level of education, interest, values and sense of professional responsibility.

Concluding remarks

The contributors to this volume adhere to the claim that, in order to achieve its goals of social justice and social rights for all, social work cannot ignore its task of social change, nor can it afford to delegate the role of ensuring that social policies do indeed reflect its desire for a more equitable society to other professions or to decision makers. They concur that social workers can play a major role in the policy formulation process and indeed have done so in the past and continue to do so today. However, too often this engagement in policy has been the domain of a small minority of social workers who have often focused exclusively on this field of practice. Intervention in policy that affects service users, be it at the agency, local or national levels, cannot remain on the sidelines of the profession. It is something that all social workers can, and should, integrate into their repertoire of intervention tools. They must be able to shape the environment in which service users exist if the need be. We call this policy practice.

By placing policy practice at the very focal point of a cross-national research project for the first time, this volume adds to our knowledge that, while the professional discourse appears to reflect this understanding to a large degree, there is still a marked gap between this discourse and the formal socialisation process and actual practice in all the countries studied here. It also reveals that the degree to which social workers engage in policy practice and the form that this takes differ greatly between the different nations. Moreover, the nature of the professional discourse and the place of policy practice in the social work education process in the various countries vary to a large degree.

It is hoped that the rich analyses offered in the chapters in this volume, and the commonalities and divergences that emerge in the overview of the case studies presented in this concluding chapter will set the stage for more extensive cross-national scholarship that can harness the advantages of comparative analysis to a better understanding of the dynamics of policy practice in social work. The country studies reveal the limited extent of systematic research on policy practice in most of them. Moreover, this research has tended to focus on questions such as: why should social workers engage in policy practice? How should they do so? And, to what degree do they undertake this type of activity, and why? This project offers a framework through which to offer responses to these questions in the different countries studied here but also to move beyond these issues to a research agenda that will focus on the diversity of forms of policy practice adopted by social workers and a better understanding of the factors that explain this engagement and its forms.

The intention is that the insights into policy practice that can be found here will not only stimulate the analytical minds of social work scholars but also serve as an impetus for greater engagement in this crucial type of activity on the part of social work educators and practitioners.

References

Adams, R. (2002) *Social Policy for Social Work*, Basingstoke: Palgrave Macmillan.

AASW (Australian Association of Social Workers) (2010a) *Code of Ethics*, Canberra: AASW.

AASW (Australian Association of Social Workers) (2010b) *Australian Social Work Education and Accreditation Standards*, www.aasw.asn.au/document/item/100.

Banks, S. (2006) *Ethics and Values in Social Work* (3rd edn), Houndmills: Palgrave Macmillan.

BASW (British Association of Social Workers) (2012) *Code of Ethics*, www.basw.co.uk/codeofethics.

Burgess, H. and Taylor, I. (eds) (2005) *Effective Learning and Teaching in Social Policy and Social Work*, London: Routledge Farmer.

Carey, L. (2007) 'Teaching macro practice', *Journal of Teaching in Social Work*, vol 27, no 1, pp 61–71.

Chandler, S.K. (2009) 'Working hard, living poor: Social workers and the Movement for Livable Wages', *Journal of Community Practice*, vol 17, pp 170–83.

Cheron-Sauer, M.C. (2008) 'Why does social policy matter to social work? A case study in developing policy leadership', address to Strength in Unity Conference, Sydney, 9 November.

'Code of Ethics for the Social Worker and Social Pedagogue' (2003) Moscow, available at: http://socpedagogika.narod.ru/Kodeks.html (in Russian).

Colby, I.C. (2008) Social welfare policy as a form of social justice', in K.M. Sowers and C.N. Dulmus (eds) *Comprehensive Handbook of Social Work and Social Welfare*, Hoboken, NJ: Wiley.

Consejo General de Colegios (1999) 'Código Deontológico de la Profesión de Diplomado en Trabajo Social', www.ifsw.org/p38000297.html.

Corral, L. (2001) 'The alarming decline of social policy in Spain', *Servicios Socialesy Política Social*, vol 54, pp 101–8.

Cummins, L.K., Byers, K.V. and Pedrick, L. (2011) *Policy Practice for Social Workers*, Boston, MA: Allyn and Bacon.

De la Red-Vega, N. (1997) 'Social policy and social work', in C. Alemán and J. Garcés (eds) *Política social*, Madrid: McGraw Hill, pp 531–52.

Denny, D. (1998) *Social Policy and Social Work*, Oxford: Oxford University Press.

Dickens, J. (2010) *Social Work and Social Policy: An Introduction*, London: Routledge.

DiRigne, L. (2011) 'Teaching social policy: Integration of current legislation and media resources', *Journal of Teaching in Social Work*, vol 31, no 2, pp 224–31.

Domenech, R. (1991) 'The evolution of social work in Spain during the 80s', *Servicios Sociales y Política Social*, vol 20, pp 14–18.

Ersing, R. and Loeffler, D. (2008) 'Teaching students to become effective in policy practice: Integrating social capital into social work education and practice', *Journal of Policy Practice*, vol 7, no 2, pp 226–38.

Eytan, S., Aran, L., Khamra, K. and Obed, W. (2009) 'Training for enlarging the role of social workers in formulating policy processes', *Social Security*, vol 81, pp 135–66 (in Hebrew).

Gal, J. and Weiss-Gal, I. (2011) 'Social policy formulation and the role of professionals: The involvement of social workers in parliamentary committees in Israel', *Health and Social Care in the Community*, vol 19, no 2, pp 158–67.

Gomá, R., Arenas, J., Figueras, C. (2009) 'An inside look at social work from different political groups', *Servicios Sociales y Política Social*, vol 86, pp 91–102.

Hamilton, D. and Fauri, D. (2001) 'Social workers' political participation: Strengthening the political confidence of social work students', *Journal of Social Work Education*, vol 37, no 2, pp 321–32.

Hardina, D. and Obel-Jorgensen, R. (2009) 'Increasing social action competency: A framework for supervision', *Journal of Policy Practice*, vol 8, no 2, pp 89–109.

Hare, I. (2004) 'Defining social work for the 21st century', *International Social Work*, vol 47, no 3, pp 407–24.

Hartnett, H., Harding, S., and Scanlon, E. (2005) 'NASW chapters: Executive directors' perceptions of factors which impede and encourage active member participation', *Journal of Community Practice*, vol 13, no 4, pp 69–83.

Haynes, K. and Mickelson, J. (2009) *Affecting Change: Social Workers in the Political Arena* (7th edn), Boston, MA: Prentice Hall.

Hoefer, R. (2012) *Advocacy Practice for Social Justice* (2nd edn), Chicago: Lyceum.

Hothersall, S. and Bolger, J. (eds) (2010) *Social Policy for Social Work, Social Care and the Caring Professions: Scottish Perspectives*, Farnham: Ashgate.

Ife, J. (1997) *Rethinking Social Work*, Melbourne: Longman.

Israel Association of Social Workers (1995) *Code of Ethics*, Tel-Aviv: ISASW.

Jansson, B.S. (2003) *Becoming an Effective Policy Advocate: From Policy Practice to Social Justice* (4th edn), Belmont, CA: Thomson, Brooks/Cole.

Jansson, B.S. (2008) *Becoming an Effective Policy Advocate: From Policy Practice to Social Justice* (5th edn), Belmont, CA: Thomson, Brooks/Cole.

Kaufman, R. (2005) 'Involvement of faculty and students in promoting the Rights To Food Security: Lessons from a social change project', *Society & Welfare*, vol 25, pp 511–32.

Kimberlin, S.E. (2010) 'Advocacy by nonprofits: Roles and practices of core advocacy organizations and direct service agencies', *Journal of Policy Practice*, vol 9, pp 164–82.

Lasswell, H.D. (1936) *Politics: Who Gets What, When and How* New York: P. Smith.

Lima, A. (2009) 'Social work profession', *Servicios Sociales y Política Social*, vol 86, pp 9–41.

Mendes, P. (2003a) 'Social workers and social action: a case study of the Australian Association of Social Workers Victorian Branch', *Australian Social Work*, vol 56, no 1, pp 16–27.

Mendes, P. (2003b) 'Teaching social policy to social work students: A critical reflection', *Australian Social Work*, vol 56, no 3, pp 220–33.

NASW (National Association of Social Workers) (2008) 'Code of Ethics', www.socialworkers.org/pubs/code/code.asp.

Pawar, M. (2004) 'Social policy curricula for training social workers: Towards a model', *Australian Social Work*, vol 57, no 1, pp 3–18.

Pierce, D. (2000) 'Policy practice', in J. Midgley, M.B. Tracy and M. Livermore (eds) *The Handbook of Social Policy*, Thousand Oaks, CA: Sage, pp 53–63.

Pierson, P. (2000) 'Increasing returns, path dependence and the study of politics', *American Political Science Review*, vol 94, no 2, pp 251–67.

Reisch, M. and Staller, K. (2011) 'Teaching social welfare history and social welfare policy from a conflict perspective', *Journal of Teaching in Social Work*, vol 32, no 2, pp 131–44.

Ritter, J. (2008) 'A national study predicting licensed social workers' levels of political participation: The role of resources, psychological engagement, and recruitment networks', *Social Work*, vol 53, no 4, pp 347–57.

Rocha, C., Poe, B. and Thomas, V. (2010) 'Political activities of social workers: Addressing perceived barriers to political participation', *Social Work*, vol 55, no 4, pp 317–25.

Sather, P., Weitz, B. and Carlson, P. (2007) 'Engaging students in macro issues through community-based learning', *Journal of Teaching in Social Work*, vol 27, no 3, pp 61–79.

Schmid, H., Bar, M. and Nirel, R. (2008) 'Advocacy roles of nonprofit human service organizations: Implications for policy', *Nonprofit and Voluntary Sector Quarterly*, vol 37, no 4, pp 581–602.

Sherraden, M.S., Slosar, B. and Sherraden, M. (2002) 'Innovation in social policy: Collaborative policy advocacy', *Social Work*, vol 47, no 3, pp 209–21.

Simpson, G. and Connor, S. (2011) *Social Policy for Social Welfare Professionals: Tools for Understanding, Analysis and Engagement*, Bristol: The Policy Press.

State of Israel, the Ministry of Welfare and Social Services (2010) *The Report of the State Commission on Reform of Local Social Care Service*, Jerusalem: Ministry of Welfare and Social Services.

Tower, L. and Hartnett, H. (2011) 'An internet-based assignment to teach students to engage in policy-practice: A three-cohort study', *Journal of Policy Practice*, vol 10, no 1, pp 65–77.

Verba, S., Schlozman, K. and Brady, H. (1995) *Voice and Equality: Citizen Voluntarism in American Politics*, Cambridge, MA: Harvard University Press.

Weiss, I., Gal, J. and, Katan, J. (2006) 'Social policy for social work: A teaching agenda', *British Journal of Social Work*, vol 36, pp 789–806.

Weiss-Gal, I., and Asher Ben-Arieh (eds) 2009) 'Social Workers and Policy in Israel', *Social Security*, 81 (Special Issue) (in Hebrew)

Weiss-Gal, I. and Gal, J. (2011) *Policy Practice in Social Work*, Jerusalem: Magnes.

Weiss-Gal, I. and Savaya, R. (2012) 'A hands-on policy practice seminar for social workers in Israel: Description and evaluation', *Journal of Policy and Practice*, vol 11, no 3, pp 139-57.

Wolfer, T. and Gray, K. (2007) 'Using the decision case method to teach legislative policy advocacy', *Journal of Teaching in Social Work*, vol 27, no 1, pp 37–59.

Zubrzycki, J. and McArthur, M. (2004) 'Preparing social work students for policy practice: An Australian example', *Social Work Education*, vol 23, no 4, pp 451–64.

Index